S0-AHE-180

LANGUAGE
OF THE
SPECIALISTS

Language

OF THE

Specialists

A COMMUNICATIONS GUIDE TO
TWENTY DIFFERENT FIELDS

Edited, and with an Introduction, by

MARIO PEI

FUNK & WAGNALLS

A Division of *Reader's Digest Books, Inc.*

88085

R
423
P 376

© 1966 Reader's Digest Books, Inc.
—Funk & Wagnalls Division.

Library of Congress Catalog Card Number: 66-22943

Contents

Contents

LIST OF CONTRIBUTORS

Anthropology..........................Herbert S. Camenson
Architecture...........Eugene Raskin, B.A., B.Arch., C.I.A.A.
Astronomy..........................Victor Goedicke, Ph.D.
Biochemistry.......................David M. Locke, Ph.D.
Business.............................James J. Flynn, Ph.D.
Computers.........................Charles A. Veldon, B.S.
Construction.........................Frank W. Stubbs, Jr.
Electronics.........................Harold A. Rodgers, Jr.
Linguistics.............................John Hughes, Ph.D.
Literature............................Martin Tucker, Ph.D.
Medicine...............................Donald G. Cooley
Military Affairs..........................Robert E. Hunter
Music.............................Caryl Daly Friend, B.S.
Painting and Sculpture...................Marve H. Cooper
                                   Michele F. Cooper, M.A.
Philosophy........................Daniel J. Sullivan, M.A.
Political Science.................Earl L. Packer, B.A., LL.B.
Psychology........................Adam Margoshes, M.A.
Sociology............................Tad K. Krauze, M.A.
                                       Leah Glass, Ph.D.
Space Research.....................Julie Ann Farrer, M.A.
Theater.............................Henry Popkin, Ph.D.

INTRODUCTION

The total number of English words is estimated at about one million. Of these, the average cultivated man probably uses about 30,000, and may be able to recognize and understand 60,000 more. Outside of a few highly specialized lexicographers and linguists, the most educated of us do not know more than one out of every ten words in the language. This ratio, incidentally, holds true for the speakers of other highly civilized languages—German, French, Spanish, Italian, Russian.

The principal reason for this startling discrepancy between what we have at our disposal and what we know and use lies in the highly specialized vocabularies of the various and numerous branches of activity to which modern man devotes himself. As these forms of activity increase and multiply, so does the vocabulary. Each field finds it necessary to borrow, adapt, combine, coin, or otherwise create the nouns, adjectives, and verbs that describe its objects and concepts, its qualities, its forms of action.

The average man normally reacts to this situation by ignoring it. He learns, perforce, the specialized vocabulary of his own field of activity, which may range all the way from dispensing ice-cream sodas or digging ditches to healing the myriad diseases to which the physiological organs of his fellow man are prone. He possesses, of course, the hard core of vocabulary which is the common possession of all speakers of the language—basic nouns such as *bread* and *water, car* and *plane;* basic adjectives such as *good* and *bad, young* and *old;* basic adverbs, prepositions, and conjunctions like *fast* and *slowly, here* and *there, when* and *how, to* and *from, by* and *at, if* and *but;* basic verbs such as *come* and *go, run* and *ride, eat* and *drink, read* and *write.* It is safe to say that even the semiliterate adult has at his disposal between 10,000 and 20,000 of these words, to which he has been exposed since childhood, and which he holds in common with all his fellow speakers, however he may misspell, mispronounce, or otherwise mishandle them. Beyond this, it is every man for himself. The physician, who has digested the manuals of anatomy and pharmacology, does not normally have much need for the vocabulary of the automotive engineer, or that of the attorney, or that of the banker. He can rest content with his basic and his specialized sets of words.

But can he? The words of the specialized fields have a way of coming at the layman from all sides, in his daily newspaper, in popular magazine articles, on radio and television, even in ordinary conversation. Complete ignorance of their form and meaning is unfortunate, to say the least. It is perfectly true that these words can be looked up in our more comprehensive dictionaries, if it is absolutely necessary. But is there not a better way of familiarizing ourselves with those words which the specialists in some of the major fields consider basic, both by reason of their importance and their frequency of occurrence?

The present volume represents an attempt to abstract

from twenty fields of specialization such terms as the specialists themselves have selected as a cross section of what the generally educated man might be expected to understand. In addition, the various experts have supplied introductions, of varying length, in which they discuss the terminology of their respective fields from the standpoint of its significance to the layman.

These twenty chapters do not, of course, furnish the layman with a specialist's knowledge. They do, however, constitute an interesting introduction to the various fields, a sort of tour under expert guidance. Above all, they supply the reader with quick and relatively easy reference to those words from the individual jargons which most often find their way into the news and into general reading and discussion.

It must be at once admitted that some of our twenty fields are more accessible than others to the general public. It will be found, for example, that the vocabulary of the theater, of literature, of military affairs, of political science, of business, lie more within the range of the educated adult than do those of astronomy, biochemistry, construction, linguistics, computers, or space. Even with the discussions and definitions given, it will be hard for the layman, without on-the-spot demonstration, to visualize the application of some of the terms of the more physical sciences. All sections, however, can be read with profit. All can be readily referred to. Some, as, for example, the vocabulary of medicine, may be found of real practical use. A few will even constitute what may be described as "fun" reading. Side by side with traditional topics of ancient and honorable vintage (Philosophy, Literature, Music, Architecture) are fields of very recent emergence, such as Electronics, Computers, and Space, giving the work what may be described as historical balance.

For myself, I can say that I have found working on *Language of the Specialists* both pleasurable and profitable. It is a book from which I have personally learned a great deal.

July, 1966.

MARIO PEI
Columbia University.

CHAPTER 1

Arrangers of the Stars

The Language of Astronomy

Victor Goedicke

The history of the language of astronomy is the history of astronomy itself. Born in the mists of prehistory, transplanted to Babylonia and then to Greece and Egypt, rescued from oblivion in the Dark Ages by the accident of having been transplanted to Arabia by a banished sect of Christians, brought from Arabia to Spain by the Moors, astronomy comes to us finally with its language strongly influenced by its Arabic-speaking custodians, and generously sprinkled with echoes of Spanish, Latin, Greek, and even Sumerian.

ARABIC INFLUENCES. In the Middle Ages astronomy was little studied or cared for in Europe, and astronomical knowledge might easily have been lost to the world except for an event which had taken place centuries earlier in another part of the world. In Constantinople, in 431 A.D., a Syrian monk named Nestorius had been accused of heresy by his fellow Christians, deposed from his post as patriarch of Constantinople, and exiled. His band of followers had settled in the valley of the Euphrates, and over

1

the ensuing centuries had sent out many missionaries to found churches and schools in many parts of Asia. They kept in their possession, throughout their wanderings, carefully recopied Syriac versions of the ancient Greek writings on astronomy, among them Ptolemy's great encyclopedia of thirteen books which contain nearly all that we know of ancient astronomy. Among the schools which they founded was a medical school at Kusistan, at the head of the Persian Gulf.

Meanwhile, in Baghdad, the triumphant Kalifs had set up a magnificent capital and brought there men of science and literature and art, among them some physicians from the school at Kusistan. When the Kalifs learned from them of the existence of the Syriac versions of the Greek scientific writings, they brought them to Baghdad and had them translated into Arabic, and on this slender thread they have come down to us. From Arabia, astronomy was transported by the Moors to Spain, where it flourished in observatories in Cordova and Toledo, and from there it spread through Europe.

This strange travelogue is reflected in many of the words of astronomy. Our word *zenith*, for example (for the point in the sky directly overhead), began as an ellipsis for the Arabic phrase *samt al-ra's*, "the direction of the head." Then, by what authorities describe as "a common scribal error" of *ni*, in place of *m*, *samt* became *cenit* in early Spanish versions of Arabic writings. In Spanish it has survived as *zenit*, but in Old French it became *cenith*, and in Middle English *senyth*, and then finally *zenith*. In the course of these travels, it has undergone some small variations of meaning. The great English poet Geoffrey Chaucer, for example, in the highly technical book which he wrote ostensibly to teach his ten-year-old son Lowys the workings of the astrolabe, uses *senyth* to mean the point on the horizon where the sun rises.

Curiously, our word *azimuth* (for the angular distance around the horizon to a point directly underneath an astronomical body) is also derived from this same Arabic word *samt*. In Arabic the word *al-samt*, or its plural form *al-summūt*, was used to abbreviate a phrase meaning "direction along the horizon." It was customary in speaking to absorb the *l* of the article *al* into the following consonant, and these words became *as-samt*, and *as-summūt*. In Old French the latter form became *azimut*, and in Middle English *azymuth*, and finally *azimuth*.

Nadir (the point directly opposite the zenith) also began as an ellipsis. *Nazīr assamt*, meaning "like the zenith," was shortened to *nazīr*, and this led to the Old French form *nadir* which has come to us unchanged. *Almucantar* (a circle in the sky parallel to the horizon) has an Arabic-through-Spanish history. *Mugantarah* is the Arabic word for sundial, and its plural is *mugantarāt*. With the article *al*, this developed into the Arabic *almuqantarāt*, and into the Spanish *almicantarat*. *Alidade* (the index of a sighting instrument) is from the Latin *alidāda*, which in turn is from the Arabic *al-'idādah*. In fact, even the modern name of Ptolemy's great encyclopedia is itself Arabic. Ptolemy called it the *Megiste Syntaxis;* the Arabs shortened this and added the ubiquitous prefix *al* to make it *Al-majisti*, which then became our *Almagest*.

But it is in the realm of star names that the Arabic influence is most strongly felt. Of 183 star names listed by George Davis,[1] 125 are Arabic (Vega, Betelgeuse, Algol), 26 are Greek (Sirius, Arcturus, Antares), 14 are Latin (Capella, Regulus, Spica), 9 are Arabic-Latin combinations (Miaplacidus, Yed Prior, Kaus Australis), and 3 are Persian (Alshain, Tarazed, Alcor). The Arabic names are of two kinds. First are the indigenous names, used by the Bedouin tribesmen, who named the stars after camels, jackals, birds, hyenas, frogs, sheep. Four stars of the constellation Lepus were, for them, four camels which had quenched their thirst in the River of the Milky Way, and five bright stars of Virgo were five barking dogs, and four stars of Corvus were a four-pole tent. An example of such an old Bedouin name which has survived is *Alphard*, from *Fard ash-Shujā*, "the lonely one," for the only bright star in the constellation Hydra.[2]

The second kind of Arabic star names are those assigned to the stars by Arabian astronomers. The principle of naming was simple. The astronomers simply adopted the ancient Greek or Babylonian names and figures for the constellations, and then named the stars to detail the anatomy, so to speak. Thus Denebola, in Leo, is *Dhanab al-Asad*, "the lion's tail," and Fomalhaut, in Piscis Austrinus, is an ellipsis for *Fum al-Hūt al-Janūbi*, "the mouth of the southern fish," and Rigel is short for *Rijl al-Jausā' al-Jusrā*, "the left foot of Orion." Most of the Arabic star names are of this second kind.

ANCIENT ORIGINS. For the names of the constellations themselves we must go to another altogether earlier period in history, and review one of the most remarkable detective stories of science.

It has long been known that although many of the figures in the constellations are based on Greek mythology, both the figures and the myths are actually of much older origin. The evidence for this is direct, and comes from a decipherment of Euphratean cuneiforms which indicates that at least most of the Greek myths have a Euphratean parallel, and which makes it probable that the Greek system of constellations was of Semitic or pre-Semitic origin. The evidence for a still more ancient origin comes from

an unexpected source: the analysis of astronomical observations described in a long poem written by Aratos, a
Greek poet, in 277 B.C. This poem, which was probably a
mnemonic for remembering the boundaries of the constellations, consists of a remarkably detailed and exact account
of the risings and settings of the stars. For example, lines
596 to 606 are:

"Not few, either, are the constellations which the Maiden at her
rising sends beneath the verge of earth. Then set the Cyl-
lenian Lyre, the Dolphin and the shapely Arrow. With them the
wingtips of the Bird up to her very tail and the farthest reaches
of the River are overshadowed. The head of the Horse sets, sets
too his neck. The Hydra rises higher, as far as the Crater, and
before her, the Dog brings up his hind feet, dragging behind
him the stern of Argo of many stars. And she rises above the
Earth, cleft right at the mast, just when the whole of the
Maiden has risen."

Now the point of this is that the way of rising and setting
of the stars fixes not only the latitude of the observer, but
also (because of the slow drift of the axis of rotation of the
earth) the epoch in history. The phenomena described in
Aratos' poem cannot at all be reconciled with his latitude
(41° N) nor his epoch. This is not surprising, since the
data in the poem are openly taken from a prose work of
Eudoxus, written about 360 B.C. What is surprising is that
the latitude and the epoch do not fit Eudoxus either, and
since Aratos attributes the constellations to ancient "men
that are no more (who) noted and marked how to group
in figures and call by a single name," and whom he calls
the "Elder Race," it is reasonable to assume that Eudoxus
too was simply reporting still older accounts.

A detailed investigation of the risings and settings described in Aratos' poem indicates that they must have been
observed from a latitude of 37° or 38°, and at a date close

to 2900 B.C. The constellation figures indicate that the "Elder Race" knew ocean-going ships, domesticated dogs, and horses. The latitude excludes the civilizations on the Nile, the Euphrates, and the Indus. Furthermore, horses were unknown in these parts of the world.

From here on it is anybody's guess. The ship described by Aratos has a high poop and a long body, and resembles the pictures of ships found in Bronze Age carvings on stone in Norway and Sweden. Experts even point out that the Vikings were known to have beached their ships always stern-first, to be prepared for a quick launching in case of attack, and that they built their ships accordingly, with a strong high poop. Perhaps one day the names of the constellations will help us to clarify a little of the puzzle of the origin of civilization.[3]

This ancient origin, whatever it might have been, has had little effect on the names we now use for the constellations. Most of the old Sumerian names come to us in translation into Latin or Greek forms. However, a few fragments of the Sumerian words survive, chiefly because the Arabs occasionally used the ancient name of the constellation to describe a bright star in the constellation. For example, *Hamal*, in the constellation Aries (the ram), is from the Arabic *al-Hamal*, "the full-grown lamb," which in turn is a modified form of the Sumerian $^{mul}LU\text{-}LIM$ $(^{kakkab}Lulimu)$, "the constellation of the ram." Altair, in the constellation Aquila (the eagle), is a short form of the Arabic *an-Nasr at-Tā'ir*, "the flying eagle or vulture," which in turn is from the Sumerian $^{mul}ID^{hu}$ $(^{kakkab}Našru^{hu})$, "the constellation of the eagle."

MODERN. More recently, many terms in astronomy have been simply invented to fill a need. Thus a spectrograph designed to study the sun is called a *spectroheliograph*, and when a motion-picture camera is used with it to make a continuous record it is sometimes called a *spectrohelio-kinematograph!* The study of the sun's surface has given us *flocculus* and *facula* to describe bright areas, and, more recently, such terms as *spicule* and *flare* to describe various kinds of solar prominences and related phenomena. *Telescope* itself is such a word; Galileo himself used *perspicillum* for the instrument which he discovered, and sometimes *organum* or *instrumentum*, and sometimes *occiale*. The word *telescope* was introduced by a rival and lesser claimant to the discovery.

In the realm of names, it has usually been the discoverer's prerogative to choose a name for his discovery, and this right has often been used to immortalize the name of a friend or a patron. Galileo tried to name the satellites of Jupiter for the Medici family, but again he lost out to a rival who also claimed the discovery. The rival, Simon Marius, proposed that the four objects which endlessly circle around Jupiter (or Jove) should have the names of the four objects of Jove's sexual desire, and he proposed a mnemonic:

> "Io, Europa, Ganimedes puer, atque Calisto,
> Lascivio nimium perplacuere Jovi,"

or, as the translator has it, in even poorer meter,

> "Io, Europa, the boy Ganymede, and likewise Calisto,
> Aroused to excess the lust of Jove."

In at least one instance the words of astronomy appear to have influenced astronomy itself. When Schiaparelli observed faint lines on Mars he called them *canali,* that is, *channels.* But this was translated into English as *canals,* carrying with it a strong connotation of being man-made, which *canali* does not. It is believed that this linguistic accident stimulated some American astronomers to undertake a search for evidence of life on Mars.

CURRENT TRENDS. Radio astronomy is currently adding new words and phrases to astronomical literature. *Microwave, antenna temperature, decameter region, Mills cross, traveling wave maser*—these and many other terms would not have been found in a book on astronomy a decade or two ago.

In all fields of astronomy there is a tendency to produce new words by contractions or abbreviations of longer words or phrases. An example is the widespread use of *quasar* for the recently discovered quasi-stellar radio sources, and the use of the abbreviation *QSG* for the still more recently discovered quasi-stellar galaxies. Many such words are still insecure. For example, at least one prominent astronomer would prefer to use the pure abbreviation *QSS* in place of *quasar*.

No account of the language of astronomy would be complete without a comment on the word *astronomy* itself. Astronomy has long been deprived of its rightful title, *astrology* (to parallel such words as *sociology, psychology,* and so forth), and astronomers are forever condemned to be titled mere arrangers of the stars!

[1] See Davis' article in *Popular Astronomy,* January, 1944.
[2] An excellent account of these names is to be found in an article by M. A. Evershed in *Observatory,* vol. 58, page 237, August, 1935.
[3] For an interesting account of the interpretation of Aratos' poem, see the article by Mrs. A. S. D. Maunder, on the origin of the constellations, in *Observatory,* vol. 59, page 367, December, 1936.

WORD LIST

ALBEDO. The fraction of the total incident sunlight which is reflected back in all directions by a planet, satellite, or asteroid, or any part of their surfaces. Latin, *albus,* white.

ANOMALY. The angular distance of a planet from its perihelion, as seen from the sun; called *true anomaly* or *mean anomaly* depending on whether it is measured according to the real position or to the mean position of the planet. **ANOMALISTIC YEAR:** the time between two successive passages of the earth through perihelion; 24 minutes 45 seconds longer than the tropical year. Greek, *anomalia*, inequality.

AP- or **APO-.** Prefix meaning from. Greek, ἀπό (or ἀπο), from.

APASTRON. The point in the orbit of a double star at which the secondary is farthest from its primary.

APHELION. The point in a planet's orbit which is most distant from the sun.

APOGEE. The point in the orbit of the moon or other body which is most distant from the earth.

ASTEROID. Any of the many thousands of small planets revolving around the sun mainly between the orbits of Mars and Jupiter. Also called *minor planets* and *planetoids*. The largest is less than 500 miles in diameter. Greek, *aster*, star, and *eidos*, form.

ASTRONOMICAL UNIT. The mean distance from the earth to the sun, widely used in describing the distances from the planets to the sun or for the separations of double stars. It is equal to 92,970,000 miles.

BINARY. A pair of stars revolving around their common center of gravity. Latin, *binarius*, from *bini*, two by two.

BURST. A sudden increase in the intensity of an isolated wavelength of solar radio-frequency radiation, lasting only a few seconds.

CARBON CYCLE. A set of thermonuclear reactions by which helium is synthesized from hydrogen with the aid of carbon. The carbon cycle is one of the two nuclear reactions responsible for the energy production in most stars.

CELESTIAL SPHERE. The infinite sphere of the sky upon which celestial objects are projected for mapping purposes. **CELESTIAL POLES:** the projection upon the celestial sphere of the extended axis of the earth; the axis points around which the celestial sphere appears to rotate. **CELESTIAL EQUATOR:** the great circle 90° from the celestial poles. **CELESTIAL MERIDIAN:** the great circle passing through the celestial poles and through the observer's zenith.

CEPHEID, or **CEPHEID VARIABLE.** A member of a class of intrinsic variable stars, important to astronomy because they provide a means of measuring the distances to star clusters and galaxies.

CHROMOSPHERE. The bright scarlet lower layer of the sun's atmosphere, just above the photosphere. Greek, *chroma,* color, and *sphaira,* sphere.

COLOR INDEX. A measure of the color of a star, defined as 2.5 times the logarithm of the ratio of the visual brightness to the photographic brightness, or as the photographic magnitude minus the visual magnitude.

COMA. The diffuse head of a comet; also an aberration of reflecting telescopes which gives off-center star images a comet-like appearance. Greek, *kome,* head of hair.

CONJUNCTION. That configuration in which two celestial bodies have the same celestial longitude or the same right ascension.

CONVECTIVE ZONE. A layer of rising and falling currents just beneath the photosphere of the sun.

COPERNICAN THEORY. The doctrine that the sun is at the

center of the universe and that the planets revolve around it.

CORONA. The faint extended outer portion of the sun's atmosphere, formerly visible only during a total solar eclipse, but now visible by means of special optical devices. CORONAGRAPH: an optical instrument for studying the sun. From the Latin, meaning crown.

COSMOGONY. The study of the ultimate origins of physical systems. Greek, *kosmogonia,* from *kosmos,* order or universe, and *gonos,* from a root meaning to produce.

COSMOLOGY. The study of the content and arrangement of the physical universe.

DECLINATION. The angular distance from the celestial equator.

DIURNAL. Having to do with the day. DIURNAL MOTION: the apparent daily motion of the celestial sphere. Latin, *diurnalis,* day by day, from *diurnus,* daily.

DOPPLER EFFECT. The apparent change in the wavelength of light received from a source which has a line-of-sight component of motion relative to the observer. It is observed in the apparent displacement of spectrum lines and is a valuable source of information about the velocities of celestial objects.

DWARF. A star of small or moderate luminosity and diameter. See HERTZSPRUNG-RUSSELL DIAGRAM.

EARTHLIGHT. Light reflected from earth to moon and back, visible on the dark portion of the moon.

ECCENTRICITY. A measure of the degree to which an orbit differs from a circle. The eccentricity of a circle is zero, that of a parabola is one, and that of a hyperbola is greater than one. The eccentricity of the orbit of the earth is 0.017.

ECLIPTIC. The sun's apparent annual path among the stars; a great circle on the celestial sphere intersecting the celestial equator at an angle of 23½°. Latin, *eclipticus;* Greek, *ekleiptikos,* pertaining to an eclipse; from *ekleipein,* to leave out.

ELONGATION. The amount by which the right ascension or celestial longitude of an object differs from that of the sun.

EPHEMERIS. A table giving the predicted positions of an object revolving in an orbit around another object. Greek, *ephemerios,* of or for the day.

EQUINOCTIAL. A word sometimes used for the celestial equator.

EQUINOX. Either of the two points on the celestial sphere where the equator intersects the ecliptic; also the time of the sun's arrival at one of these points. The **VERNAL EQUINOX** refers to the sun's passage from south to north, and the **AUTUMNAL EQUINOX** to its passage from north to south. Latin, *aequinoctium,* from *aequus,* equal, and *nox,* night.

FACULA. A small spot on the sun's surface, brighter than the rest of the photosphere. Latin, dim. of *fax,* a torch.

FILAMENT. A solar prominence seen in projection against the sun's surface.

FLARE. A sudden outburst of monochromatic emission over a large area of solar surface.

FLASH SPECTRUM. The spectrum of the solar atmosphere as viewed briefly during total solar eclipse, at the instant when the moon covers all but a sliver of the sun's edge. Optically, this thin sliver substitutes for the image of the slit of the spectrograph.

Flocculus. A high, bright, chromospheric facula. Latin, *floccus,* a lock of wool.

Galactic. Having to do with our galaxy. **Galactic Cluster:** a group of several dozen to several thousand stars having common origin and space motion, and found near the central plane of our galaxy.

Galaxy. Originally the Milky Way, the array of billions of stars apparently merging into a luminous band extending across our sky. More recently, any independent system of tens or hundreds of billions of stars, isolated in space, of which our own system is one. Greek, *galaxias,* from *gala,* milk. The systems other than our own are sometimes called **Extragalactic Nebulae. Spiral Galaxy:** a galaxy consisting of a central nucleus with (usually two) spiral arms. **Elliptical Galaxy:** a galaxy lacking spiral arms and showing an elliptical outline. **Barred Spiral:** a galaxy whose spiral arms attach to the ends of a transverse bar rather than directly to the nucleus.

Giant. A star characterized by its high luminosity. See **Hertzsprung-Russell Diagram.**

Gibbous. Between quarter phase and full phase of the moon or a planet. Latin, *gibbosus,* humped or hunched, from *gibbus,* a hump.

Globular Cluster. A relatively compact group of 10,000 to several hundred thousand stars.

Hertzsprung-Russell Diagram. A graph in which the spectral types of stars are plotted against their absolute magnitudes; thus a graph showing the relationship between temperature and luminosity. Most stars appear in a band (called the main sequence) running from upper left (high temperature and high luminosity) to lower right (low temperature and low luminosity), or in a second band (called the giant branch) running from the center of the diagram to the upper right (low temperature and high luminosity). Stars near the bottom of the main sequence are called dwarfs, and the scattered stars which occur in the lower left (high temperatures and low luminosities) are called white dwarfs. The scattered stars at the extreme top of the diagram (very high luminosities) are called supergiants.

Hour Angle. The angle at the celestial pole between an hour circle and the celestial meridian.

Hour Circle. A great circle passing through the celestial poles.

Inclination. The angle between an orbital plane and a plane of reference.

Intercalation. The practice of sometimes inserting days or months in a calendar to secure agreement of dates or seasons.

Libration. The seeming oscillation of the moon around her axis, by which portions of her surface near the edge of the disc are alternately brought into sight and swung out of sight.

Light Year. The distance which light travels in a year, approximately six trillion miles. See **Parsec.**

Limb. Apparent edge of an astronomical body as seen from earth. **Limb Darkening:** the falling off of surface brightness from center to limb.

Magnitude. The brightness of a star or other astronomical object. **Apparent Magnitude:** brightness as seen from the earth. An arbitrary group of bright stars are assigned magnitude "one," and the magnitude of any other star is defined by the equation $\text{Log } l_2/l_1 = 0.4(m_1 - m_2)$.

Barely visible naked-eye stars are of magnitude 5 or 6. **ABSOLUTE MAGNITUDE:** the apparent magnitude which a star would have if it were at a distance of ten parsecs.

MARE. A large, dark, comparatively smooth area of the moon, containing relatively few craters and no mountains. Latin, *mare*, sea.

MEAN SUN. A fictitious body having a uniform eastward motion on the celestial sphere equal to the annual average motion of the true sun. **MEAN TIME:** time measured by the motion of the mean sun.

NADIR. The point on the celestial sphere directly below the observer. Arabic, *nazīr*, from *nazīr assamt*, corresponding to the zenith.

NEBULA. An irregular mass of diffuse gas, usually glowing from the light of nearby stars. **PLANETARY NEBULA:** a nebula surrounding a star, usually in the form of a hollow sphere, once believed to be a step in the formation of planets. Latin, *nebula*, a cloud, mist, vapor.

NODE. The point on the celestial sphere at which an orbit (as of a planet or satellite) intersects a reference plane (as the ecliptic).

NOVA. A star which increases its luminosity by many thousandfold in a few hours, and which ejects material from its surface into space.

NUTATION. A small oscillation or "wobble" in the earth's axis, with a period of 19 years, caused by the moon's tendency to pull the earth's equatorial bulge into line with its gravitational attraction.

PARALLAX. The apparent difference of direction of an object when seen from the two ends of a base line. **GEO-CENTRIC PARALLAX:** the parallax obtained from a base line on the earth, used for determining the distance to objects in the solar system. **HELIOCENTRIC PARALLAX**: the parallax obtained by using the earth's motion around the sun to give us a much longer base line, used for determining the distances to stars. Greek *parallaxis*, from *para*, beyond, and *allassein*, to change.

PARSEC. The distance at which a star's parallax would be one second of arc. It is equal to 3.26 light years, or 206,265 astronomical units, or about 19 trillion miles. A synthetic word from *par*allax and *sec*ond.

PENUMBRA. The region of semishadow in an eclipse; also, the less dark outer region of a sunspot.

PERI-. Prefix meaning around or near.

PERIASTRON. The point in the orbit of a double star at which the secondary is closest to its primary. **PERIGEE** and **PERIHELION**, the points closest to the earth and to the sun, respectively, are similar.

PHOTOSPHERE. The layer of the sun's surface which we normally see; the sun's visible surface.

PRECESSION (of the equinoxes). A slow westward motion along the ecliptic of the position of the vernal equinox, caused by the gyroscopic motion of the earth's axis of rotation.

PROMINENCE. A large projecting cloud of chromospheric material, usually in rapid motion. Prominences were formerly seen only during total solar eclipses, when the moon blotted out the bright light of the sun, but are now studied routinely outside of eclipses with the aid of specially designed optical equipment.

PROPER MOTION. The motion of a star perpendicular to the line of sight.

QUASAR. Contraction for the recently discovered quasi-stellar radio sources.

RED SHIFT. The displacement of spectral lines toward the red end of the spectrum, an invariable feature of the spectra of other galaxies, interpreted as indicating high velocities of recession.

RETROGRADE. Motion counter to the prevailing norm; westward motion on the celestial sphere, or clockwise motion as seen from above the North Pole.

RIGHT ASCENSION. Angular distance east from the vernal equinox, expressed usually in units of time.

ROCHE's LIMIT. The least distance at which purely gravitational cohesion can prevent the tidal disruption of a secondary by a primary; that is, the smallest distance from a planet at which a moon could survive.

SAROS. The 18-year cycle of eclipse recurrences. Greek, *saros*, a Chaldean cycle.

SCARP. A lunar cliff.

SCHMIDT TELESCOPE. A telescope having a spherical mirror and a correcting lens as its principal optical elements.

SIDEREAL. Having to do with the stars. Latin, *sideralis*, from *sidus*, a star. **SIDEREAL PERIOD:** period of motion with respect to the stars. **SIDEREAL TIME:** time measured by the angle between the vernal equinox and the observer's meridian. **SIDEREAL YEAR:** the exact period in which the earth completes one revolution around the sun, equal to 365 days, 6 hours, 9 minutes, and 10 seconds, and differing from the year in ordinary use, which is called the **TROPICAL YEAR.**

SOLSTICE. Either of the two points on the ecliptic at which the sun is farthest from the celestial equator; also the moment of the sun's arrival at such a point. Latin, *solstitium*, from *sol*, the sun, and *stitium*, from *statum*, p. p. of *sistere*, to make stand still.

Sub-Dwarf. A star slightly below the main sequence on the Hertzsprung-Russell Diagram.

Supergiant. A star of very high luminosity. See Hertzsprung-Russell Diagram.

Supernova. A cataclysmic stellar explosion, so violent as to hurl all or most of the star out into space, as opposed to a nova, in which only the surface layers are ejected.

Surge. A rapid, short-lived solar prominence associated with a solar flare.

Synodic. Relating to the Nodes (q.v.). **Synodic Period:** period of revolution with respect to some relative rather than absolute standard of reference, as the sun instead of the fixed stars.

Syzygy. Either of the two points in the orbit of the moon or other heavenly body at which it is most nearly in line with the earth and sun. Greek, *syzygia; syn-*, together, and *zygon*, a yoke.

Trojan Group. A group of asteroids which remain approximately equidistant from Jupiter and the sun.

Tropic. Either of two small circles on the celestial sphere, at a distance of 23½° on either side of the celestial equator and parallel to it, which the sun just reaches at its greatest declination north or south. **Tropical Year:** the time required for the sun to move from either equinox around to the same equinox, equal to 365 days, 5 hours, 48 minutes, 46 seconds. This is the year in ordinary calendar use.

Umbra. The region of total shadow in an eclipse; also, the dark central portion of a sunspot.

Zenith. The point on the celestial sphere directly overhead.

ZODIAC. The broad belt of constellations through which
the sun passes in its annual motion around the ecliptic.
Greek, *zodiakos,* from *kyklos,* circle, and *zodion,* dim. of
zoon, an animal. **ZODIACAL LIGHT:** the faint glow pre-
ceding and following the sun and symmetrical about
the ecliptic.

Airspace of the Stars

Zodiac. The broad belt of constellations through which the sun passes in its annual motion around the celiptic. Greek, zodiakos (from kyklos, circle...
sun... in annual. Zodiacal. Factor: the faint glow pre-
ceding and following the sun and symmetrical about
the ecliptic.

CHAPTER **2**

"For None Are There That Can Compare . . ."

The Language of Military Affairs

ROBERT E. HUNTER

Since military affairs have been an important part of human activity for a few thousand years, it is not surprising that the words of the profession in common use today are derived from many of history's major languages. Thus, we find many military words that can be traced back to ancient Roman, Greek, or even earlier. There are words in military affairs whose origins are lost, or which originated with Norse and Saxon tribes. Again, there are words that have made their way to English through a dozen languages, so that, with two words both derived from Latin, one, *reconnoiter*, might have a French lilt, another, *junta*, the flavor of Spanish.

The grand words of military affairs—the words of the philosophy and direction of warfare—tend to be of Greek origin. The three pillars of military thought—tactics, strategy, and policy—all are derived from the ancient tongue of philosophers. One may even include here the art of logistics, a relative newcomer to military terminology, but formed on a Greek root.

Many of the rest of traditional military terms boast of Latin antecedents. *Victory* and *peace* both come from Latin. So do *army, navy, cavalry,* and a host of others. But some escaped: thus we may sometimes reject a Latin root for another, as in the case of the word *war*—derived from the Old High German—instead of the Latin *bellum* (though we do use words like *bellicose*). Or we may use both the northern European-derived *weapons* and the Latin-based *arms. Military* itself comes through the French from the Latin word for soldier (while *soldier* comes from an Old French word).

Warfare had been elaborated to a highly professional craft by Roman times. The concepts in use then have direct relevance for us today. In just two sentences in the first chapter of Caesar's *Conquest of Gaul,* for example (S. A. Handford translation), one may count no fewer than eleven words that have contemporary significance in military affairs, namely, *alliance, sacrifice, concessions, victories, rank, stronger, rivals, dependencies, surrender, hostages,* and *hostile.* Such is the firm legacy of language and concepts left to military affairs by ancient civilizations.

We must make a very clear distinction between those words that developed from ancient words which were, themselves, related to military affairs, and those words, no matter how distinguished their pedigrees, which have acquired military meanings only in modern usage. Thus the word *strategy,* one of the words in military affairs hardest to define precisely, has played a role in military affairs over thousands of years. When used by the ancient Greeks, *strategia* referred to *generalship.* On the other hand, *operation,* a word closely linked with *strategy* today, appears to have attained military significance only within the past two centuries, appearing in English in a military sense about the middle of the eighteenth century. The basic vocabulary of military affairs, today, is divided between those words, such as *army, navy, tactics, weapon, war, force, victory,* and *peace,* that have been growing and developing as military words for centuries, and those words that have entered military language only during the last few centuries of growth and elaboration of the art of warfare. Thus the word *division* was co-opted into military affairs by the English at the end of the sixteenth century; a *marine* began to be thought of as a soldier carried on shipboard at the end of the seventeenth century. The word *campaign* comes from the French word for field, or country, and was introduced into English in the seventeenth century to indicate the period of time during warm months when an army was "in the field."

As more words were developed and used for military purposes, they began to be used unchanged in many languages. While English has swallowed foreign words such as *junta, coup d'état,* and *Blitzkrieg,* the invasion of foreign tongues by English military language has paralleled the general permeation of English words into other languages.

With the development of new words for the military profession, some older words have undergone a transformation from their earlier military meanings. Some of these words remain in use, although their modern applications may sound a bit quaint. Thus a *cavalry* division—derived from the Latin word for horseman and filtered through all modern European languages—may never encounter a flesh-and-blood horse. Its horsemen are more likely to ride tanks or even more elaborate vehicles, such as helicopters, although the principle of the mobile weapon has been retained.

The meanings of other words may change, not because

the concepts and techniques of warfare change, but because of imprecision in the use of language. For example, the word *decimate* has come to indicate a large proportion of casualties in a military force or population. But the word is actually taken directly from a Latin word based on the number ten (as is our word *decimal*). In the ancient Roman army, mutinous troops were sometimes punished by having one tenth of their members, chosen by lot, put to death. Hence, *decimate*, or to take one tenth. When this word was appropriated into English in the seventeenth century, *decimate* retained the original meaning (the practice not having fallen into complete disuse), but in the last three centuries the word has lost its precise meaning and has become a general, descriptive term.

Still other words may retain their meaning within the context of military thinking, but lose precision for the layman. The word *barrage*, for example, may evoke a vision of the great artillery bombardments that were a standard part of the war on the Western Front during the First World War. But a barrage is not a bombardment, as such, but a barrier: indeed, the word is based upon the French word *barre*, or in English *bar*. An artillery barrage is designed to be a barrier to enemy activity; any destruction that occurs in the process is secondary. To be clear about *barrage*, however, one might summon up another vision from both World Wars: the tethered blimp, or "barrage balloon," designed to be a barrier against low-flying aircraft.

Though the general vocabulary of military affairs has developed steadily over a few thousand years of activity, there has been a revolution in terminology since the Second World War. Much of this revolution results from the great development of technology, the hundreds of new weapons—and methods of employing them—that have been introduced into every modern army. But the change is deeper than that. For now military affairs, particularly in America, are no longer the province only of the military professional or occasional layman. As in many other academic fields, there has been a sudden growth of interest and investigation into every aspect of military affairs. While there was only a handful of peacetime strategists two decades ago, there are now hundreds, annually churning out millions of words. World War II brought warfare to civilians everywhere; World War III, if there ever is one, might eliminate civilians altogether. With the advent of nuclear weapons, suddenly everyone has a real stake in military affairs. Moreover, billions and more billions of dollars are being spent every year, not to fight a war which will soon be over and forgotten, but to provide for strength to prevent that or any other war. Governments, particularly the American government, are spending vast sums of money to study war, how to prevent it, how to prepare for it, how to conduct it, how to control it, and how to stop it.

With the growth of interest in military affairs, there has also grown a new jargon. This is not a special case. In field after field, an increase of interest and knowledge has led to the need for new words, not only to express old concepts better and more subtly, but also to express new concepts and new techniques. Like every academic élite, the élite that makes military affairs the subject of its study needs a shorthand, a vocabulary all its own. English scholars may be horrified; communication to laymen may be impeded; but the vocabulary becomes steadily larger and more specialized, as requirements of speed and innovation place their demands on the English language.

During the past few years, this development of military jargon, at least in the West, has been almost entirely American, and has made good use of American methods of creating words. Verbs are often changed into nouns; adjectives and prefixes are grafted onto nouns, with a liberal use of hyphens (*counter-city, test-ban, para-military*); older, general words take on more limited, specific meanings (e.g., *missile*); and the old military standbys, abbreviations and initials, are dusted off and pressed into service (*tacnuk, GCD*). The list of specialized words that follows this section is composed mainly of this new jargon: those English words created, modified, or merely called up for duty in the field of military affairs.

Perhaps nowhere else do abbreviations and initials play such an important role as in military affairs. One might speculate whimsically that without initials, warfare and the military profession would both have long since ceased to exist! Some military initials become words, with their original meanings nearly lost. How many people outside America realize that the word by which American soldiers are universally known—GI—stands for the hardly descriptive Government Issue? *Radar,* a universally accepted and recognized word, started out as *R*Adio *D*etection *A*nd *R*anging. The famous PT-109 was a Patrol Torpedo boat, while within the caverns of the Pentagon, there are words made up of initials whose origins are completely lost to mankind. Everyone in the Navy knows that the CNO (sound the letters) is the Chief of Naval Operations (who would ever mouth the longer title?), while within the British services, an official will quite properly be addressed by the initials of his title only, in the best James Bond tradition. "Good morning, DGS," will merit a courteous reply by the Director General, Ships, of the Royal Navy.

But with a little effort, even the layman can begin to decipher the code of military abbreviations, particularly if he has an inkling of the function or purpose of the object or person thus glorified. Therefore, CINCPACFLT (sink-pack-fleet), the Admiral who commands the American Navy in the Pacific, is clearly Commander-in-Chief, Pacific Fleet. Or, in South Vietnam, MACV—actually pronounced as two words, Mac-Vee—stands for Military Assistance Command, Vietnam. This system can create its own embarrassments. In World War II, for example, the abbreviated title of the Commander-in-Chief of forces in the United States was hastily changed when it came to light as the demoralizing and unpatriotic CINCUS (sink us).

The average civilian may never encounter this forest of initials, but he had better be prepared to understand MLF (Multilateral Force), NATO (North Atlantic Treaty Organization), and ICBM (Intercontinental Ballistic Missile), if he wishes to be reasonably well informed about the prospects for his surviving the nuclear age.

The game becomes difficult when names are selected more or less arbitrarily, for purposes of secrecy or public relations. In the former instance, some names may seem fairly obvious—after the fact. Thus *Overlord* appears a fitting code name for the master plan for the invasion of Normandy in 1944, as does *Anvil,* the invasion of southern France that might have given a hammer-and-anvil look to battle maps. But why S-1 for the first atomic bomb? Perhaps to keep a secret.

When one gets into the area of the naming of weapons, however—good military public relations—then even the initial-makers must take a back seat. Perhaps during the Battle of Britain the British were heartened by the *Hurricanes* and *Spitfires* which, as fate would have it, lived up to their names. The *Polaris* missile, which assured the U.S. Navy of a role in America's nuclear strategy, was named for the North Star, guide and friend of mariners since time began. The *Minuteman* missile evokes memories of a sturdy and dependable band of early Americans, but whether it can be fired in a minute is a well-kept Air Force secret. *Atlas* may no longer carry the world on his shoulders, but this missile did loft several Americans into space, along with the nation's prestige. There are the *Bull-Pup* and the *Hound Dog,* to dog the enemy's heels, as well as the *Sidewinder* to strike at him while his back is turned. But let us not forget the *Skybolt* and the *Thor,* neither of which can today be found in the lightning-and-thunder business.

Finally, we should note the relationship between warfare and games (was it not Caesar who talked of the die's being cast?). Indeed, most games of skill involve strategy and, as in card games, an element of the unforeseen as well. The strategy of war has sometimes, though simply, been compared to the strategy of chess, a game whose pieces are representative of a medieval nation at war (King, Queen, Bishop, Knight, Castle, Pawn). One of the roots for the word *chess* is the Sanskrit for a military force of the period, and for a game played with pieces representing this force: elephants, chariots, horsemen, and foot soldiers. The terms *movement, deployment, stalemate, rank, file,* and others are found in chess as in traditional military language.

Chess is not the only game so endowed with military terms. In contract bridge, for example, we find the term *preemption;* in poker, the term *bluff.*

That military strategy is similar in some ways to games played between individuals has been enshrined in the now popular (but century-and-a-half old) activity of *wargaming,* in which individuals assume the roles of various protagonists in a conflict in order to test the validity of strategies and tactics. To turn the process around, the German translation of wargame, *Kriegspiel,* is also the name of a novel variation of chess.

WORD LIST

ABC. Atomic, Biological (Bacteriological), and Chemical weapons. These three types of modern superweapons are often grouped together for purposes of expressing deterrent capabilities, or for negotiating arms-control agreements. The latter two types of weapons are generally intended for disabling or destroying people, plants, or animals, rather than real property, thereby decreasing an enemy population's ability to wage war. Anthrax germs spread over enemy territory would be a B weapon. Nerve gases would be a C weapon. When the Federal Republic of Germany joined the Western European Union and NATO, it agreed not to manufacture ABC weapons in its territory.

ABM. Antiballistic Missile System, currently being developed by both the United States and the Soviet Union. Such a system would include radar detection of incoming ballistic missile reentry bodies, discrimination between warheads and decoys, and destruction of incoming warheads by Antimissile Missiles (AMMs), either with nuclear or high–explosive warheads. In 1966, the United States had not yet decided whether to construct and deploy an ABM system.

ACCIDENTAL WAR. Any war that begins by accident rather than by design. Safeguards against accidental war have become particularly important since the advent of nuclear weapons, because of the tremendous destruction that a single accident could cause, the difficulties of commanding and controlling complex weapons system, the difficulties of determining rapidly whether an attack is deliberate or accidental, and the rapid escalation of warfare that is possible under modern conditions. A plane that dropped a nuclear weapon by mistake in Western Europe might trigger an accidental war. See SECOND-STRIKE, INVULNERABILITY, CATALYTIC WAR, FAIL-SAFE.

AIRLIFT. The transporting of military equipment and troops by air. The airlift is a modern means of greatly increasing the mobility of combat units. In the fall of 1963, the United States Army and Air Force airlifted more than 15,000 troops to Europe in a dramatic demonstration of troop mobility.

ALLIANCE. A grouping or coalition of nations for the purpose of achieving some common objective that could not be achieved by any of the nations singly. In modern military affairs, alliances have extended into peacetime, as opposed to the traditional limitation of military alliances (with forces under central command) to wartime. Principal military alliances today are the North Atlantic Treaty Organization—NATO (1949), and the Soviet-dominated Warsaw Pact (1955). Western alliances of lesser importance include the Southeast Asia Treaty Organization—SEATO (1954), and the Central Treaty Organization—CENTO (1955). The concept of the military alliance in war-time is as ancient as the art of war itself. The English word comes from the Old French, and was originally derived from the Latin word "to bind to," or "fasten to."

ARMS CONTROL. The attempt to place limits upon the development, deployment, and use of weapons, particularly those of a highly destructive or indiscriminate nature, in order to increase international stability. The Limited Nuclear Test-Ban Treaty of 1963 is a form of arms control. Arms control may or may not include partial disarmament, but is usually considered a prerequisite for proceeding to general and complete disarmament.

ARMS RACE. The active competition among nations in developing and building up armaments. During the 1950s and into the 1960s, there was a very active arms race between the United States and the Soviet Union, particularly involving the development of nuclear weapons and delivery systems. One object of arms control measures is the prevention and control of arms races.

ATOMIC BOMB. A weapon that produces a tremendous release of energy through the fission (division) of nuclei of certain isotopes of either uranium or plutonium. Original detonation released energy equivalent to 20,000 tons of high explosives (TNT). Used twice against Japan during the Second World War, it was first developed by the United States (1945) and subsequently developed by the Soviet Union (1949), United Kingdom (1952), France (1960), and the People's Republic of China (1964). Serves as triggering device for thermonuclear (fusion) weapons. "Atomic" is a misnomer, since all chemical reactions are atomic. The atomic bomb should be called a "nuclear fission" bomb.

BALLISTIC MISSILE. A warhead-carrying projectile powered by a rocket motor only during the first part of its flight, with the resulting impetus carrying the warhead on to its target in an arcing trajectory. Technically, any projectile with a period of unpowered flight (such as a bullet fired from a rifle) is a ballistic missile, but the term is now generally reserved for the special case of certain nuclear weapons systems. Ballistic is derived through Latin from the Greek word for "to throw." In ancient armies a *ballista* was a machine for throwing projectiles against the enemy.

BLAST EFFECT. One measure of the destructiveness of weapons, usually used in reference to nuclear weapons. The blast effect is the amount of physical damage, as opposed to radiation and thermal damage, that results from a nuclear explosion. Often measured in terms of types and extent of damage at given distances from **GROUND ZERO,** or the point at which a bomb is detonated.

BUTTON. A slang expression indicating the means for starting a nuclear war. Derived from a popular misconception that in the age of computers, one need only "push a button" in order to start war. Compare "when the button is pushed (or mashed)" to the earlier expression, "when the balloon goes up."

CAPABILITY. The military potential of a nation, usually expressed in terms of specific weapons and the ability to produce them. The "missile-gap" of the late 1950s was based upon intelligence estimates of the Soviet Union's ability to build missiles. See **INTENTIONS.** Capability can also indicate that a nation has the means to wage a particular type of war, such as having a nuclear capability, or a conventional capability.

CATALYTIC WAR. A war precipitated between two or more powers through actions involving an outside power, whether by deliberate design of the outside power or by accident. In a situation of nuclear instability, an attack by a small nuclear power against a great nuclear power might bring on general nuclear war between the great powers. One argument for the French *force de dissuasion* is that its limited capability might be sufficient to start a general nuclear war between the United States and the Soviet Union if France's interests were mortally threatened. Catalytic is a term borrowed from chemistry, and is based upon the Greek word for "able to dissolve." See ACCIDENTAL WAR, STABILITY.

CEP. Circle of Error Probability: a measure of the statistical accuracy of launched missiles. The CEP is the radius of the circle within which 50 percent of the missiles launched toward a given point can be expected to impact.

CITY-BARGAINING. A concept in modern nuclear war theory related to the conduct and control of a nuclear war after it has begun. A selective nuclear strike against one of the enemy's cities might induce him to cease his nuclear strikes against one's own territory, at the peril of further destruction to enemy cities. Thus the United States, in a nuclear war with the Soviet Union, might "bargain" by destroying one Soviet city in response to a Soviet nuclear attack, particularly against one or more U.S. cities, to try to bring the nuclear war under control. See CONTROLLED RESPONSE, SELECTIVE RESPONSE.

CIVIL DEFENSE. Protection of the civilian population of a nation under attack. The concept has generally come to describe measures taken to protect civilian populations from the effects of aerial bombardment. In the nuclear age, civil defense usually refers to protection either against the immediate blast effects or the delayed radioactive fallout of a nuclear explosion. Civil defense thermal or radiation fallout shelters are an essential part of an ABM system (q.v.) that might involve nuclear explosions over friendly territory. See HOSTAGES.

COMMAND AND CONTROL. The concepts, organization, and equipment involved in both the commanding of military action and the controlling of its scope and direction. With the efforts to harness any potential nuclear war, control has come to assume a much greater importance than ever before. Much of the contemporary sophisticated nuclear policy depends upon effective command and control, with all the complexities of organization and communication that they require. A nation that has a SECOND-STRIKE deterrence policy (q.v.) must have secure command and control arrangements. See CONTROLLED RESPONSE.

COMMITMENT. Either the act of consigning (e.g., troops) or of guaranteeing performance. In the first sense, the decision of a commander to employ forces in battle is a commitment. The United States committed ground forces in the war in Korea. In the second sense, commitment indicates determination to follow through on a policy decision, particularly when this involves a promise by one ally to defend the interests of another. The United States is committed to the war in South Vietnam, and is also committed to the defense of Europe. This latter commitment, often expressed in an American nuclear guarantee to Europe, has been one of the central pillars of NATO since its inception. See HOSTAGES.

CONFRONTATION. The act of two nations' challenging one another, often in military terms, or of two military forces' coming face to face. There was a serious confrontation between America and the Soviet Union during the October 1962 crisis over Soviet missiles deployed in Cuba.

CONTROLLED RESPONSE. A response, to an attack, that remains under careful command and control throughout (contrast with SPASM). Efforts to limit war, especially where there is an acute danger of escalation or nuclear war has already begun, depend to a great extent upon the ability of nations to retain control over their "answers" to provocation. With Selective and Flexible Response, Controlled Response forms a cornerstone of modern efforts to exert rational control over the conduct of warfare. See also FAIL-SAFE, LIMITED WAR, COMMAND AND CONTROL.

CONVENTIONAL WAR. Any war that does not involve modern weapons of mass destruction (ABC weapons), or that does not entail principally guerrilla actions. The conception of conventional war, or conventional weapons, necessarily changes as the popular conception of warfare changes. At present, a "conventional" war would be of the World War II (pre-Hiroshima) or Korean variety. "Conventional" weapons, on the other hand, might include just about anything, except the ABC weapons. The distinction is drawn between conventional and other types of war and weapons primarily to permit the setting of limits that all participants in a conflict can recognize and accept without there having to be a specific agreement.

COUNTER-CITY STRIKE. A nuclear attack against an enemy's cities. Counter-city strike is applicable in two principal instances: 1. as a second-strike strategy of deterrence, where the attacker maintains a limited number of invulnerable weapons systems which could still pose a threat of unacceptable damage to the enemy regardless of the enemy's actions (finite deterrence); 2. as a first-strike strategy, where the attacker has a small, vulnerable strike force (such as that of France), and could only hope to achieve deterrence by posing a threat of initiating a catalytic nuclear war or of bringing on "doomsday." See SECOND-STRIKE, FIRST-STRIKE.

COUNTERFORCE STRIKE. A nuclear attack against an enemy's forces (particularly his nuclear delivery systems), instead of his industrial areas or cities. Counterforce strike is applicable in two principal instances: 1. as a first-strike strategy of deterrence, where the attacker has a large number of vulnerable delivery systems, and would have to destroy an enemy's nuclear forces on the ground in order to escape destruction of his own forces or cities; 2. as a second-strike strategy, where the attacker wishes to spare the enemy's cities, in order to try to bring nuclear war under control. See FIRST-STRIKE, SECOND-STRIKE.

COUNTERINSURGENCY. Military operations designed to put down rebellion that has not become a formal civil war. Counterinsurgency usually entails operations against guerrilla forces. Insurgency is derived from the Latin words meaning "to rise up," and was introduced into English at the beginning of the nineteenth century.

COUP D'ETAT. The overthrow of a government by illegal or violent means. A French phrase meaning, literally, blow or stroke of state. Adopted into English at the beginning of the nineteenth century. South Vietnamese governments have been overthrown by frequent coups d'état.

CREDIBLE. Believable, or reliable. Used in deterrence theory to indicate a threat—for example, to retaliate against a nuclear attack—that an enemy (or a friend seeking reassurance) will believe could and would be carried out.

D-DAY. The date of the beginning of a military operation (in French, *Jour J*). The most famous D-Day was June 6, 1944. See H-HOUR.

DAMAGE ASSESSMENT. The process of determining how much damage has been inflicted upon an enemy, particularly in an air attack, in which case the assessment is based upon analysis of aerial reconnaissance information.

DAMAGE LIMITATION. The attempt to minimize the damage suffered in an attack by an enemy. Damage limitation is the essential purpose of an ABM system.

DECOY. In nuclear warfare, a dummy warhead included in a missile reentry body or launched from a plane in order to confuse enemy defense systems. One problem of an ABM system is the discrimination between those parts of a ballistic missile reentering the atmosphere that are decoys and those that are real warheads.

DELIVERY SYSTEMS. The physical means for directing nuclear weapons against an enemy, whether by missile, airplane, sampan, or suitcase. See WEAPONS SYSTEM.

DEPLOY. To place military force where it can effectively be brought to bear against an enemy. Thus ground troops are deployed in the field, Polaris submarines at sea. Deploy is descended through Old French from the Latin word for unfold. Related to "display." Adopted in French and English as a military term in the late eighteenth century.

DETERRENCE. In modern military terminology, the whole body of theory and policy related to the forestalling of hostile enemy action by convincing potential enemies of the sureness of retaliation to an unacceptable degree. Derived from the Latin words meaning "to frighten off." Used in English first with respect to behavior of criminals. Applied to military affairs only recently, although the concept is as old as war itself. Deterrence is used most often with respect to nuclear warfare and has many elaborate and complicated nuances and variations. Deterrence is essentially negative; when it fails, then actual military operations, defensive or offensive,

come into play. See FIRST-STRIKE, SECOND-STRIKE, COUN-
TER-CITY, COUNTERFORCE, CREDIBLE, UNACCEPTABLE
DAMAGE.

DIFFUSION. The spreading of the possession of nuclear
weapons among many nations. See PROLIFERATION, DIS-
SEMINATION. Also a process for separating isotopes of
fissionable materials for nuclear weapons manufacture
from nonfissionable isotopes while both are in a gaseous
state (the gaseous diffusion method). Diffusion is derived from the Latin word for the act of pouring out or
away.

DISSEMINATION. The providing of nuclear weapons or information regarding the technology of their production
to one nation by another. Dissemination is derived from
the Latin words for "to spread abroad." See DIFFUSION,
PROLIFERATION.

DIVISION-SLICE. The total number of a nation's military
forces deployed in a given area divided by the number
of divisions these forces either constitute or support.
Term often used to indicate the relative effectiveness of
forces of different nations where the size of actual combat divisions is different. For example, the American
division-slice in Europe is much larger than the Soviet
(i.e., each American division would, in theory, be more
effective).

EARLY-WARNING SYSTEMS. A series of radar-equipped systems for detecting and giving warning of airplane or
missile attack. In North America, Early-Warning Systems include BMEWS (Ballistic Missile Early-Warning
System, which also includes an installation in Britain),
the DEW Line (Distant Early-Warning), and the Pine
Tree Line. All are linked through elaborate communications systems to command and control centers.

ECM. Electronic countermeasures, for jamming air or missile defense systems. ECM are generally based upon the interception and deception of enemy defensive radar signals.

ESCALATION. The step-by-step expansion of the range, scope, or type of military action. A conventional war may escalate into a nuclear war. Escalation is derived (coined) from the Latin word for ladder, and has only recently entered the military vocabulary. Escalade—referring to scaling ladders—has been a military term for some time, appearing in English in the sixteenth century.

FAIL-SAFE. A procedure designed to prevent accidental nuclear war, introduced by the United States Air Force Strategic Air Command (SAC) in the 1950s. A bomber could not fly into enemy territory, or drop its bomb, without specific orders to do so. If these orders were not received, the bomber would return home without dropping its weapon. Therefore, a failure—such as in the failure to receive a radio message—would be a failure on the "safe" side, that would not accidentally trigger a nuclear war. Similar systems have subsequently been extended to other nuclear weapons systems. See ACCIDENTAL WAR, PERMISSIVE LINK.

FALLOUT. Residual radioactive particles from a fission weapon that descend to earth following detonation of the weapon, potentially producing burns, disease, death, or mutation, depending upon concentration and nature of radioactive isotopes. See TEST-BAN, CIVIL DEFENSE.

FBM. Fleet Ballistic Missile—Polaris missiles based at sea, with ranges of 1500 (A-2) and 2500 (A-3) nautical miles.

FINITE DETERRENCE. A theory of deterrence against nuclear war premised upon the maintenance of a relatively small and more economical number of invulnerable nuclear weapons delivery systems that could survive any attack and then cause unacceptable damage to the enemy. Essentially a counter-city deterrence strategy (few weapons), appropriate for second-strike deterrence (invulnerability).

FIRE-CONTROL SYSTEM. The equipment, men, and organization devoted to the physical direction and firing of a weapon against a target, as an antiaircraft gun against an airplane, or a ballistic missile against a city. Fire-Control Systems for very modern weapons systems make effective use of electronic computers.

FIRE-POWER. A measure of the armaments that could potentially be employed by a military force. Since most modern weapons are based upon some sort of explosive force, the term fire-power has become more or less all-inclusive. The fire-power of a fighter plane may be measured as so many rounds of ammunition fired, at a given number of rounds per second.

FIRST-STRIKE. The first attack in a nuclear war, by either side. A first-strike, to have any chance of success, must be a counterforce strike against the enemy's nuclear weapons systems; otherwise, the attacker lays himself bare to a retaliatory attack against his own cities that could prove unacceptable. A first-strike strategy might be adopted where an attacker has a vulnerable force, and must strike first (i.e., before being struck) if at all; where an attacker wishes to achieve "victory" through surprise attack, particularly against a strategically inferior nation (preventive war); where an attacker wishes to preempt a threatened enemy attack; or where a strategically inferior nation wishes to bring about catalytic war involving other powers. As a policy of deterrence, a first-strike strategy is unstable, since vulnerability of weapons systems means that decisions concerning retaliation must be taken quickly, if at all. See MASSIVE RETALIATION, SPASM, WARNING TIME, PREEMPTION, PROVOCATION, ACCIDENTAL WAR.

FLEXIBLE RESPONSE. A military action, in response to an enemy attack, that is appropriate in type, size, and location to the initial attack. In nuclear theory, this implies that a target system can be altered to suit changing conditions of warfare. In general, a flexible response capability implies the existence of a range of military force sufficient to permit a variable strategy to meet changing conditions. A flexible response capability would permit greater control of wars in progress, help prevent automatic escalation into nuclear warfare, provide a measure of deterrence at all levels of warfare, and permit a more economical, effective waging of wars once they have begun. With a flexible response strategy, a limited conventional war, for example, could be fought with forces appropriate to such a war, or a limited nuclear attack could be met by an appropriate, tailored response. See CONTROLLED RESPONSE, SELECTIVE RESPONSE.

FORCE DE FRAPPE (DE DISSUASION). The French nuclear striking force. Later renamed the dissuasion force, in order to stress the deterrent role cast for it.

FORCE GOALS. The projected size and composition of a military force, in terms of equipment, men, and organization. Often used with regard to NATO, where the establishment and fulfillment of force goals have presented problems throughout NATO's history.

FORCES-IN-BEING. Those military forces available for action at the beginning of a conflict (D-Day), as opposed to forces that would have to be mobilized. This is an important distinction in modern warfare, where, unlike the First and Second World Wars, the outcome of a conflict may depend solely upon those forces that can be brought to bear in a few hours.

FORWARD STRATEGY. A strategy that provides for the defense of an area or country as far forward as possible. The establishment of a Forward Strategy for NATO, in order to include the defense of Western Germany, involved one of the most important early strategic and political decisions of the NATO alliance.

GCD. General and Complete Disarmament. Any of a number of proposals for disarmament advocated at various times since the Second World War by several nations, principally the United States, the United Kingdom, and the Soviet Union. Disarmament itself is a concept with a long history.

GENERAL NUCLEAR WAR. Large scale strategic nuclear warfare involving the major nuclear powers. Possibly still subject to rational control, particularly with the further development and deployment of invulnerable nuclear delivery and command and control systems by the major nuclear powers.

GIGATON. A measure of energy released equivalent to one billion tons of high explosive (TNT). The combining form *giga-* means one billion times (10^9) a specified unit; from the Greek *Gigas,* giant.

GO NUCLEAR. Slang for "to begin to use nuclear weapons," perhaps as a result of escalation of a smaller conflict.

GRAND STRATEGY. The overall plan, involving the total resources of a nation, for achieving policy objectives for which a resort has been made to military force. The dividing line between strategy and grand strategy is unclear, and is constantly changing. In general, however, one may place under grand strategy the overall organization and plan to wage war, including military, economic, and psychological warfare. The British blockade of German ports during the First World War, a major cause of German defeat, is usually considered to have been grand strategy of the economic warfare variety. The concept of grand strategy is a relatively new one that has come to prominence in the twentieth century.

GUERRILLA WAR. A war conducted by irregular forces operating independently in small groups, behind enemy lines or in areas nominally controlled by the enemy. Guerrilla also refers to one engaged in such operations: a partisan. Guerrilla is adopted from Spanish, and is a diminutive form of the word for war. Introduced into English in the early part of the nineteenth century.

GUIDANCE SYSTEM. The means for directing missiles and aircraft to target. A guidance system may be of any one of several varieties, including: heat-seeking, radio, radar, and sonar, all of which are subject to jamming by an enemy; stellar guidance, which relies upon star-sighting; television scanning; and inertial guidance, which is almost impossible to jam. American ballistic missiles usually rely upon the self-contained inertial guidance, and theoretically could also use a supplementary, or terminal, guidance system for the last part of their ballistic flight.

HARD TARGET. A target constructed to resist a considerable overpressure (perhaps 100 pounds per square inch) from a nuclear explosion.

HARDENED AND DISPERSED. Referring to missiles (such as the Minuteman) placed in underground silos that are both well protected (hardened) to resist nuclear attack, and set far apart (dispersed) to make their destruction more difficult, and make the missiles less vulnerable. A second-strike deterrent strategy (or a variation of it, finite deterrence) is dependent upon missiles, such as those hardened and dispersed, which can survive a large-scale nuclear attack and then be delivered against enemy targets.

HARDWARE. Military equipment; in particular, the equipment involved in nuclear delivery systems. See SOFT-WARE.

H.E. WEAPONS. High Explosive Weapons of conventional (non-nuclear) composition; generally TNT.

H-HOUR. Hour of the beginning of a military operation. See D-DAY.

HOSTAGE. Person held captive by an enemy as a pledge of good conduct by the hostage's own nation. An ancient practice, which in the nuclear age includes every civilian population potentially threatened by nuclear destruction. In Europe, American troops and their families are, in effect, hostages to insure the continuing commitment of America to defend Europe (with nuclear weapons, if necessary), if Europe were attacked. The term hostage was adopted through the Old French from the Latin word for hostage. Appeared in English in the thirteenth century.

HOT-LINE. A direct line of communication between military commanders or political leaders for rapid consultation in an emergency. The most famous Hot–Line is that established between Washington and the Kremlin, to permit U.S.-Soviet communications, particularly in the event of an accident involving nuclear weapons. This particular Hot-Line tends to decrease the likelihood of an accidental nuclear war.

HYDROGEN BOMB. See THERMONUCLEAR WEAPON.

ICBM. Intercontinental Ballistic Missile (range generally greater than 3000 miles). In the American nuclear arsenal, ICBMs include the Atlas, Titan, and Minuteman. Because of the targets it can cover, the Polaris missile based at sea (FBM) can also be considered an ICBM. See MISSILE.

INCURSION. Invasion, particularly a sudden or unexpected one. The United States sent forces to Korea to repel the Communist incursion into South Korea. Derived from the Latin word for "to incur, run in, invade." Used in English as a military term since the mid-fifteenth century.

INFILTRATE. To pass troops or subversive agents through enemy lines singly or in small groups, where they either reform into regular military units, operate as guerrilla bands, engage in sabotage, or the like. Can also describe any kind of stealthy, piecemeal invasion, as the infiltration of an army or government by agents loyal to a foreign power. Infiltration of North Vietnamese-trained troops into South Vietnam has been one of the major problems of the war in Southeast Asia.

INFRASTRUCTURE. The fixed installations that an armed force requires in order to operate. Infrastructure includes airfields, fuel dumps, communications systems, headquarters, supply depots. The term is taken from the French railroad term for the fixed parts of the railroad system, such as bridges, gradings, and tunnels (*infra*, below). The development of infrastructure has been particularly important to NATO, where the ability to maintain, supply, move, and operate forces must be insured before the beginning of any European war.

INTENTIONS. Actually determined plans of action. Often used in comparison with capabilities in evaluating possible courses of enemy action. For example, the Soviet Union had the capability to produce a large number of ICBMs during the 1950s, but their actual intentions were to produce far fewer. The assumption by Western intelligence that Soviet intentions would be equal to their capabilities produced the widely held belief that the Soviets possessed a large lead in the production of ICBMs.

INTERDICTION. Prohibition. In military terms, to prevent an enemy from using some of its forces by destroying them or the means of deploying or supplying them. Interdiction forces are those assigned the task of prohibiting enemy use of military force, particularly in the case of air defense systems, communication systems, supply or troop concentrations. In nuclear warfare, interdiction forces would destroy air or missile defenses in order that strategic forces could strike primary military, industrial, or city targets.

IRBM. Intermediate Range Ballistic Missile (range generally between 1000 and 2500 miles). The American nuclear arsenal has included the IRBMs Thor and Jupiter. See MISSILE.

INVULNERABILITY. The ability of military forces to survive attack. Particularly used with regard to nuclear strike forces that can survive almost any nuclear attack, and then be employed. Relatively invulnerable missiles (or, more properly, missiles with relatively low vulnerability), such as Polaris and Minuteman, are essential to second-strike deterrence, finite deterrence, and mutual deterrence. An invulnerable missile is one that can survive (underwater or underground) an overpressure in the range of 100 pounds per square inch (psi). See HARDENED AND DISPERSED.

JUNTA. A ruling or administrative council, often composed of military officers, in the absence of a properly constituted civilian government. The military junta has become commonplace in South America, the Middle East, and Southeast Asia. Term adopted directly from Spanish (and descended from the Latin word for "to join") at the beginning of the nineteenth century.

KILOTON. A measure of energy released equivalent to 1000 tons of high explosives (TNT). Formed from the Greek word for one thousand.

KRIEGSPIEL. Literally, *wargame*. Military moves are simulated either on paper by individuals representing commanders of opposing forces, or in the field with the deployment and maneuver of actual military forces. Wargaming is especially valuable for testing, by means short of actual combat, such things as the validity of military theory, the effectiveness of equipment, and the quality of training. Adopted directly from the German (early nineteenth-century development, in Switzerland), although usually translated into the English wargame.

LIMITED WAR. A war that is deliberately limited in scope and extent through the communication to an enemy of specific restraints placed upon one's own forces. In modern warfare, Korea was a limited war, in that the United Nations Command placed specific constraints upon its own actions—such as not attacking airbases in Manchuria—in order to prevent the spread or escalation of the conflict. More generally, limited war can refer to any conflict limited in scope.

LOCAL WARS. Wars that remain confined to a local area and do not spread to other countries or become world-wide. The intermittent fighting between Pakistan and India was—when it broke out—a local war.

LOGISTICS. The important branch of military affairs dealing with certain functions in support of actual combat forces. Although the definition of logistics varies and is rarely used with precision or consistency, it has included such functions as supply, transportation, quartering of troops, evacuation of wounded, and, according to some definitions, even the development of weapons systems. Logistics is adapted from a French word based partly upon the word for "to lodge," and partly upon the Greek word for reckoning, or accounting.

MASSIVE RETALIATION. A nuclear doctrine elaborated in the United States during the late 1940s and early 1950s, under which a Soviet nuclear attack against the United States or Europe, or a major ground attack against Europe, would be met by a large-scale bombardment of the Soviet Union with American nuclear weapons. Abandoned by most major powers, today, but still attractive to France and some smaller powers as a deterrent policy. See SPASM.

MILITARY ALPHABET. An alphabet in which every letter is represented by a word, in order to insure precise communication of information, particularly where codes, initials, or abbreviations are being used. The alphabet currently used by the Western powers is designed so that each word can be pronounced reasonably well by non-English-speaking people. This alphabet makes it possible, for example, for everyone in NATO to use the same military alphabet. Alfa, Bravo, Charlie, Delta, Echo, Foxtrot, Golf, Hotel, India, Juliett, Kilo, Lima,

Mike, November, Oscar, Papa, Quebec, Romeo, Sierra, Tango, Uniform, Victory, Whiskey, X-ray, Yankee, Zulu.

MEGATON. A measure of energy released equivalent to one million tons of high explosive (TNT). Formed on the Greek word for great.

MISSILE. In modern military terminology, a warhead-carrying projectile that is both pilotless and self-propelled. Most missiles are equipped with some form of guidance. Propulsion may be by jet or ramjet, but most commonly by rocket motor, in which both fuel and oxidizer are stored and burned, thus making the missile independent of the atmosphere. Missile is derived from the Latin word for missile weapon, itself based on the word for "to send." Hence, any projectile is a missile, although there has been a severe restriction of meaning in contemporary usage. Missiles in use by American forces, today, range from the battlefield antiaircraft Red-Eye, to the many-thousand-mile-range Titan II.

MIXED-MANNED. Composed of men of more than one nation's military forces. The United States' proposal for a multilateral force for NATO included surface vessels that would be mixed-manned with sailors from several nations.

MOBILITY. A measure of the extent and speed at which military forces can be moved from one place to another. Mobility of forces has always been an essential ingredient of strategy, and relative mobility often determines the outcome of battles. Considerable emphasis is now being placed upon increasing the mobility of military forces, particularly in order to bring outside force to bear in local war situations. Mobility is derived from the Latin word for "mobile, movable," but it did not enter the military vocabulary until the late nineteenth century.

MRBM. Mid- (or Medium-) Range Ballistic Missile (range generally between 200 and 1000 miles). In the American arsenal, the Pershing and the Redstone are MRBMs.

MULTILATERAL FORCE (MLF). A proposed military force to be composed of 25 surface ships, each carrying eight Polaris 2500 nautical-mile missiles, and manned by crews of mixed nationality. Command and control of the force would be shared by all participating NATO nations, although the United States, at least initially, would retain an ultimate veto over the use of the nuclear armed missiles. The MLF was conceived by the United States as a means of limiting the spread of nuclear weapons and of strengthening the bonds of the NATO alliance. Proposal moribund in 1966. Multilateral means having many sides.

MULTINATIONAL FORCE. A proposed nuclear force within NATO composed of elements of the nuclear weapons delivery systems of participating nations. Command and control of national forces, however, could be reserved by a participating nation at any time. French reluctance prevented this force from coming into being, although the United States and the United Kingdom (1963) assigned to NATO the forces intended for the Multinational Force (renamed the Inter-Allied Force).

MUTUAL DETERRENCE. A situation in which two or more nations are deterred by one another. In the nuclear age, mutual deterrence is achieved with a high degree of stability only when contending nuclear powers both possess an invulnerable second-strike deterrent capability and there is a degree of strategic parity. Mutual deterrence, in the absence of technological breakthroughs that destroy it, produces nuclear stalemate, or deadlock.

NEUTRON BOMB. A theoretical nuclear weapon that would release great quantities of neutrons, thereby destroying life in an enemy nation, but causing no physical destruction because of the absence of blast effect at ground level.

NO-CITIES DOCTRINE. A modern nuclear doctrine elaborated in the United States, whereby an enemy would be given an incentive to spare American cities in a nuclear attack by having his own cities spared. See SELECTIVE RESPONSE, COUNTERFORCE STRIKE, SECOND-STRIKE.

NUCLEAR THRESHOLD. The point, in the escalation of any conflict, beyond which nuclear weapons would be employed; i.e., the war would GO NUCLEAR (q.v.).

OPTIONS. The various courses of action open to a military commander or policy maker. This term has been used, to a great extent, in wargaming, in decisions regarding which weapons to develop, and in the development of the doctrine of flexible response.

OVERKILL. The portion of a nuclear arsenal that could be delivered on a target beyond that necessary to demolish or "kill" the target.

OVERPRESSURE. The increase in air pressure against a target resulting from the blast effect of an explosion. Used to describe both the destructive capabilities of nuclear weapons and the degree of vulnerability of potential targets. See SOFT TARGET, HARD TARGET.

PACIFICATION. The quelling of a revolt or guerrilla war. American and South Vietnamese troops are attempting the pacification of areas of South Vietnam dominated by the Viet Cong (Vietnamese Communists).

PARA-MILITARY. Any extra-military actions in support of military operations. When related to counterinsurgency operations, para-military forces might be expected to carry out such seemingly nonmilitary duties as providing medical care for civilians, assisting with agricultural development, and in general winning over, by nonmilitary activities, civilian noncombatants in a military (particularly guerrilla) campaign. *Para*, derived from the Greek word for "beside" or "beyond."

PAUSE. In NATO strategy, the period following the containment, by conventional forces, of a conventional attack in Europe. During this period, the aggressor would have time to consider whether to continue attacking, and thus risk nuclear retaliation, or to cease hostilities. Similarly, forces sufficient to force a pause would enable NATO commanders to deliberate carefully over the use of nuclear weapons, rather than having to use them immediately. See SPASM, TRIP WIRE.

PENETRATION AIDS. Equipment carried in the reentry body of a missile or in an attacking aircraft to confound enemy defense systems.

PERMISSIVE-LINK. One element in the mechanism of a nuclear weapon that must be completed or supplied before the weapon can be armed or launched. An early permissive-link system consisted of "keys" that had to be inserted in nuclear weapons by one or more responsible officers in order to arm the weapons. More sophisticated permissive-link systems might require reception of a coded radio signal from highest command headquarters by a receiver physically integrated into a nuclear weapon's arming or firing mechanism. A permissive-link system increases the effectiveness of command and control, and decreases the chances of accidental nuclear war. See FAIL-SAFE.

POLICY. The highest designs and plans of government, the object and end of military affairs. Grand strategy, strategy, and tactics are all geared to achieve the policy, or objectives, of a particular government or quasi-government (such as an insurgent council of war). Policy (like the word politics) is derived through Latin from the Greek word for government or constitution, whose root means city or state. See GRAND STRATEGY, STRATEGY, and TACTICS.

POLITICO-MILITARY. Referring to theory, policy, or actions that combine political effort with military effort. Concerned with the melding of military and political methods and ideas to attain ultimate policy objectives. In the war in South Vietnam, for example, politico-military activities are essential in order to create sufficient political stability within the country for military actions to have any real COUNTERINSURGENCY (q.v.) value.

PREEMPTION. An attack designed to forestall an attack against one's own forces or cities. Preemption differs from preventive war if there is some reason—such as the existence of some sort of provocation—to believe that an enemy is preparing to attack. A preemptive attack is designed to "beat the enemy to the punch." See FIRST-STRIKE.

PREVENTIVE WAR. A war waged against a militarily inferior power before that power has an opportunity to achieve strategic parity with the attacking nation. Unlike a preemptive attack, a preventive war requires no provocation to justify it but is fought only for its value in the long run. There was some support for an American preventive war against the Soviet Union during the period when the U.S. had a monopoly of nuclear weapons; this might have eliminated the possibility of a later war, at poorer odds for the United States. There was a similar suggestion with regard to the People's Republic of China, about the time of the Korean War.

PROLIFERATION. The increase in the number of nations possessing nuclear weapons. (When weapons possession *diffuses* among many nations, perhaps through *dissemination* of information, *proliferation* takes place.) Many strategists consider the proliferation of nuclear weapons capabilities to be the central problem of international military affairs during the late 1960s and 1970s. Proliferation is based upon the Latin word for offspring, and has long been used in biology to denote budding or division.

PROVOCATION. A challenge or stimulus. An excuse, real or fabricated, for starting a war. In nuclear terms, the possession of vulnerable weapons by a nation might be provocative, since, as they must be used at the start of a nuclear war in order to be effective at all, these weapons might inspire a preemptive attack. See FIRST-STRIKE.

R. & D. Research and Development. In the military sense, the process, prior to actual production, of creating new weapons, equipment, and weapons systems. In the American defense establishment, the process is sometimes extended to R.D.T. & E., for Research, Development, Test, and Evaluation.

REENTRY BODY. The fore-end of a ballistic missile, capable of withstanding the tremendous heat of friction during reentry of the missile, following its arcing, ballistic trajectory, into the atmosphere. The reentry body, protected by a heat-shielding nose cone, contains the warhead, and may also contain decoy devices, penetration aids, and a terminal guidance system.

RETALIATION. An attack on an enemy in response to his initial attack. It may be a response in kind or, particularly in a nuclear war, it may take some other form in order to bring the war under control. Derived from the Latin words meaning "re-such-like," and referring to punishment similar to the original injury.

ROLES AND MISSIONS. The duties assigned to particular military forces; the place within overall strategy that particular forces occupy. The U.S. Navy, for example, has both a nuclear and a conventional role, and missions that include nuclear strikes against enemy targets, interdiction of enemy forces, air support for ground actions, and the securing of sea lines of communication.

SCENARIO. The manner in which a military action is expected to unfold. Particularly useful in wargaming and in projecting the probable responses of an enemy to a given course of action. Scenario is borrowed from the theater and is derived from the Greek word for stage or scene.

SECOND-STRIKE. An attack in a nuclear war by a nation that has already absorbed a first-strike. A second-strike can be directed either against an enemy's cities (see FINITE DETERRENCE), or against his forces in an attempt to bring the war under control and spare cities. The essence of second-strike is the ability of a nation to "ride-out" a nuclear attack, through the possession of invulnerable, sophisticated weapons systems, and still cause unacceptable damage to an enemy. A second-strike strategy, as a policy of deterrence, tends to increase nuclear stability: since decisions regarding retaliation do not have to be made within the limits of warning time, a preemptive attack against a second-strike force would be to no avail, and use of a second-strike force alone could not possibly

save the attacker from unacceptable damage in retaliation. A large second-strike force might appear to be
capable of a FIRST-STRIKE (q.v.) and, hence, be provocative. But if the enemy also has a second-strike force,
then the large force becomes, instead, a means for bringing a war under control (through sparing of cities) even
after the war has progressed to the point of second-
strikes. See MUTUAL DETERRENCE, HARDENED AND DIS-
PERSED, INVULNERABILITY, HOT-LINE, NO-CITIES DOC-
TRINE, CONTROLLED RESPONSE, FLEXIBLE RESPONSE,
SELECTIVE RESPONSE.

SELECTIVE RESPONSE. An answer to an enemy attack that is
highly discriminate in choice of targets and method of
attack, in order to gain maximum value from the employment of force, or to communicate intentions to an
enemy (e.g., the desire that cities be spared in any
nuclear exchange). A selective, controlled response can
be useful in preventing further escalation, or in deter-
ring an enemy from further ventures. A selective nuclear
response against one enemy city, for example, might
serve as a warning of ability and willingness to attack
cities generally, unless the enemy ceased its own provocative activities. See CITY-BARGAINING, FLEXIBLE RE-
SPONSE.

SOFT TARGET. Any target capable of surviving an overpressure of only a few pounds per square inch. Cities
are generally considered to be soft targets.

SOFTWARE. A slang expression sometimes used to indicate
the organization and command and control arrangements that accompany HARDWARE (q.v.).

SPASM. An immediate nuclear response to an enemy attack
(real or imagined), made necessary by the attacked
nation's either lacking sufficient ground forces to contain

a major enemy ground attack, or lacking an invulnerable second-strike capability that could survive a major nuclear attack. One of the primary reasons for preventing the proliferation of nuclear weapons capabilities is the danger of spasm responses by nations with primitive delivery systems. These responses might lead to catalytic, or accidental, nuclear war. Derived from the Greek word for "to tug." See MASSIVE RETALIATION, FIRST-STRIKE, WARNING TIME.

SPECIAL FORCES. An American term for soldiers especially trained for types of warfare involving other than conventional infantry or armored engagements. In particular, Special Forces might take part in para-military, counterguerrilla, or counterinsurgency operations, or serve as instructors in these fields.

SRBM. Short-Range Ballistic Missile (range generally less than 100 miles). An American SRBM is the Corporal missile.

STABILITY. In a military sense, the degree to which war can be expected not to occur. In the nuclear age, military stability is increased by mutual deterrence, and the possession by all major nuclear powers of invulnerable second-strike deterrent capabilities. An approximate parity of strategic forces, in general, tends to contribute to the enhancing of military stability. Stability is derived from the Latin word meaning "to stand."

STRATEGY. The art of planning the major military operations of war. Although the distinction between tactics and strategy is not a clear one, and subject to constant redefinition, strategy is generally concerned with the larger movements of forces, with decisions regarding their employment, and with other activities, including political and economic efforts against the enemy (though here, the definition of strategy begins to overlap with that of grand strategy). With the development of warfare, the concept of strategy has grown and expanded as well. Strategy is derived from the Greek word for generalship. See POLICY, GRAND STRATEGY, TACTICS.

SUBSYSTEM. A component part of a weapons system. In the case of a missile weapons system, the subsystems might include command, communications, resupply, platform, missile, fire-control, launch, guidance, reentry body, and warhead.

SWORD AND SHIELD. A NATO strategy, elaborated during the 1950s, whereby conventional forces would serve as a shield against Soviet attack (see TRIP WIRE) and nuclear weapons would serve as the sword, for retaliation against any major assault on NATO European countries. Since 1962, there has been an effort in NATO to reverse the roles of conventional and nuclear forces with respect to Sword and Shield.

TACNUK. Tactical Nuclear Weapon. A fission weapon of low yield, often considered to be of an explosive power of less than ten kilotons. Includes battlefield nuclear weapons, such as the American Sergeant and Honest John missiles, and weapons with an interdiction role.

TACTICAL NUCLEAR WAR. A war fought with small nuclear weapons directed, not against cities, industrial areas, or strategic nuclear forces, but against battlefield troops, airfields, communications, and enemy tactical nuclear weapons. Many strategists believe that a tactical nuclear war could not be fought without escalating immediately into a strategic nuclear war, particularly in an area as densely populated as Europe.

TACTICS. The art of the actual ordering and employment of military forces in battle, from the lowest level up to the point, which is ill-defined, when the direction of operations falls within the province of STRATEGY (q.v.). Tactics is derived from the Greek word meaning "to set in order." See POLICY, GRAND STRATEGY.

TAKE OUT. Slang for destroy (e.g., a city, or an enemy nuclear force).

TEST-BAN. An agreement prohibiting the testing of nuclear weapons. In 1963, a Limited Nuclear Test-Ban Treaty was signed by most nations of the world (notable exceptions: France and the People's Republic of China), prohibiting the testing of nuclear weapons in the atmosphere, under water, or in space. The Limited Test-Ban Treaty was concluded in order to reduce the amount of accumulated fallout in the atmosphere, to slow down the arms race, to inhibit the development of nuclear weapons by powers not already possessing them, and to increase the chances of further agreements to increase international stability.

THERMONUCLEAR WEAPONS. Weapons producing tremendous energy through the fusion, at ultra-high temperatures, of the nuclei of certain isotopes of hydrogen and other light elements (hence, the name "Hydrogen Bomb," or "H-Bomb," applied to these weapons). The basic weapons in the nuclear arsenals of the United States, the Soviet Union, and the United Kingdom, with potential delivery by either bombers or missiles. First thermonuclear reactions achieved by U.S. in 1952, Soviet Union in 1953 (first deliverable weapon), and United Kingdom in 1957. Largest weapon detonated (USSR) believed to have been in the order of 100 megatons.

TRIP WIRE. A concept elaborated for NATO during the 1950s, and later modified, whereby only enough conventional forces would be maintained to force a potential aggressor to make a fairly large-scale conventional attack against Western Europe before provoking nuclear retaliation. Once overwhelmed, these trip-wire forces would presumably have touched off a major nuclear war.

UMBRELLA. A guarantee of protection granted to one nation by another. In nuclear terms, a guarantee to retaliate against certain kinds of threats or attacks against an ally by an enemy nation. Western Europe, for example, is protected by the American nuclear umbrella.

UNACCEPTABLE DAMAGE. That amount of potential destruction to an enemy's forces, industrial areas, or cities that would deter it from provoking an attack that would result in that amount of destruction. Unacceptable damage, along with CREDIBILITY (q.v.), is the cornerstone of most nuclear deterrence theories.

WARGAME. See KRIEGSPIEL.

WARNING TIME. The amount of time between receipt of the first indications of an actual nuclear attack and the attack itself. With the advent of ICBMs, warning time may have decreased to a matter of a few minutes (perhaps four minutes for the United Kingdom, fifteen minutes for the United States). Because of this development, the invulnerable, second-strike deterrent capability has increased in importance, for purposes of preventing accidental nuclear war, obviating the need for a spasm response, and permitting attacked nations to make rational decisions without being constrained by the brief warning time.

WEAPONS SYSTEM. An integrated system, extending from command to weapon detonation, that includes all components (subsystems) necessary for employment of the weapon. A concept developed since the Second World

War for purposes of producing, deploying, employing, and supporting certain weapons (e.g., nuclear delivery systems) rapidly, efficiently, and effectively, with high priority placed on command and control arrangements.

YIELD. The destructive power of a weapon. In nuclear weapons, yield is measured in tons, kilotons, megatons, or gigatons of high explosive (TNT).

CHAPTER **3**

Farther than Infinity, Longer
than Forever

The Language of Philosophy

DANIEL J. SULLIVAN

In its beginnings with the Ionian Greeks, philosophy
simply took over the language of everyday speech and
adapted it to its own ends. Thus, what Democritus named
"atoms" were originally the "seeds" of Anaxagoras. Empedocles called the primal elements "roots" and used the
terms "love" and "strife" to describe the forces of attraction
and repulsion. As philosophical thought became more complex and more refined, everyday terms took on specialized
connotations which transcended the original content of
meaning; for example, *nous,* or mind, which in Anaxagoras
was a mechanical and material principle, became an immaterial power in Plato; *psyche,* or soul, the breath in the
body in popular belief, became the *attunement* of the body
for the Pythagoreans and the incorporeal principle of life
for the Platonists. Technical neologisms are very rare in
ancient philosophy, and even the most specialized terms
conceal metaphors based on some primitive sense observation.

61

The early Greek philosophers were, for the most part, gifted and leisured amateurs, but with the coming of the Sophists in the fifth century B.C., learning was put on a professional level. Language came under systematic and scientific investigation, and for the first time a clear-cut and conscious distinction was made between a thing and its name, between the laws of nature and the conventions of language.

In the exuberance of their new discoveries, the Sophists overemphasized the versatility of language, and in reaction to the extravagances and word trickery of the rhetoricians, Socrates worked out the techniques of definition. Plato, his pupil, went on to elaborate what is really the first technical vocabulary of any consequence. Two of his dialogues, *Euthydemus* and *Cratylus,* deal with the mysteries of language.

We owe to Socrates the refining of many of our key terms in ethics: words like *virtue, friendship, temperance, courage.* To Plato we owe the first technical exploration of words like *idea, form;* we also owe to him the first sketch of the language of psychology and the delineation of the various levels of knowing in the mind. To Aristotle, above all, must go the credit for firming up the special language of philosophy, a technical elaboration to which philosophy is still indebted, and which is still reflected in everyday speech. We owe the technical term *matter* to Aristotle, and such everyday words as *informed, information, abstract, substantial, accidental, generic, specific.*

The technical vocabularies of Plato and Aristotle, Latinized, dominated the philosophy of the West until recent times and are by no means negligible even today. The Platonic language, more flexible and literary than the Aristotelian, persisted naturally wherever Platonism found its adherents: in Byzantium and among the Greek Fathers of the Church; with Plotinus in the West and his semi-disciples Augustine and Scotus Erigena. Through Augustine particularly, Platonic language became incorporated in the philosophy and theology of the early and middle Middle Ages. It enjoyed brief periods of revival in the Renaissance and early modern times.

In the Arabian world, in the Latin West of the later Middle Ages, and in early modern times the technical language of Aristotle was practically synonymous with the language of the learned world. Through the Stoics, especially Cicero, and through Boethius (d. 525), it had some currency even in the earlier Middle Ages, but what really established Aristotle in the western universities was the rediscovery of Aristotelian science, by way of the Arabs, in the thirteenth century. Practically speaking, Aristotelian science was the only science until the seventeenth century, and with the time lag characteristic of academic circles, continued to be taught well into the eighteenth. The philosophy that we call modern did not find its way into the universities until the very end of the eighteenth century. What was usually taught as philosophy in the European universities up until that time was some form of debased Aristotelianism, either a Catholic or a Protestant scholasticism. Even modern philosophy, through men like Leibnitz and Wolff on the continent and John Locke in England, inherited and perpetuated a good deal more of the Aristotelian philosophy and vocabulary than it is sometimes willing or able to recognize.

Nevertheless, one of the distinguishing marks of modern philosophy, starting with Descartes, is the return to a common-sense vocabulary in the everyday vernacular. The limpid clarity of Descartes' prose mirrors his doctrine of clear and distinct ideas, and John Locke's deceptively simple language reflects his declaration of war on "the learned but frivolous use of uncouth, affected or unintelligible terms."

As in the first age of philosophy, the new philosophy of the modern age remained in the hands of gifted amateurs until, in the eighteenth century, the German philosopher Wolff, a disciple of Leibnitz, married the new philosophy to the older scholastic forms and brought it into the schools. With Emmanuel Kant, a professor of philosophy at the University of Königsberg, philosophy once more took on a vocabulary and a structure which could be assimilated only through systematic study. Philosophy and the language of philosophy became more and more complicated and obscure with those who came after Kant, culminating in the despairing cry of Hegel on his deathbed: "One man has understood me, and even he has not."

The Cartesian ideal of clarity never quite died out in France and the English-speaking world, where the language of philosophy has remained fairly intelligible to the ordinary reader. Exception must be made of those philosophers for whom the passion for originality dictates the invention of a totally new and idiosyncratic technical language—the only distinction which, on analysis, some of these innovators can boast.

The last generation of philosophers has seen an endeavor to reduce philosophy to a particular kind of logic. Because of the ambiguities of everyday speech, a set of arbitrary symbols is proposed as an alternative, specialized language. To get rid of the further distortion of grammatical forms, a special calculus is employed to manipulate the symbols. The resultant complex is called symbolic logic; it is also called mathematical logic because mathematics is regarded as an extension of this kind of logic.

Symbolic logic is usually combined with certain philosophical presuppositions (often unspoken), such as the contention that only experiences that are directly verifiable through the senses are valid. Philosophy then becomes the logical analysis of statements of fact, and whatever is outside this type of analysis (such things as poetry, religion, metaphysics) must be regarded as nonsense. Philosophy, in short, is a highly specialized enterprise, employing a private language, known only to the initiates. It is, in fact, the science of logic, and philosophy in its older sense is either a fraud or a delusion.

Philosophy, however, has a habit of burying its undertakers, and in England, particularly, such men as Wittgenstein and Ryle, while remaining in the current of linguistic analysis, are restoring the primacy of everyday speech, "ordinary language," as somehow indicative of the way things really are.

Two other tendencies in contemporary philosophy have also tended to free philosophical discussion from the limitations of an esoteric vocabulary or the strictures of a symbolic method. One of these trends is the movement, especially strong in Germany, called *phenomenology*. Whereas modern philosophy has tended to concentrate so strongly on the preconditions of knowledge that it never gets around to the business of actual knowing, the phenomenologist says that we should bypass or at least postpone these concerns and start with the actual things we are exposed to, dwelling patiently on the phenomena present to our gaze until they deliver up their secret of meaning.

Another closely allied trend is the *existentialist* movement, which also stresses the importance of the immediately given, the dynamic actual existent, as against *static essences* and *sterile abstractions*.

Phenomenology and existentialism, to which we can add the classical humanism of men like Hutchins, Adler, Barr, Wild, Weiss, are a response to the urgency of contemporary problems: given man's present-day capacity for self-destruction, he no longer has time to play academic games; neither can he leave the fate of the world to the political naïveté of the professional scientist. And so while the academic philosopher has frequently abdicated his field to the poet, the novelist, and dramatist, the existentialist especially has taken up the traditional role of the philosopher in the examination of the global as well as the personal, the moral as well as the psychological, aspects of reality. The existentialist is normally non-academic and not infrequently he utilizes literary forms such as the novel and the play in order to elaborate and dramatize his philosophical insights. Once more, in short, philosophy talks the language of everyday speech.

Philosophical terms are sometimes classified according to the traditional divisions of philosophy: logic, epistemology, metaphysics, ethics, etc. However, the very names of the branches of philosophy offer difficulties of definition and are a subject of intense controversy. Thus, for some philosophers, ethics is a branch of psychology; psychology is sometimes made a branch of metaphysics; metaphysics itself may be regarded as a pure invention of the imagination. Even if agreement existed on the fields within philosophy, terms nevertheless cut across boundary lines: *accident*, for example, is a basic term for both logic and metaphysics; *good* and *evil* are significant terms for both metaphysics and ethics; *evolution* may be a physical, biological term, or it may be given cosmic and metaphysical scope. Therefore, because of the elasticity of philosophical boundaries and the multidimensional character of many terms, it has been thought preferable to list words in an alphabetical order.

The meanings given are primary and usually have universal acceptance. Definitions are free, of course, and if a philosopher like Engels wants to define *freedom* as "necessity" no one can stop him. Highly arbitrary and eccentric meanings, however, have been excluded. Some terms, such as *idea, nature, body,* are of enormous complexity, and their varying usages often reflect quite distinct philosophical positions. Like the knucklebone from which the paleontologist is said to reconstruct the entire skeleton of the dinosaur, many philosophies can be reconstructed merely from the way they define key words such as *idea, body, nature, being, cause.* Some effort has been made to suggest the versatility of such terms, although it is no exaggeration to say it would take a book to elaborate them properly; indeed, libraries have been written on each of them. Some terms, again, like the word *realism,* may change so much in the course of centuries as to be unrecognizable. Some attempt is made to mark these changes. Terms that are especially treacherous are also indicated.

WORD LIST

ACCIDENT. A being which cannot exist except as an aspect of some other being. The smile on a cat, the dimensions of a box, the color of a rose are called accidents. Aristotle and others have tried to classify all the possibilities of these secondary ways of existing. Aristotle's list: quantity, quality, relation, acting, being acted on, time, place, posture, ornamentation.

ACT. In metaphysics, the fullness of being, the actual as against the possible. In a secondary sense, operation. In its primary sense, Socrates would be said to be a man in act; that is, his primary being is to be a human being; in the secondary sense, he would be said to act as a philosopher or as a patriot.

AESTHETICS or **ESTHETICS.** The philosophy of art, concerning itself with the theoretical problems and standards of values as they relate to beauty and the arts. Only recently separated out as a distinct branch of philosophy, the name was coined by the German philosopher Baumgartner (d. 1762) from the Greek *aisthanomai*, to perceive, to feel, to become sensible. Sometimes now considered, along with ethics, as a branch of a wider philosophy of values called AXIOLOGY (q.v.).

ANALYTICAL PHILOSOPHY. See POSITIVISM.

ANTHROPOMORPHISM. The doctrine which depicts God or the gods as being like humans in shape or personality. Sometimes, by extension, to any metaphor comparing nonhuman to human; for instance, the depiction of the universe as a man on a large scale. From the Greek *anthropos*, man, and *morphe*, form.

A POSTERIORI. Of knowledge: knowledge based on sense experience. Of reasoning: from effect to cause. A posteriori proofs for the existence of God are those which start from some observation of the senses, such as the fact of change, and argue back to the ultimate cause of that fact. From the Latin, meaning "from that which comes after."

A PRIORI. Of knowledge: knowledge held independently of any sense experience. Of reasoning: from cause to effect. An example of an a priori proof for the existence of God is Descartes' argument from the idea of a perfect being to the necessity of its actual existence. For the German philosopher Kant, a priori is a specialized term signifying the structural forms within the mind. Just as a mold shapes the metal poured into it, so the mind shapes the raw material of experience, giving it the a priori forms of space, time, substance, cause, etc. Kant also called these forms CONCEPT and CATEGORY (q.q.v.). From the Latin, meaning "from that which is before."

ATOMISM. The doctrine that matter is composed of ultimate, irreducible particles called atoms. Theory first formulated by the Greek philosophers Leucippus and Democritus (fifth century B.C.). Greek atomism was the first formulation of one of the distinctive and recurrent patterns of philosophy: the quantitative, mechanical kind of explanation which sees the universe and everything in it as a kind of machine made up of interchangeable parts. From the Greek *a*, not, and *tomos*, cut.

AXIOLOGY. A recently coined word meaning the science of values in general. Major subdivisions are the field of aesthetics, which considers values in the world of art, and ethics, which treats of values in the world of morals. From the Greek *axios*, worth, and *logos*, science.

BEHAVIORISM. A name popularized by the American psychologist, John B. Watson, to describe his idea of the proper function of psychology: to study the outward and visible signs of man's behavior, as a scientist would describe a physical specimen of any kind. In practice the method tended to degenerate into pure physiology. Behaviorists have popularized the expressions *conditioning* and *conditioned reflex*. The United States and Russia (home of Pavlov and his salivating dogs) are two areas where behaviorism retains a serious following.

BEING. Whoever can say what being is, in all its implications, will have exhausted the science of metaphysics, which Aristotle called the primary philosophy. Being, for Aristotle, was both the richest and poorest of concepts: the richest in that it covers all reality, from God through man, animals, and atoms, down to pure possibilities; the poorest in that all that it declares in common of these things is that they are *not nothing*. Parmenides (b. 510 B.C.) is the first philosopher on record to isolate the notion of being. He gave it a rigidity which forced him to say that all reality is an unchanging, undifferentiated One. Everything is either the one thing, being, or *no thing*, nothing. Aristotle modified this position by putting possibilities within the realm of being; possibilities are *not nothing* and so they are *real*, even though they are not as real as fully existent beings. See META-PHYSICS, ONTOLOGY.

BODY. One of the most common and difficult words in philosophy. It is sometimes explained as matter, an even more difficult word. In the attempt to say what is really real about bodies, that is, what remains as ultimate behind all appearances and changes, these are some of the answers that have been given: various combinations of qualities, such as taste, color, moist and dry, hot and cold (the early Greek philosophers, the alchemists); quantity, which is inert, colorless, tasteless, etc., as in the early atomic theories; numbers (Pythagoreans); mathematical symbols (Jeans); collections of sensations (Berkeley, Hume); shadowy reflections of the eternal ideas (Plato and Platonists); a union of matter (non-sensible) and form (Aristotle and the Aristotelians). Part of the difficulty here lies in the fact that the question, "What is a body?" is susceptible to both scientific and philosophical answers, and the boundary lines are not always very carefully observed. Whoever gives a clear answer to this question, either in science or philosophy, will make a name for himself. See also MATTER.

CATEGORICAL IMPERATIVE. The phrase is from Kant and refers to the moral law, which has the character of an absolute command: duty must be done solely for the sake of duty. Conditional obligation, which relates to the means rather than the goal of moral action, can be referred to as a **HYPOTHETICAL IMPERATIVE**. The "categorical" in categorical imperative is taken from the language of logic, where it refers to an absolute or unconditioned statement.

CATEGORY. From the Greek word meaning statement. In logic and metaphysics the ultimate classes of reality. For Aristotle (whose list is tentative and exploratory) there are ten categories: substance and the nine accidents (quantity, quality, relation, acting, being acted on, time, place, posture, ornament). Kant gives a new division of categories corresponding to the A PRIORI (q.v.) conceptions supplied by the mind as a frame to sense experience. Kant's division is no longer accepted even by those whom he has influenced otherwise.

CAUSE. The definition of cause will vary in meaning and emphasis depending upon its philosophical context. Standing at first vaguely for any kind of influence of one thing on another, a cause came to mean anything which had to do directly with bringing about a change. Aristotle's enumeration of four types of cause as principles of change has put a permanent mark on philosophy. The four causes may be summarized as *that out of which* (material), *that to which* (formal), *that by which* (efficient), and *that for the sake of which* (final). Many contemporary philosophers, following in the path of Hume and John Stuart Mill, deny that cause has any meaning other than a statement of a hitherto unvarying sequence of antecedent and consequent. In other words, things we call cause and effect have followed one another consistently so far, but this does not imply any necessity that they will do so tomorrow; in plain English, there are no causes.

CONCEPT. See IDEA.

CONCEPTUALISM. See IDEA.

COSMOLOGY. The science of the cosmos; that branch of philosophy which concerns itself with theories about the origin and structure of the universe. Also called the *Philosophy of Nature* (the study of being as material and changing) and, an older name, *Cosmogony* (*cosmos + gonos,* begetting).

COSMOS. The word appears in the *Odyssey* in a phrase meaning to range things in order. In time the term took on overtones implying beauty, especially the beauty following on order, and in this sense it came to stand for the order and symmetry of the universe. By the fifth century B.C. it was used as a simple synonym for universe. Empedocles (d. 461 B.C.) was the first philosopher to use it in this sense.

CREATION. To bring existence out of nonexistence. Often associated with the theological notion, but the last century has seen the emergence of religiously indifferent philosophies of creation in Bergson, Whitehead, and the existentialists.

DETERMINISM. The theory that human actions are never free but are necessitated from within (psychological determinism) or from without (physical, economic determinism).

DIALECTIC. From the Greek word meaning "to converse." In the beginning, the process of discovering and testing truth by discussion. Zeno (b. 490 B.C.), who elaborated the famous paradoxes about the impossibility of change, is called by Aristotle "the father of dialectic." The peak of its development as a question-and-answer method of investigation can be seen in the early and middle dialogues of Plato.

Although really a precursor of logic, the term dialectics is still sometimes used in a broad and loose sense for logic in general. It had a highly specialized meaning in nineteenth-century philosophy starting with Hegel, for whom the processes working themselves out in reality follow the laws of thought unfolding in the mind. The World Soul is conceived as thinking out its thoughts (thesis, antithesis, synthesis), and these thoughts are the successive phases of reality. The world, in short, mirrors a kind of great cosmic dialectic. "What is rational is real, and what is real is rational."

Karl Marx, standing the idealism of Hegel on its head, reinterpreted the processes of reality as a *dialectical materialism;* that is, a dynamic materialism unfolding according to a certain internal logic.

DUALISM. A very elastic term which scholars cannot resist whenever they find two of anything. One of its widest applications refers to the division of reality between God and creation. A very ancient dualism is Zoroastrianism which sees the universe made up of two antagonistic realities, good and evil, light and darkness. In epistemology dualism may refer to the opposition between sense data and the objects they represent. Probably its most common use in modern philosophy is to describe the division of reality, following Descartes, into mind and matter, thought and extension. See also MONISM and PLURALISM.

EMPIRICISM. In general, the doctrine that all knowledge starts in the senses (Aristotle, Aquinas, Locke) often contrasted in modern philosophy with RATIONALISM (q.v.), which holds that the source of knowledge is in the reason, independent of any contribution from the senses (Plato, Descartes, Spinoza). Philosophers like Hume and Mill who hold that sensation is the only kind of knowledge are sometimes called *extreme empiricists*.

EPICUREANISM. The doctrine of Epicurus (341-270 B.C.) that pleasure is man's highest good. Epicurus held for a gradation of pleasures, with pleasures of the mind superior to pleasures of the body. This distinction tended to be blurred with his disciples and Epicureanism has come to mean, at least popularly, a life dedicated to an undiscriminating pursuit of sense pleasure. See HEDONISM.

EPISTEMOLOGY. The branch of philosophy which deals with the nature and explanation of knowledge. Other names: *critics, criteriology* (as dealing with the criteria of truth and certitude), *noëtics,* the *science of first principles,* the *philosophy of knowing.* From the Greek *episteme,* knowledge, and *logos,* science.

ESSENCE. What a thing is basically; its primary kind of being. Used in both a narrow and a wide sense. In a narrow sense, only of substances, natures capable of independent being, such as man, dog, flower. In a wide sense, for the "what-is-it-ness" of anything whatsoever. A Latin term that is thought to be a corruption of the Greek phrase, "What is it?"

ETHICS. The philosophy of morals. From the Greek *ethos,* meaning character or disposition. Some contemporary philosophers make Ethics a subordinate branch of AXIOLOGY (q.v.). From the Greek *axios* meaning worthy, precious.

EUDEMONISM. The ethical doctrine that makes well-being the ultimate goal of man's actions. The right living of the human life will eventuate in happiness. From the Greek words *eu,* well, and *daimon,* guardian spirit.

EVIL. In early religion and philosophy, a positive principle dividing the world with the contrary principle of the good. In Zoroastrianism identified with darkness and matter. A later version: the Manichaeism which attracted St. Augustine. The classical definition of evil in Western philosophy: the absence of a good that ought to be present.

EVOLUTION. The doctrine that interprets reality as a continuing process, an unfolding, a development. The term stretches from the field of biology to unlimited cosmic dimensions. Types of the latter in philosophy: **EVOLUTIONARY MECHANISM,** which says that physico-chemical processes are enough to account for the evolution of the world to its present complexity (Thomas Huxley, Spencer). **EVOLUTIONARY VITALISM,** which affirms a directive life principle, an *élan vital,* within reality; Bergson's *creative evolution* is an example. **EMERGENTISM,** which says that new dimensions of reality emerge from old, synthesizing into still newer forms, as in the sequence: matter, living matter, mind (Alexander, Whitehead).

EXISTENCE. The actuality of being, the affirmation *that* a thing is, in contrast to essence, which gives the abstract *what* of a thing.

EXISTENTIALISM. A movement in modern philosophy started by the Dane, Søren Kierkegaard (1813-1855). Later exponents: Jaspers, Heidegger, Sartre, each of whom says he has nothing in common with the others. Existentialism takes its name from the re-emphasis on the priority of existence over essence, in rebellion against academic philosophers who are supposed to live by choice in a tidier world of bloodless abstractions, of essences. Sartre says that man does not embody an essence which reflects a pre-existent pattern, but that he first exists and then by the exercise of his freedom gives himself a distinctive structure or essence.

FORM. For Plato, the idea, the independently existing archetype, such as treeness, whiteness, triangularity. For Aristotle, the positive, determining principle which gives things their basic way of being, and which combines with the limiting principle of matter to make up physical bodies. The mathematically minded philosophers tend to stress the formal, determined, permanent aspects of reality as against the changing and the indeterminate. The Greek word for form, *eidos*, like *idea*, is rooted in the Greek verb *idein*, to see.

FREEDOM. A "red light" word, to be carefully examined in the philosophical context in which it occurs. The classical descriptions of the levels of freedom, one or more of which are mirrored in the terminology of most philosophers, are as follows:

1. Freedom from coercion. Simple absence of constraint: as free as a bird.

2. Freedom of choice: the area of immediate decision, which is strongly affected by circumstances; the millionaire is freer than the wage-slave, the general has more freedom than the private, the libertine has a wider field than the monogamist.

3. Freedom of autonomy or self-rule: the inner freedom of the man who realizes to the full his inner capacities of self-discipline and development: the artist, the sage, the saint.

GOOD. Vaguely described as the object of all desire. A term interchangeable with BEING (q.v.) for the classical philosophers (Plato, Aristotle, and their disciples). This means that any being, by the very fact that it is a being, presents an aspect of desirability (not necessarily desirable to man). Also linked with the notion of perfectibility—a thing is good when it is finished, complete. It has been something of a contemporary fashion to prefer the word *value* to good.

HEDONISM. The ethical doctrine that the end of man is the securing of the greatest possible amount of pleasure for himself. Pleasure may be conceived of quantitatively (Bentham) or qualitatively (J. S. Mill, Santayana). *Hedone* is the Greek word for pleasure.

HUMANISM. A form of naturalism which emphasizes man and his welfare. Often called *humanistic naturalism,* it stresses the self-sufficiency of man and rejects any tie of man to anything supernatural. It has roots back in "the religion of Humanity" proclaimed by Comte, the founder of positivism. Also it has strong ties with pragmatism and with the instrumentalism of John Dewey. Philosophic humanism should not be confused with the literary humanism of the Renaissance.

HYLOMORPHISM. The doctrine (Aristotelian) that all bodies are made up of two complementary principles: matter (*hyle*) and form (*morphos*). See FORM and MATTER.

HYLOZOISM. The first Greek philosophers held that the matter of which all reality is composed is itself alive, and so they were called *hylozoists*. Because they root life and consciousness in matter itself, Marxist philosophers have been called latter-day hylozoists, a label they militantly reject. From the Greek words for matter (*hyle*) and living (*zoos*).

IDEA. A key word in any man's philosophy, the kind from which the whole skeleton can be reconstructed. One of its early senses is found in the medical writers where it means basic bodily qualities. The atomists used it to describe the shape of the atom, and by extension, for the atom itself. Finally, it came to stand for anything that persists through change and is therefore susceptible to being named or defined. Plato extended the term to the self-subsistent, immaterial, eternal archetypal existents, which for Plato are "the really real." Any reality in this corporeal world is a participation, a faint reflection from the ideal world.

Aristotle put the ideas of Plato back into the corporeal world, where they become the forms which, circumscribed and limited by matter, make up bodies. In knowing, the intellect separates out (abstracts) the forms from the matter that individualizes them, and they then exist in the mind as universals.

Plato's position came to be called (through the sixth-century Latin philosopher Boethius) the doctrine of REALISM (q.v.) (also *Platonic realism, absolute realism*), because he makes ideas independently real. Aristotle is also a realist because he gives the ideas reality in the mind (with a foundation in things); he is called a *moderate realist,* however, because he gives the ideas less reality than Plato.

In modern philosophy, idea tends to be synonymous with any state of consciousness representative of things "outside." In English and American philosophy this usually means a sense awareness of some kind. Any idea that cannot be traced back to a sensation is fictitious. Kant gave to the mind the function of casting the raw material of experience into the form of universals. This view is called CONCEPTUALISM. See INNATE IDEA.

IDEALISM. Primarily the doctrine that reality is made up solely of ideas (variously defined) and the mind or minds that think these ideas. Reality, in brief, is exclusively mental (Berkeley, Hegel). There is a secondary and much less important sense in which the term refers vaguely to any philosophy which sees an optimistic future for man, or which goads him to high aspirations. In this latter usage, the term is best avoided when referring to philosophers.

IDEOLOGY. An early nineteenth-century neologism meaning the science of ideas; the study of the nature and origin of ideas. The term became broadened to signify the set of ideas characteristic of an age or a social class. It also acquired mildly abusive overtones as implying dangerous ideas or as suggestive of visionary, ivory-tower thinking as against the empiricist's disciplined and restrained concentration on facts.

IMMANENT. Usually contrasted to transitive or transcendent. An immanent act is one which comes to completion in man; for example, an act of reasoning. The term is also used to signify the indwelling of God in the universe. God conceived of as independent and above all other being is called *transcendent*.

IMMATERIAL. It took Greek philosophy close to three centuries to arrive at the notion of immateriality, and 2300 years later there are still a great many philosophers who say the term has no meaning. It is first found clearly elaborated in Plato, for whom it described the condition of the ideas: changeless, universal, timeless, dimensionless, without quantity, in short everything that bodies are not; hence, incorporeal (non-bodily), immaterial (non-material).

INNATE IDEA. An idea which is inborn, which appears in man's consciousness just because he is man. Such ideas are independent of all external experience, except that our inner awareness may be triggered off by some external stimulus.

INTELLECT. A power distinct from the senses, whereby man can perceive the ideas or forms which provide the meaningful patterns within reality. From the Latin, *intus* and *legere,* meaning to read within.

INTENTIONAL. A technical term in mediaeval Aristotelianism referring to the nonphysical kind of existence things can have in the intellect; for example, tree exists in my mind as "treeness." The term has been revived in modern times by the German philosopher Brentano, through whom it has entered the vocabulary of the phenomenologists, especially Husserl. Not to be confused with the everyday use in which it refers to an act of the will.

INTUITION. Direct insight in knowing. Used of both senses and intellect. When it is applied to the intellect, there is usually an implied contrast with empiricism. From the Latin, *in* and *tueor,* to gaze or look at.

LOGICAL POSITIVISM. See POSITIVISM.

LOGIC. Traditionally, the art or science by which the intellect puts order in our concepts with a view to reaching the truth. **FORMAL LOGIC** examines the forms of thought to insure correctness in the actual thought forms. **MATERIAL LOGIC** investigates the content of thought in order to determine its truth. This side of logic is often absorbed into epistemology and the science of method. See also **SYMBOLIC LOGIC.**

MATERIALISM. The doctrine that the only kind of being that is real is corporeal. A persistent type of philosophy, it has many contemporary forms. Among them, **MECHANISTIC MATERIALISM**: reality consists of ultimate corporeal units arranged on the model of a machine. Also called *physical realism.* **DIALECTICAL MATERIALISM**: the

materialism of Marx and Engels, given an inner dynamism by combining the notion of a material universe
with the Hegelian notion of an organic development
through a dialectical process. Also called *historical materialism.*

MATTER. In Aristotle, the principle of indeterminacy,
which by limiting form makes possible the existence of
individual bodies (hence called the principle of indi-
viduation). PRIME MATTER: the principle of possibility
(as *pure possibility*, an abstraction). SECOND MATTER:
the visible, quantified body.

The Greek term for matter was *hyle.* Originally it
meant forest, and also what comes out of the forest.
Only with Aristotle was the term extended to cover the
limiting principle within corporeal being. The keynote
is that of indeterminacy: just as anything might emerge
from the hidden depths of the forest, so can things
emerge from the realm of possibility. The Stoics popularized the term *material* as an alternative for *corporeal.*

METAPHYSICS. The philosophy of being, the study of being
in its universal, noncompartmentalized aspects. Called
by Aristotle, *first philosophy* or *theology* (since it takes
the mind back to God as the ultimate explanation of
change, causality, etc.). Kant eventually demonstrated
the impossibility of metaphysics as a legitimate branch
of knowledge, only to spawn a whole new generation of
metaphysicians.

The name metaphysics came about by accident. The
rediscovered corpus of Aristotle's writings were brought
to Rome as booty by the Roman general Sulla in
the first century B.C. They were given to a Greek
scholar, Andronicus of Rhodes, for editing. The treatise
on being was placed after the treatise on physical na-

ture and labeled simply, "After the Physics." *Meta* is the Greek preposition meaning after: *meta ta physica*. The name was an apt one and has persisted, since the natural progression of the mind is from the knowledge of things apparent to the senses to the intelligible principles which explain them.

MIND. The seat of consciousness. It tends to be a vague word. The Platonist is more apt to use it than the Aristotelian, who uses it occasionally as a synonym for intellect or reason. The word translates the Latin *mens* and the Greek *nous*.

MONAD. An ultimate unit of reality; a term usually associated with Leibnitz, for whom reality is an aggregation of ultimate units, monads, of varying degrees of spirituality from the unconscious body monads to God, the supreme Monad. From the Greek *monas, monados* meaning unit.

MONISM. The view that reality is fundamentally and essentially one. Early Greek theories of reality were monist, culminating in Parmenides, who made all reality an undifferentiated being which he called The One. Spinoza makes all reality a single substance (with an infinite number of aspects) which he calls God or Nature. The term is generally set against dualism or pluralism. Monistic theories of reality tend to be final, absolute, whereas pluralistic philosophies, such as the pragmatism of William James, tend to stress process, development, evolution, change.

NATURE. A set of operations by which a thing comes into being. This is another "red light" term, varying greatly from one philosopher to another, but usually indicative of his general position. It can have the following meanings (with many subordinate shades of meaning): an individual, bodily thing, considered as an independent unit; the sum total of individual, bodily natures (for the early Greeks Nature was made up of natures); creation as distinct from the Creator; all reality, including God; the visible universe contrasted with the invisible (supernature or the supernatural); God as identical with reality (Spinoza's *Deus sive natura*, God or Nature). From the Latin word for the Greek word physics, *nata* meaning "things born."

NATURALISM. In modern philosophy it is generally used with an implied contrast to *supernaturalism*. It stands for a kind of philosophical one-worldism: the only reality is what falls within my immediate experience; this is called nature, and there is nothing else, no supernature.

NOMINALISM. The relegation of the Platonic idea and universals in general to the category of fiction, of names (*nomina*) signifying nothing.

OBJECTIVE. A very ambiguous term because it is based on the term *object*, and few philosophers agree on just what the term *object* means. For one school, objective means existing independently of any knowing mind, as against subjective, which implies that you cannot get outside the knowing mind, which is the subject. The doctrine that things have an existence independent of any knowing mind is called *objectivism*. See SUBJECTIVE.

ONTOLOGY. Literally the science of being. From the Greek *on, ontos* (being) and *logos*. See METAPHYSICS.

PHENOMENON. In general, what is immediately perceived by either the sense or intellect. Specialized meanings: 1. The immediate imprint on the senses which is the sole object of knowledge (Hume). This is sometimes called **PURE PHENOMENALISM.** 2. The product of the raw data of experience plus the formal constructive activity of the mind (Kant). This composite is contrasted with the NOUMENON, the thing-in-itself, which is beyond man's grasp, since the intellect always transforms what comes into it. 3. The recent school of phenomenology (Husserl, Heidegger, etc.) uses the term *phenomenon* to signify the complete reality of a thing as it is delivered to consciousness—the fact immediately and fully given in its essential reality. From the Greek word meaning appearance.

PHILOSOPHY. The early philosophers were called wise men, *sophists*, a term that covered any kind of skill, from bridge-building to the making of riddles. The word philosopher is attributed to Pythagoras, who is supposed to have declined the title of *wise* man, since "no man but only God is wise. Call me rather," he said, "a philosopher, a lover of wisdom." Until the Middle Ages philosophy continued to mean loosely all branches of learning, though medicine and mathematics particularly separated off early as distinct fields of investigation. Cicero defined philosophy as "the knowledge of things divine and human and their causes." Most definitions of philosophy stress the overall interest of the philosopher and his concern with the remote and ultimate rather than the immediate causes of things. The German word for philosophy, *Weltanschauung*, world view, is in this respect much more expressive than the English word. It is sometimes thought necessary to spell out the philosophic dependence on reason alone, as against religious or other explanations. Aristotle identified philosophy with metaphysics. Philosophers who say metaphysics is an illusion are apt to deny the existence of philosophy as a distinct kind of knowledge. The positivist, for instance, says that the business of philosophy is simply to put in order and unify the findings of the various positive sciences. Some logicians, too, say that philosophy, stripped of its verbiage, reduces to logic. From the Greek *philos*, love, and *sophia*, wisdom. See META-PHYSICS, POSITIVISM.

PHYSICS. Originally from the Greek meaning growth or birth. Then, with the Ionian philosophers, the implication of definite structure. It remained a synonym for natural philosophy until the separation of physics as a science from the philosophy of nature in the nineteenth century.

PLURALISM. The view that the universe is made up of a number of irreducible, ultimate principles; for example, the infinity of atomic particles in the early Greek atomists. William James's pragmatic philosophy is pluralistic because it stresses the unassimilable differences that mark off each thing from every other thing. See MONISM.

POSITIVISM. The name given to his philosophy by A. Comte, who depicted the intellectual development of man as occurring in three stages: a theological or mythical stage; a metaphysical or abstract period; and finally, a positive era, the age of science, which brought man down to earth. Working in the tradition of Hume, Comte held that the only valid knowledge was what could be directly verified in the senses or positive facts. The business of philosophy is simply to order and synthesize the findings of the positive sciences. The name positivism has been extended to all who similarly describe the nature and limits of knowledge. Some philosophers in this current are J. S. Mill, Poincaré, Wittgenstein, G. Moore, Russell. Pragmatism has been strongly affected by this doctrine and according to some is one of the species of the genus positivist. (Most pragmatists would disavow the label.) More recent varieties have been called *logical empiricism, logical analysis, analytic philosophy, logical positivism.* Various representatives: The Vienna Circle (Schlick, Carnap), Wittgenstein, Ayer, Ryle, Bridgman.

POTENCY. Primarily the principle of possibility, and always a correlative of act. Sometimes used as a synonym for MATTER (q.v.), though strictly speaking it has a wider application, since it applies to immaterial as well as material being. The everyday sense in which it means power is secondary for philosophy.

PRAGMATISM. A philosophical attitude as much as a body of doctrine. Pragmatism stresses the practical as against the theoretical. It tests the truth and value of a doctrine by its personal and social utility, its workability. Epistemologically, it is strongly empirical in the Hume-Mill tradition. From the Greek *pragma,* a fact, a deed, a thing done. The term was invented by C. S. Peirce, who later redesignated his own version as *pragmaticism.* William James is the great popularizer of pragmatism. Dewey's **INSTRUMENTALISM** is a later version, stressing the social environment and the experimental method.

RATIONALISM. The opinion (especially in modern philosophy) that reason reaches truth independently of sense experience. Sometimes used in the meaning that man's reason is self-sufficient in the pursuit of truth and therefore does not need religious revelation. In modern philosophy the term is used usually in contrast to EMPIRICISM (q.v.).

REALISM. In modern philosophy, the doctrine that things have a real existence, independent of any knowing mind. A further breakdown, **REPRESENTATIVE REALISM**

—things are real, but in knowing are represented in the mind by ideas. In mediaeval philosophy, the term had reference to the reality or otherwise of the Platonic ideas. See IDEA.

REALITY. What is actually existent, as against appearance. Philosophies differ basically according to the way they answer the question, "What is really real?"

SCHOLASTICISM. The philosophy taught in the mediaeval and early modern universities. Erroneously identified sometimes with Aristotelianism, which was actually a fairly late arrival in the European universities. The term is often used with overtones of contempt. The word *dunce* illustrates the radical change in values from earlier times; the word is from the name of the famous philosopher Duns Scotus, and it was once deemed a compliment to be called a Duns.

SEMANTICS. The science that studies the meanings of words and symbols (Carnap, Richards).

SEMIOTICS. A close cousin to SEMANTICS (q.v.). The word was given currency by C. S. Peirce. It means the science that studies signs. Based on the Greek word *semeion* (*semeiotikos*), sign (of signs).

SOLEPSISM. The opinion that the individual is the sole, existing reality. The problem of the knower imprisoned in the circle of his own ideas is also called the EGOCENTRIC PREDICAMENT. From *solus*, alone, and *ipse*, self.

SOUL. Originally it meant breath, but it slowly came to stand for the living principle in any living thing. In Plato, for whom "man is a soul imprisoned in a body," it is a distinct, immaterial substance. For Aristotle it is the immaterial principle which organizes the living body. In modern philosophy, mind, ego, consciousness, person, knower, self, spirit, entelechy, brain, thinking substance, have all been given as synonyms for soul. The English equivalent of the Greek *psyche*, principle of life.

SUBJECTIVE. Within the subject's consciousness. **SUBJECTIVISM:** nothing is real apart from states of consciousness (Berkeley). See **OBJECTIVE.**

SUBSTANCE. A being whose nature is to exist on its own, as an independent center of existence; for instance, man, bird, tree. The Latin root, *substare*, to stand under, gives a secondary meaning: to stand under accidents as a kind of support.

SYMBOLIC LOGIC. A logic which substitutes symbols for everyday words and its own technique for manipulating symbols for everyday grammar. For some of its exponents, it is supplementary to, for others it has superseded, the traditional logic. It is particularly the logic proper to mathematics, and is often called *mathematical logic*. Another name is *logistics*. Foreshadowed by Leibnitz, its real origins are with Boole (1815-1864) and De Morgan (1806-1871). Continental pioneers are Schroeder, Frege, Peano. In America, C. S. Peirce (1839-1914). The modern *Summa* of symbolic logic is the *Principia Mathematica* of Whitehead and Russell (pub. 1910).

TELEOLOGY. The view that there is a design or purpose in the universe, that things move toward an intelligently foreseen end. From the Greek *telos*, end, and *logos*, science.

THEODICY. A word coined by Leibnitz as an alternative to natural theology, but with the special implication of a science which justifies the ways of God in spite of the existence of evil.

TRANSCENDENTAL. Terms such as *one, true, good, thing, something*, which are coextensive with being itself; they transcend categories, the divisions within reality. In the philosophy of Kant, transcendental is a specialized term relating to the A PRIORI (q.v.) forms which regulate thought and which are independent of, transcend, the raw material of experience. Philosophies in the Kantian tradition are often called transcendental.

TRUTH. A very complicated notion which philosophers are apt to define in various and sometimes clashing ways, unless they give up and say it can't be done. John Locke follows the traditional Aristotelian distinctions, which cover many of the common uses of the word. Logical truth, or the truth of knowing, is the agreement of the intellect with things; Aristotle: "to say of what is, that it is, and of what is not, that it is not." The truth of being (ontological truth), which is the transcendental truth of the metaphysician, is the conformity of a thing with its ideal pattern; St. Augustine: "The true is what is." Moral truth is the truth of speech, the conformity of the spoken word with the thoughts of the speaker; "to tell the truth."

UNIVERSAL. The Latin version of IDEA (q.v.), from *unus,* one, and *vertere,* to turn, i.e., combined into one.

UTILITARIANISM. The name given by Bentham and publicized by John Stuart Mill, to the ethical doctrine that actions are good because they are useful. On the social plane, this becomes "the greatest good to the greatest number" principle.

VALUE. A bracketing of the notions of good and beauty, which seems to be losing popularity since it adds a further dimension of vagueness to terms that are already sufficiently difficult.

VOLUNTARISM. The philosophical position which affirms the priority in man of will over intellect. Philosophies which emphasize the primacy of power in human affairs (e.g., Nietzsche) are apt to be in the voluntaristic pattern.

WILL. The power of choice in man. The choices here are limited: man's will is free (in some sense nondetermined) or not free (determined). See FREEDOM.

CHAPTER **4**

Names for the Molecules of Life

The Language of Biochemistry

DAVID M. LOCKE

From time to time the specialized language of some branch of science leaks through into the world of the general public. These occasions are usually of one of two types: some awe-inspiring new finding in an area of fundamental research has altered our basic ideas about life and the universe, or some useful new discovery in an area of applied research has made a powerful impact on the realm of kitchen, laundry room, or garage.

In such instances, technical words which form the specialized vocabulary of the particular science involved are likely to appear in the popular press and, particularly in cases of useful new products, may enter the vocabulary of the general public. Thus, the horrifying demonstration in 1945 of man's new-found control over the heart of the atom brought into newspapers and magazines a long list of scientific terms—isotope, electron, nucleus, proton, and neutron, for example—and the reader was even likely to find himself puzzling over such complications as "neutron cross section," "thermal neutron," and "neutron flux." Likewise, at a somewhat more mundane level, research on the controlled combustion of hydrocarbons in the 1920's made household words of an otherwise obscure organo-metallic compound called "tetraethyllead," the antiknock compound used in ethyl gasoline, and the branched-chain hydrocarbon known as "isooctane," a standard used to determine "octane ratings."

It is probably true, however, that even the most fre-quently used of these popularized scientific terms carry a certain strangeness or foreignness for the average ear. The man in the street is likely to be sufficiently familiar with one of these words to know in general what sort of thing it refers to, but is probably uncertain of its exact meaning and spelling; he may, in fact, hesitate to use it in his own speech. Perhaps no automobile owner ever hesitated to order "ethyl," and it is quite possible that most drivers recognize the word "tetraethyllead" when they see it, but how many of them would be able to give this answer when asked what antiknock material is added to ethyl gasoline? And how many would have any idea at all of the chemical nature of tetraethyllead? Or be able to spell it correctly?

To overcome this hesitancy of the general reader to appropriate scientific terms for his own vocabulary, it is not necessary for him to become an expert in the scientific field itself. All that is needed is to have some knowledge of the specific meaning of the word, some very general feeling for the scientific context in which it originated, and some idea of how it is put together from its compo-nent parts (if it fits the pattern of verbal complexity usual in scientific terminology).

In the case of tetraethyllead, for example, the reader probably knows that it is a gasoline additive. With the additional information that is it an organometallic com-pound—that is, part metal and part organic chemical—he is on his way toward understanding. Especially so, if he knows that organic chemicals are the general class of carbon-containing compounds that were once thought to be formed only by living organisms, but which are now produced every day in staggering amounts in laboratories and factories, like gasoline itself, and plastics, synthetic fibers, and drugs. An analysis of the word tetraethyllead gives additional relevant details. "Tetra-" is a common scientific prefix which is derived from the Greek and means four, while "ethyl" is an organic chemical grouping consisting of two carbon atoms and five hydrogen atoms. It occurs in ethyl (or drinking) alcohol and gets its name from the fact that it is also part of the molecule of ordinary *eth*er. Putting this information all together gives us the following definition: tetraethyllead—an organometallic compound containing one atom of lead and four ethyl groups per molecule. Knowing this background makes it much easier to spell and use the word correctly.

The purpose of this article is to give background information about the vocabulary in a field of biochemistry which is now producing discoveries as startling and significant as was the unleashing of the power of the atom in 1945. This field is biochemical genetics, the unraveling of the complex biochemical processes by which hereditary characteristics are recorded in the genes, passed on to succeeding generations, and translated into physical traits. This is the fundamental process which makes life possible, and a complete understanding of its working may well give man a new dimension of control over nature.

Popularized accounts of this research already have appeared in many newspapers and general-circulation magazines. More are sure to come. These accounts all refer to certain key chemical compounds which play essential roles in the process of genetic transcription. The mysterious acronyms DNA and RNA are seen frequently, and we will probably hear more and more in the next few years of words like nucleic acid, protein, enzyme, nucleotide, and amino acid. A complete list of the major chemical compounds involved in the field of biochemical genetics is included here.

Before presenting this list, however, it would be helpful to include some very general remarks about the naming of chemical compounds. Inorganic chemicals, largely materials of mineral origin, are most frequently named as two words, indicating roughly that they are made up of two contrasting parts. Thus we have familiar names like sodium chloride, hydrogen peroxide, and hydrochloric acid. Organic chemicals, the carbon-containing class of chemicals mentioned above, are sometimes named in the same way. What is probably the commonest example of this has already been mentioned, ethyl alcohol. Another is the organic acid found in vinegar, acetic acid.

But much more frequently organic chemicals are named by running together in one long name the names for the different component parts of the molecule. We saw how this was done with tetraethyllead. The most common way of running words together to name organic chemicals is called a substitution system. In this process one portion of the molecule is considered as the main part and its designation is placed at the end of the word, while the rest of the molecule is considered as being substituted into it, and modifiers describing these parts are placed earlier in the word. This is somewhat similar to the German practice of making a long word by combining a noun and one or more modifiers, which is not surprising, since this method of naming organic chemicals was developed by nineteenth-century German chemists.

A substance whose molecules contain six carbon atoms,

five hydrogen atoms, and one chlorine atom is named, according to this system, chlorobenzene. In this case the benzene ring, a closed circle of six carbon atoms each bearing a hydrogen atom, is considered as the main part of the molecule. A chlorine atom is then considered to be substituted for one of the hydrogen atoms, and the combining form "chloro-" indicates this substitution. A closely related ring system is called toluene, and substituting into it three (indicated by the combining form, tri-) nitrogen dioxide groups (combining form, nitro-) produces trinitrotoluene or TNT.

This system has been preserved because it works extremely well and allows the chemist to name very complex substances. In naming substances by this system, however, the chemist produces extremely long and complicated names which look to the layman like gibberish. The secret to making these long names more understandable is to look at them as the chemist does, not as one long word, but as a combination of shorter words joined together. Thus: tetra, ethyl, and lead; chloro and benzene; and tri, nitro, and toluene.

Of course, it isn't easy for a nonchemist to tell how the long words should be broken up into smaller ones. Some of the smaller units, like "ethyl," occur frequently and can be easily recognized. Another such common unit is "methyl." This is very much like "ethyl," not only in its sound but chemically as well, except that it contains only one carbon atom and three hydrogens, instead of two and five. Methyl is used most familiarly in the phrase methyl (or wood) alcohol, and in fact its name comes from the Greek words *methy* (wine) and *yli* (wood). Many of the other common chemical prefixes have origins in Greek or Latin terms. "Iso-", for instance, is based on the Greek *isos* or equal. (Remember that an isoceles triangle has two equal sides.) It is used chemically to indicate a compound which is just like another except that the iso- form has its carbon atoms arranged in a branched chain instead of a straight one. The straight-chain form is indicated by the prefix *n-* for normal. This is the explanation for the "iso-" in isooctane mentioned above in connection with gasoline. *Oct*ane itself indicates that the carbon chain of the molecule has eight atoms in it (Greek, *octa-*, eight). Incidentally it is isooctane which has good antiknock characteristics and an "octane rating" of 100. The straight-chain form, *n*-octane, is very poor in this respect. The prefixes which are probably the most commonly used in naming chemical compounds are based on the Greek words for the numbers. These prefixes are: mono-, di-, tri-, tetra-, penta-, hexa-, hepta-, octa-, and so on.

Another factor that helps to break the long words up into simpler ones is the chemists' habit of using numerals to indicate how the individual chemical units are joined together in the molecule. When these numerals occur in the middle of a word, they naturally indicate how it can be broken up. Thus it is a lot easier for a nonchemist to see how to split up 4-ethyl-5-methyloctane than simply ethylmethyloctane.

Sometimes, too, these substitution names get so very long and complicated that even the chemists prefer to adopt a simpler name. So there are special names made up specifically for some frequently used compounds, and these are called common or trivial names. Most anyone, given a choice, would prefer to call 17,21-dihydroxypregn-4-ene-3,11,20-trione by its trivial name of cortisone. Chemists exercise great ingenuity in thinking up new trivial names, and sometimes they try to use a bit of humor. One compound was called cubane because a drawing of its molecule looks like a cube. Another one was named congressane because a drawing of it was used as a symbol of one of the recent international congresses of chemistry.

In biochemistry most of the chemicals dealt with are organic chemicals, and many of them are named according to the rules of organic chemical nomenclature. Many of them however are given trivial names of their own. This may be a matter of convenience, as is the case with cortisone, because the regular name is very long and awkward to use. In many cases, also, the compound may have been isolated and its biological activity studied before its exact chemical structure was known. In this case a compound has to be given a trivial name because it is not possible to give it a regular systematic name. The common names of chemicals of biological origin usually indicate the source of the compound. Thus *corti*sone comes from the adrenal *cortex*. Cholesterol, another common biological chemical, was first found in gallstones and gets its name from the Greek words *chole* (gall) and *stereos* (solid). Sometimes, however, a common name is chosen to give an indication of the compound's major biological function. ACTH, for example, is adrenocorticotrophic hormone, the hormone which stimulates (Greek, *trophe*, food) the adrenal cortex.

These, in general, are the ways in which chemical compounds are named. Now let us consider the specific chemical substances which are involved in biochemical genetics and, in particular, in the biochemical aspects of what has come to be called "The Code of Life." With each term is given its definition, role in the process of genetic transcription, and derivation. For brevity a number of technical words are used in the definitions. These words are defined, in turn, in the appropriate alphabetical listing. By follow-

ing a chain of such definitions you will build up an understanding of what the individual words mean and how they
fit together in their scientific context.

WORD LIST

ADENINE. A purine base found in NUCLEOTIDES (q.v.).
Adeno- refers to gland and is from the Greek *aden*.

AMINO ACID. A relatively small molecule characterized by
the fact that it contains both an amino (basic) group
and a carboxylic (acid) group. Twenty different amino
acids are combined in different relative amounts and
in various arrangements to produce all the different
proteins in the body. (A supplementary list of these
twenty amino acids is included at the end of this article.) The arrangement of amino acids in a particular
protein—and hence the biological activity of the protein
—is directed by the arrangement of nucleotides in the
RNA which has acted as a template for the production
of the protein. The word amino is derived from am-
monia, to which the amino group is closely related
chemically. See NUCLEOTIDES and RIBONUCLEIC ACID.

CYTOSINE. A pyrimidine base found in nucleotides. The
prefix cyt- is a combining form meaning cell and is from
the Greek *kytos* (hollow vessel).

DEOXYRIBONUCLEIC ACID or DNA. A nucleic acid whose
nucleotides contain the sugar deoxyribose and the bases
C, T, A, and G. These are the nucleic acids which constitute the genes and preserve the genetic information
from generation to generation. The name reflects the
fact that the nucleotides of this type of nucleic acid all
contain deoxyribose. See RIBONUCLEIC ACID (RNA).

DEOXYRIBOSE. A five-carbon sugar found in nucleotides.

Contains one less oxygen atom per molecule than does RIBOSE (q.v.), hence the name, de- -oxy- -ribose.

DIPEPTIDE, TRIPEPTIDE, etc. Two, three, etc., amino acids joined together by peptide bonds. The prefixes are from the Greek. See PEPTIDE.

ENZYME. A protein which acts as a biological catalyst. Enzymes control every important chemical reaction that occurs in a cell. Enzymes are not only the product of the operation of the genetic mechanism but also they help to regulate it. The word is from the Greek *enzymos,* leavened.

GUANINE. A purine base found in nucleotides. Named from *guano,* a common source (along with other animal excrement) of this material.

NUCLEIC ACID. A long, chain-like molecule containing many subunits called nucleotides. Nucleic acids are found in all living things, including viruses, and in large part comprise the genetic machinery of the organism. The name is derived from the facts that these substances have acid properties and were first found in cell nuclei (Latin, *nuc-,* nut).

NUCLEOTIDE. A molecule made up of three parts: a nitrogen-containing base, a sugar, and phosphoric acid. Although each nucleic acid contains a large number of individual nucleotides, the nucleotides in any one nucleic acid are generally of only four different kinds. It is the particular arrangement of these four kinds of nucleotides in the nucleic acid which determines the genetic message which it carries. The name nucleotide is made up from *nucle*us plus -otide, a special ending closely related to another ending -oside. The ending -ose is characteristic for sugars, as in sucrose, and -oside is added to a word to indicate that a sugar is part of the molecule. The suffix -otide is used to indicate that both a sugar and phosphoric acid are part of the molecule.

PEPTIDE. Two or more amino acids joined together by a chemical linkage (or bond) with the loss of one molecule of water for each linkage established. The word is derived from the Greek *peptein*, to cook or digest. Peptides are the product of partial digestion of proteins.

POLYPEPTIDE. An unspecified, perhaps unknown, number of amino acids joined together by peptide bonds. It is usually reserved for molecules smaller than proteins. Poly- is a prefix meaning many, from the Greek word *polys*.

PROTEIN. A long-chain molecule made up of amino acids joined together. One of the fundamental constituents of all cells. Individual proteins form structural elements in the cell and act as the biological catalysts that regulate the processes which keep the cell alive. Proteins are the products of the operation of the genetic mechanism and the means by which the genetic information is put to work in the body. The word protein is derived from the Greek *proteios*, meaning primary.

PURINE. A class of bases very similar to the pyrimidines but containing an additional ring of two nitrogens and one carbon. This is the second class of bases found in nucleotides. Purine gets its name from the Latin words *purus* (pure) *uricus* (uric), because it may be prepared from uric acid, which in turn can be isolated from urine.

PYRIMIDINE. A class of organic bases characterized by the fact that they all contain a ring consisting of four carbon atoms and two nitrogen atoms. This is one of two general types of bases that occur in nucleotides. Barbiturates also are pyrimidines. The name pyrimidine is derived from the name of a closely related coal-tar base, pyridine, which in turn is based on the Greek word *pyr*, meaning fire.

RIBONUCLEASE. A specific protein made up from 124 amino acids. The first enzyme to have its complete sequence of amino acids determined. Splits apart or hydrolyzes RNA into its component nucleotides. Named (as are most hydrolyzing enzymes) by adding -ase to the designation for the substrate, thus *ribonucle*ic acid *-ase*. The ending is taken from the name diastase, the first enzyme whose existence was clearly established.

RIBONUCLEIC ACID or RNA. A nucleic acid whose nucleotides contain the sugar ribose and the bases adenine, cytosine, guanine, and uracil. The ribonucleic acids are generally involved in the transfer of genetic information from the genes in the nucleus of the cell into the other parts of the cell. The name reflects the ribose content of the nucleotides of these nucleic acids. MESSENGER RNA, or mRNA (also called TEMPLATE RNA). A form of RNA which picks up a portion of the genetic message from DNA and carries it into the parts of the cell where protein is produced. There it acts as a template for the manufacture of protein. TRANSFER RNA or tRNA (also called SOLUBLE RNA or sRNA). A form of RNA which combines specifically with individual amino acids and transfers them to template RNA where they are assembled in the proper order to form the protein indicated by the genetic message from DNA. Transfer RNA consists of smaller molecules than the other forms of the nucleic acids and this makes it more easily put into solution (soluble).

RNA POLYMERASE. An enzyme which catalyzes the joining together or polymerization of nucleotides to form RNA. An important enzyme, it is used in the preparation of artificial RNA, and played a key role in the research which took the first steps in solving the genetic code. Named, as is general for enzymes (except for hydrolyzing enzymes), by adding -ase to a word indicating the action of the enzyme.

RIBOSE. A five-carbon sugar found in nucleotides. Name was created as a variation on a closely related sugar called arabinose.

SUBSTRATE. A general term for a substance which is acted on or altered by an enzyme. The name is from the Latin *substratus,* spread under.

THYMINE. A pyrimidine base found in nucleotides. From the Latin *thymus,* it refers to the thymus gland.

URACIL. A pyrimidine base found in nucleotides. Name related to urea.

SUPPLEMENTARY LIST

The following are the principal amino acids found in proteins.

ALANINE. Probably derived from *al*dehyde, and including the ending *ine,* a characteristic ending for amino acids and several other chemical groups.

ARGININE. May be derived from the Greek *arginoeis,* meaning bright or white.

ASPARTIC ACID. An amino acid closely related to asparagine.

ASPARAGINE. Named from *asparag*us, first source of this amino acid.

CYSTEINE. From the Greek *kystis,* bladder.

GLUTAMIC ACID. Related to glutamine.

GLUTAMINE. Named from gluten, a protein found in flour.

GLYCINE. From the Greek *glykis,* sweet.

HISTIDINE. Hist- is a general prefix referring to tissue. From the Greek *histos.*

ISOLEUCINE. Related to leucine.

LEUCINE. From the Greek *leukos,* white.

LYSINE. From the Greek *lysis,* a loosening, from *lyo,* loosen, dissolve.

METHIONINE. From *methyl* plus thio-, a prefix indicating the presence of sulfur.

PHENYLALANINE. From phenyl-, a prefix indicating the substitution of a benzene ring minus one hydrogen atom plus alanine.

PROLINE. Probably from *pyrrolidine,* the ring system to which this amino acid is related.

SERINE. From *sericin,* a protein from silk.

THREONINE. Probably from *threose,* a sugar to which it is chemically related.

TRYPTOPHAN. Probably from *trypsin,* a digestive enzyme.

TYROSINE. From the Greek *tyros,* cheese.

VALINE. Probably from *isovaleric* acid, to which it is chemically related.

CHAPTER 5

As Artists See Us

The Language of Painting and Sculpture of Today

MARVE H. COOPER, MICHELE F. COOPER

Any vocabulary of art has intrinsic difficulties, because art itself has its own inherent, visual language. A group of defining words is necessarily secondary to the art itself and should perhaps be called a secondary vocabulary. Words, of course, can never replace the artistic experiences of either artist or viewer, and the definitions which follow are presented with that understanding. These words are simply defined in an attempt to translate some aspects of visual experience into clear English.

The words in this list have been chosen in an effort to explain, rather than identify, the various aspects of art in the last one hundred years. A limitation of time has been placed because there are virtually thousands of artistic terms which might apply to art, which, after all, goes back to the prehistoric time when man first decorated his ax handle; art histories and dictionaries are readily available for historians. It is the art of our own times that now deserves our attention and understanding.

An additional reason for limiting this vocabulary to recent art is that despite the tremendous amounts of discussion and writing, there is little precise understanding of either the terminology or the art itself. We are an oral civilization which of late finds words most convenient, but frequently we are careless in our use of them. The words here attempt to describe, however semantically, the exigencies of modern art. It is also important to realize that however precisely we may attempt to define contemporary words, these definitions are really just assumptions that are subject to change.

Most of the vocabulary derives from French, German, and Russian, because in the last half-century there has been a preponderance of movements, schools, and styles coming from these countries.

WORD LIST

ABSTRACT ART. Probably the most notoriously vague term ever to become popularized in the vocabulary of all art. Best said, the reference pertains to that which is not obviously represented, using only lines, colors, generalized or geometrical forms. This, however, does not define an abstract work of art, but only superficially refers to its appearance. When a work of art attempts to speak of nature in terms of symbols (as a computer refers to people with numbers), we may say this is an abstraction. But when a painting—even if it begins at a point in nature and slowly departs from the original subject to make a new statement—has no dependence on the original subject for its justification, we can no longer call it an abstraction; its reference is then only to itself. This might best be compared to program music, in which descriptive notes, seemingly explanatory, add little or nothing to the music itself; even the musical notations on paper are abstractions of the sounds; the sounds themselves are pure and finite.

The first deliberate abstract watercolor by Kandinsky —which is comprised of lines, forms, and areas of color in juxtaposition to each other without any representational purpose—dates from 1910, the same year he wrote his *Concerning the Spiritual in Art*. Two years later, the Czech Kupka exhibited a canvas inspired directly from music entitled "Fugue in Two Colours: Warm Chromatic," whose elements have, by themselves, an inherent, intrinsic value. Then Mondrian employed the method of making successive abstractions of a given subject, such as a tree, or a façade of a cathedral, each time moving farther and farther away until all natural appearance disappeared.

Abstract Expressionism, spearheaded by Jackson Pollock, was sometimes referred to by such titles as the School of New York, the Tenth-Street School, or Action Painting. Pollock attempted through his unconventional method of painting to produce a pictorial extension of his own personality. In doing so, there would be no need to look or refer to anything except the canvas in front of him. See CONCRETE.

It should be noted that most of the protagonists of these movements had little or no relation to each other. See works of Kline, Rothko, Motherwell, Still, Gottlieb, Hofmann, and Willem de Kooning.

ACADEMIC. Term from Plato's Academy used by fifteenth-century Italian Humanists to characterize their discussion meetings; Vasari founded Florence's first Academy of Fine Arts in 1563. Since nineteenth-century conservatism, however, the Academy has been attacked for dullness, conventionality, and prejudice. Also connotes imitation of the classical.

ACTION PAINTING. Any method of applying the paint without the usual brush or knife technique; a spontaneous spilling or spattering of the paint. Pollock discovered this unorthodox method in an attempt to project his innermost personality into the visual effect.

AESTHETICS. Describes both the sensitive perception of art by feeling and a branch of philosophy dealing with the beautiful and with doctrines of taste. Persons highly sensitive to art and beauty, especially artists, poets, musicians, etc., are regarded as "aesthetes."

ART NOUVEAU. Mainly a style of architecture and interior design which spread across Europe and America in the 1890's, characterized in its designs by smooth, vegetable-like, flowing lines on furniture, decorative objets d'art, hangings, etc. See the drawings of Beardsley. French, literally "new art."

ASHCAN SCHOOL. A group of nineteenth-twentieth-century New York painters, whose subjects, treated "realistically," emanated from the sordid side of city life; the epithet refers to one manifestation of the subject matter, the ashcan. See KITCHEN SINK and works of George Bellows.

ASSEMBLAGE. A recent manner of working predicated on the belief that there is no limitation to the materials or found objects usable for a work of art. Most assemblages come somewhere in between painting and sculpture, and are frequently in high relief.

BAUHAUS or STAATLICHES BAUHAUS. School founded in Weimar, Germany, in 1919 by Gropius, then a leading architect, in order to group the schools of fine arts and crafts in a positive reorganization after Germany's defeat in the First World War. Its artistic ideas had manifested objectivity and rationalism. Leading figures were Feininger, Klee, Kandinsky, and Moholy-Nagy. German, literally "state building house."

BLAUE REITER, DER. (The Blue Rider) Title of a small Kandinsky painting taken by a group of German Expressionist painters in Munich, which included Jawlensky, Marc, Klee; its aim was to unite young modern artistic forces of all kinds, and they expanded their circle to include the German Die Brücke Group.

BRÜCKE, DIE. A federation of Dresden, Germany, artists, founded in 1905, which linked itself to all revolutionary elements of the period. This dates the beginning of German Modern Art, and is equivalent to French Fauvism and Expressionism. German, literally "the bridge."

CALLIGRAPHIC. Refers to the free and rhythmic use of pen markings which approximate handwriting. In painting it signifies free, loose, single-stroke brushwork. Pollock, Kline, and Tobey recently used calligraphic techniques because of their immediacy and spontaneity. Calligraphy has always been important in Oriental art.

CARTOON. Now a drawing with humor or satirical intentions; previously a full-size drawing, usually in full detail, ready for transfer to the wall, canvas, stained glass, or tapestry.

CHIAROSCURO. The "science" that deals with light and shade, used often to give forms the appearance of three-dimensionality. Typical is the example of the ball depicted with strong light coming from one side and eventually ending with the other side in almost total darkness. Italian, literally "light-dark."

CLASSICAL. Usually suggests an established excellence derived from studying antique exemplars, such as Greek art. The classical style is sometimes described as having simplicity, harmony, and proportion.

CLOISONISM or SYNTHETISM. In painting and sculpture the equivalent of the Symbolist Movement in French poetry, which attempted to construct a personal language of symbols or depict the real world.

COLLAGE. A picture built wholly or partly of pieces of paper, cloth or other materials; the device was much used by the Cubists, who used pieces of newspaper in painted pictures. Matisse used cut colored paper entirely in some works. From the French *coller,* to stick.

COMPOSITION. The combined elements of a picture into a dynamic visual whole, seen to be more than the sum of its parts. It might be said that composition, along with line, color, form, etc., is the "language" used to make a work of art.

CONCRETE. A term invented to replace the term "Abstract Art" by Theo Van Doesburg in 1930 in a review by him less than a year before his death. Since that time, "Concrete" has been used in preference by many twentieth-century artists. The best clarification between Abstract and Concrete Art is found in Jean Arp's reference to "Concrete Art": "We do not want to copy nature. We do not want to reproduce. We want to produce like a plant that produces a fruit and not to reproduce. We want to produce directly and not through interpretation." As there is not the slightest trace of abstraction (implying, of course, the abstraction of some thing or some aspect of visible nature), we call it Concrete Art.

CONSTRUCTIVISM or TATLINISM, after the principal exponent, Tatlin. A Russian movement in sculpture which grew out of collage and was replaced by Socialist Realism by 1921. Its manifesto states that space, and not only volume, is important. As sculpture, it used nontraditional material, such as plastic, or industrial methods, such as welding. See works of Pevsner, Moholy-Nagy, and Gabo.

CONTOUR. See OUTLINE.

CONTRAPPOSTO. Designates a pose in which the parts of the body are twisted, sometimes distorted, into opposite directions. Widely used by the sixteenth-century Mannerists. See works of Modigliani, Matisse, and El Greco.

CUBISM. Developed by Braque and Picasso from a planimetric analysis of Cezanne's late works and the doctrine of treating nature by geometric shapes: the cylinder, sphere, cone, square, etc. The word was coined by mocking critics, calling the works "Cubist bizarreries." Cubist period generally considered from 1902-14. Recent theorists define (1) Analytical Cubism (1902-12) as the intermingling of geometric facets of natural forms and backgrounds and the flattening of planes, clearly defining forms; and (2) Synthetic Cubism (1912-14) as the elimination of all imitation of physical nature, with artist using his own palette of colors and creating plastic forms which are metaphors and equivalents of natural objects. Among Cubists, see works of Leger, Picabia, Gris, Villon, Duchamps, and Gleizes. Cubist movement shows the crux of the modern painter's dilemma of resolving the dialectic between the illusionistic three-dimensionalism and the awareness of the two-dimensional picture plane.

DADA. A movement of reaction to the materialism and boredom of bourgeois society which began in Zürich during the First World War and lasted until 1922; its philosophy was deliberately anti-art with the intent to outrage and scandalize. A characteristic production was

a "Mona Lisa" decorated with a mustache by Duchamps. French, literally "hobby horse."

DE STIJL. A Dutch style, it was an intellectual expression
of plastic ideas, with utter simplicity, excluding pictorial representation in favor of objective analysis of
picture space. It utilized basic geometric forms and primary colors. The movement took its name from a Dutch
magazine devoted to Mondrian and Van Doesburg Neo-
Plasticism (1917-28).

DIMENSIONAL, THREE. Traditionally, the realistic depiction
of objects with the appearance of a recession in distance
from foreground to background by such illusionistic
devices as perspective, chiaroscuro, or the transposition
of colors into the canvas (RAYONISM, q.v.).

DIMENSIONAL, TWO. Concerned only with the flat picture
plane on the canvas, that is, with height and width.

EXPRESSIONISM. The search for total self-expression and
emotional impact which negates the intellectual approach to art. The principal exponents were German, or
at least Nordic like the Norwegian Munch, whose hysterical art was a foundation for the movement.

FAUVISM. Artists of this movement, including Matisse,
Derain, and Vlaminck, were introduced at the Paris Sa-
lon D'Automne of 1905 with works of distortion and flat
patterns painted in violent color. The furor it caused
generated the nickname "Les Fauves," meaning wild
beasts.

FIGURATIVE. A painting or sculpture that uses in its principal motif human and animal figures. The term has
been used wrongly to describe any work that is realistic.

FOUND OBJECT. In Surrealist theory, the artist could find
any object, such as a machine part, and having almost

no concern with its intended function, see only its pure form as something of interest.

FUTURISM. Specific movements against the static art of Cubism dating from about 1910, which stressed the representation of dynamic movement; best described by a sentence from a Futurist manifesto (1910): "A galloping horse has not four legs; it has twenty and their movements are triangular."

GEOMETRIC ABSTRACTION. The preoccupation with geometric construction of forms in many nonrealistic art movements to varying degrees of "abstraction." Some of the movements are Cubism and Neo-Plasticism; some of the artists are Kandinsky, Mondrian, and Malevitch.

GOLDEN SECTION or **GOLDEN MEAN** or **SECTION D'OR.** A theory dealing with a basis of proportions, with major and minor divisions of lines into two unequal parts in balance. Said to correspond with certain laws of the universe, which artists utilized by calculation or intuition. "Section D'Or" was the name of a Paris exhibition held in 1912.

GRAPHIC. That aspect of visual arts deriving its effect from drawing; the arts of drawing have what is called a "graphic quality."

IDEAL ART. Seeks to represent an idea, rather than to deal with the material of art. In the Platonic sense, a true dog is the "idea" of dogness, not the visible dog in the gutter, and art's function is to mirror only the Ideal forms. In Neoclassicism the human figure was used to symbolize the highest aspirations of the mind; this led to the preoccupation of artists with the nude.

IMPASTO. The layer or layers of pigment in a painting; a thick and paste-like application. From the Italian *impastare*, to knead.

IMPRESSIONISM. The word first used by a critic as an abuse to describe Monet's "Sunrise: An Impression." Originating in the 1860s, this is usually considered to be the beginning of modern art movements. Its two main objectives were to capture nature through the constantly changing circumstances of light, and to use only the spectrum range of colors, those that can be seen as light hues through the prism. The artists insisted on painting on the spot in order to get a "fleeting impression," as opposed to making sketches and returning to the studio. See works of Monet, Pisarro, Renoir, Sisley, Cezanne, and, later, Seurat's POINTILLISM (q.v.).

KITCHEN SINK SCHOOL. A satirical title given to modern British social realism painting, whose subjects stem from chores associated with the kitchen sink. See works of John Bratby.

LINEAR COMPOSITION. A composition which depends for its effect on the pattern made by lines and outlined forms, rather than on the masses of tone and color.

LITERARY ART. Art whose subjects are derived from or dependent on fiction, such as myths, tales, stories, etc. Delacroix drew on Shakespeare, for example, and Blake illustrated Dante's *Divine Comedy*.

LUMINISM. In painting it determines the effects of light; particularly important to Impressionism.

MALERISCH. A theory set down by H. Wolfflin to explain the polarity of Painterly vs. Linear. The latter clearly defines the forms by contour and approaches a flat, singly-colored area. The former is an expression of form by the relation of colors which run imperceptibly into each other. German, literally "artistic."

MASS. Any large area of color, light, shade, etc., that is not a clearly described form.

MEDIUM. Suggests the particular material with which a picture or sculpture is executed, such as oils, watercolor, pastels, marble, clay, wood, even ink. Recently new mediums have arisen, such as welded steel, polymer, plastics for sculpture, and acrylic for painting.

METAPHYSICAL ART. Broadly, art based on incorporeal, supernatural or visionary inspiration, as in Klee, Blake, Ernst, and de Chirico; the latter and Carro launched the Scuola Metafisica in 1917, which believed that art must narrate something not within its outline.

MOBILE. A form of sculpture invented in 1932 by Alexander Calder, consisting essentially of free forms or objects connected by wires or rods, which, with a touch or a breeze, will revolve to give an ever-changing sequence of planes, solids, and contours in movement. **STABILES,** rather than being suspended from above, are suspended from a solid, grounded mass.

MONUMENTAL. As distinguished from a memorial monument, it is the painting or sculpture (or other form of art) which has a thoroughly planned conception and which is completely worked out; the word does not refer to size.

MOSAIC. Composed of small cubes of stone or glass set in mortar or fine cement to decorate floors, walls, or vaults. The designs may contain figures or may be floral or abstract. The mosaics in Ravenna and Istanbul, of Byzantine origin, are especially famous.

NABIS, THE. A small group of French artists (including Bonnard, Vuillard, and Maillol, between 1889-1899) who, on Gauguin's advice, painted in flat, pure colors in an orderly arrangement. Hebrew, literally "prophets."

NATURALISM. The objective use of nature, with no subjective interpretation. Objects are depicted in their entirety and with accuracy.

NEO-PLASTICISM. The doctrine of pure art dealing with the use of horizontal or vertical right angles, primary and noncolors. Mondrian developed this from Cubism. It rejects illusion and allusion. It asserts the primacy of the picture plane. Even without illusionistic devices, however, the forms still retain solidity.

NEUE SACHLICHKEIT. German, literally "new objectivity." See VERISM.

OPTICAL ART. A movement (1963-65) that reached its peak in the New York exhibition "The Responsive Eye." Optical illusion, long an artistic consideration, now focuses on the viewer's retinal, "optical" experience. The term "Op" art was probably chosen because the movement followed "Pop" art.

ORGANIC. Refers, especially in sculpture and architecture (as with Frank Lloyd Wright), to growing harmonies with all parts of the work, almost as if it grew out of nature. See CONCRETE.

ORPHISM or **ORPHIC CUBISM.** Term invented about 1912 by Apollinaire which extolled the supremacy of pure color in painting, as well as simultaneous contrasts which give pictorial dynamism; its only law was that of color relationships, and it was free from representation. See works of Delauney.

OUTLINE or **CONTOUR.** The outermost edge, which, in drawing or painting, forms the boundary of one shape, defining it in relation to another. On the other hand, an outline is no more than a boundary made up of lines.

PATINA. A discoloring of the surface of bronze or stone sculpture, either artificially or through time.

PERSPECTIVE. A mathematical system of representing three dimensions or spatial recession on two-dimensional surfaces with such devices as chiaroscuro and the principle that although parallel lines never meet theoretically, they appear so to the eye. Introduced early in the fifteenth century. **AERIAL PERSPECTIVE** deals with the changes in tone and color values observable in objects receding from the viewer.

PICTURE PLANE. That surface of two dimensions, height and width, on which the painter works. Coming to terms with this flatness began with Gauguin and was refined by Mondrian. It is now quite important, as many modern painters reject any illusion that might indicate a plane behind the first picture plane.

POINTILLISM or **DIVISIONISM.** A term used by the Neo-Impressionists to describe a semiscientific method of applying two adjacent primary color dots and having them mix in the spectator's eye; for example, a blue dot next to a yellow dot creates the illusion of green. See works of Seurat.

POP ART. A noisy "movement" at its height in 1964-65. While there were no unifying ideas of purpose, almost all adherents used artifacts as their subjects. Whether to criticize contemporary life or to regard it as beautiful has not yet been made clear at this writing. Historically, Pop Art may be seen as an outgrowth of Dadaism.

PRIMARY COLORS. Red, yellow, and blue, from which all other colors may be derived. Primary colors are much more popular in contemporary painting, for they can be experienced more immediately and directly.

PURISM. The use of purely defined form and color. Term used now only in reference to objective art which at-

tempts to eliminate all nonessentials to the artist's purpose, primarily decoration and sentimentality.

RAYONISM. The approach to painting through the creation
of forms by precise laws of the radiation of colors and
light; created by the Russian Larionov in 1911. Attempts
to create a three-dimensional effect.

REALISM. The repudiation of Ideal Art; signifies the search
for natural appearances, though these may reflect the
seamier sides of life. See works of Courbet.

RELIEF SCULPTURE. Projects in varying depths from a flat,
vertical background which is not free-standing.

SKETCH or STUDY. The artist's "thinking out" of his problem
by drawing or fast visual notations. Used by both sculptor and painter as a plan, usually for more monumental
works.

SOCIAL REALISM. The painting of unidealized everyday
life, generally focusing on the common, ordinary people's viewpoint. See ASHCAN SCHOOL, KITCHEN SINK.
Distinct from Socialist Realism, the official or academic
art of the USSR, which is intended as "revolutionary
romanticism."

SUPREMATISM. Started by Malevitch, this form of extreme
Cubism dealt only with the purest of geometric forms:
the circle, triangle, and cross. See Malevitch's "White
on White."

SURREALISM. Movement based on "super-reality," referring
to dreams and fantasies of the subconscious or super-
conscious. Apollinaire invented the term in 1924 for the
artists who sought to liberate these aspects of their
psyches. See works of Ernst, Dali, and Tanguy.

SYNTHETISM or SYMBOLISM. Movement whose object was
to construct in painting a synthesis of the real and the

imaginary and so develop a language of personal symbolism.

TONDO. Painting or sculptural relief of circular form, reflecting recent interest in shaped canvases, which culminated in a 1965 Guggenheim Museum exhibition, "The Shaped Canvas."

TRIPTYCH. A painting of three hinged panels. Previously, the two wings were subservient to the central panel, but recently they are of equal importance.

TROMPE L'OEIL. Device consisting of pasting elements of newspapers, wallpaper, cigarette packs, cloth, or other materials to the canvas to deceive the eye by disrupting logic or for poetic relationships. French, literally "to deceive the eye." See COLLAGE.

VERISM. Social purpose art of the 1920's of some German Expressionists, calling for a new objectivity or stricter truth of realistic appearances of objects.

VORTICISM. A movement in England (1912-14) comparable to Paris' Cubism and Italy's Futurism. Ezra Pound coined the word to mean something almost totally nonfigurative or abstract—machine forms, for example—and characterized by flat, plane-like systems of arcs and angles organized radially from a central focal point; hence, the "vortex," which attempts to draw the spectator into a whirling recession.

WELDED SCULPTURE. Lately popular, it is the construction of sculpture through the process of welding metals together; uses either raw materials or found metal junk, such as auto bumpers; the sculptor may or may not retain the material's original identity.

CHAPTER **6**

Man in Groups

The Language of Sociology

Tad K. Krauze, Leah Glass

The word *sociology* was coined by Auguste Comte, the father of the discipline of sociology. This was the first technical term in the new field.

As sociology has developed since the late eighteenth century, its tasks and goals have been clarified. Sociology is a discipline which has as its goal the understanding of the social processes and social organization which form the basis of the social life of man. Sociology is a *theoretical* discipline seeking not only increased knowledge, but also the integration of that knowledge into the body of theory which explains how social relationships and values influence behavior, and how behavior, in turn, modifies the social structure. Sociology is not a *practice* in the sense of social work, engineering, or psychotherapy, in which an already existing body of knowledge is studied for its usefulness in direct application to existing problems. However, the theories and findings of sociology may well form a substantial part of the body of information used in applied social and behavioral sciences.

The subject matter of sociology is the social life of man,

the way social life is organized, develops and changes, and the ways in which social organizations have consequences for the individuals within them as well as for other units of organization in society.

Three broad areas of sociology can be delineated as theory, methodology, and subfields.

Theory deals with the development of logically connected propositions which have been tested and verified and which lead to more general propositions concerning society, propositions which are thus applicable to more and more segments under specified conditions. In another sense, theory concerns a general orientation or frame of reference from which one can deduce a series of propositions which have explanatory power for specific areas of social life.

Theories of varying scope exist in sociology, and some of them are applicable to only a limited segment of society (theories about marriage and the family); some are applicable to a limited social problem (differential association theory in criminology); some are applicable to only certain size groups (small group theory). However, theories developed in one area of inquiry may have a broader applicability because the concepts involved cut across many areas of social life (role theory). Finally some theories attempt an all-encompassing explanation of society (structural functionalism) while others are content with more modest attempts (role theory).

Theory may also be conceived of as dealing with social units of varying scope from micro-sociology to macro-, with a range that moves from the social relationships that exist between two people, to families and small groups, to collectivities, to social structures, and finally to the organization of society as a whole.

Methodology properly begins with sociological epistemology, with the question of how facts about social life become known. From this, one constructs rules of evidence and methods of inquiry which take into consideration the peculiarities of sociological information and which assign or develop methods for particular problems or particular classes of problems. These methods are then applied to the particular research questions as a general method (historicism, survey, etc.), each of which has specific techniques (content analysis, sampling, interviewing, etc.).

Because sociology is a scientific discipline, and a young one, it has, at times, been intensely concerned with varying aspects of methodology. Its earlier concern was whether or not sociology could employ a scientific method at all, in the same sense as the natural or physical sciences. More recently it has been involved in the development and application of various techniques—scales, sampling, statistics, computer simulation.

Subfields of sociology are areas of inquiry delineated by a social problem, by a specific aspect of social life (medical sociology, occupational sociology) or by a specified area of inquiry. These subfields have arisen in several ways: in response to urgent social need for a better understanding of a particular social problem (delinquency, mental health); as a development from theoretical concepts which focus on a particular area of inquiry and require more information as well as more theory in that area (role theory); and, finally, the availability of funds as well as the opening of research possibilities in a particular field spurs increased activity in that field. Each subfield, working in a circumscribed area of inquiry, concerns itself with both theory and methodology and thus feeds into the mainstream of general sociology and, in turn, derives its theory and methods from the main body of theory and methodology.

Together, theory, methodology and research, and the subfields comprise the field of sociology.

Sociology, as a theoretical discipline, requires a terminology which is precise and unambiguous. Clear and exact terminology facilitates the formulation of theory, permits research analysis, and provides a common basis of understanding among members of the field and related disciplines. Without precise terms, theories cannot be developed, research analysis flounders in ambiguities, and communication among members of the profession leads to intellectual chaos.

The development of a precise language is particularly essential in a discipline such as sociology because the subject matter is one with which everyone is familiar. The techniques of influence, the emblems of rank, child-rearing practices, etc., exist among all people from preliterate societies to contemporary ones. Because everyone is familiar with and actively participates in society, strong opinions are held concerning the subject matter of sociology. The very terms used in everyday speech are value-laden.

The existence of everyday terminology poses several other problems for the use of these terms in sociology. These terms may vary in their meaning in everyday usage, so that the criterion of precision and clarity of meaning is not served. Or, the meaning of a term may be very broad; but sociological analysis may require that a broad term be separated into its component parts so that it is possible to speak about them separately. Also, the sociologist may wish to speak about different kinds of a phenomenon (group), and there he must either supply adjectives (peer group, reference group, etc.) or he must coin a new word (collectivity). New words are also coined in order to name processes which the sociologist observes or infers and for which a word does not exist. The coining of a new word, while adding to the vocabulary of the field, has the virtue of clarity since there are no preconceived notions concerning its meaning.

Despite the aim of precision and clarity, sociological terminology is sometimes overlapping so that the meaning of a term may vary. This happens in several ways: different sociologists may use different terms to mean substantially the same thing, or they may have a somewhat different definition for the same term. Terms used by one writer, or a school of writers, are generally clear in meaning. However, as one traces the use of a term over a long period of time and through many writers, the meaning may change, particularly when the term in question is a relatively broad one (social organization). Some terms, however, coined once, retain their original meaning (Sumner's folkways). Sometimes a word used by a writer drops out of usage and is only resurrected by historians of sociological theory. In other cases, new words are incorporated into the writing of other sociologists. Overlapping terminology may also occur as part of a struggle of ideas between different schools of sociology. When basic theoretical differences exist between writers, their key concepts, and therefore the meaning they attach to key terms, will differ.

Another source of overlapping terminology in sociology lies in the transfer or use of terminology from other disciplines. For example, value means something quite different in economics from its meaning in sociology. A further, more significant difficulty lies in the use of the same term by closely related disciplines, or in the borrowing or use of terms which originated in such closely related disciplines. For example, anthropology studies "cultures," while sociology studies "societies," or "social structures," yet the term culture is also used in sociology. Terminology in anthropology was developed to facilitate the analysis of preliterate societies. When these terms are adapted to complex social structures, they cut across existing sociological terminology. For example, the term subculture comes from anthropology and represents an attempt to break down complex social structures along the cultural dimension. However, it is often difficult to distinguish a subculture from a collectivity or group or occupation. The existence of overlapping terminology reflects the fact that sociology is still a young field which has not completely codified its terminology.

WORD LIST

ACTION. A term introduced into sociology by Max Weber and used extensively by Talcott Parsons to specify those aspects of behavior which are the special concern of the sociologist, as distinct from aspects of behavior which are not relevant to his analysis. Action refers to behavior to which the individual attributes subjective meaning. It is behavior which is directed toward a goal and may be either subjective or objective.

ALIENATION. Used in sociology, refers to either an objective or subjective state in which the individual is, or perceives himself as, separated from significant aspects of the social structure or from social interaction. In its subjective aspect, alienation is related to hopelessness, isolation, and dejection.

AUTHORITY. The socially or institutionally denoted right given to certain individuals or administrative units to administer rules in specified areas of social behavior. Authority is based on the ability to gain the assent of others. Authority is usually but not always legitimated. See LEGITIMACY.

ANOMIE. A term first introduced into sociology by Emile Durkheim. It refers to a situation in society in which the norms which generally regulate behavior are no longer operative. Anomie is accompanied by a state of social and personal disorganization or upheaval. Anomie is most frequently used in reference to society itself; however, it is also used in reference to individuals experiencing the effects of anomic social structures.

BUREAUCRACY. A term associated with Max Weber, who used it to describe a type of administrative and governmental organization which develops in a "rational-legal" society. Bureaucracy is characterized by a graded hierarchy of officials culminating in a central authority, the rationalization of tasks, fixed and limited areas of jurisdiction, the creation of a system of central files and record-keeping.

CHARISMA. Refers to extraordinary genius, state of grace, or power of personality ascribed to an individual, which forms the basis of his ability to influence others and to acquire and maintain a position of leadership. Persons regarded as charismatic by their followers are thought to have almost superhuman qualities, and it is on this basis that they are accepted as leaders.

CLASS. A relative position of individuals in the social structure, based on income, education, and occupation. It is usually referred to as social class, and one speaks of upper, middle, and lower class.

CONFLICT. A struggle between individuals, or groups within a society or social group, over values, ideologies, status, power, or scarce resources.

CONFORMITY. Behavior which is in compliance with the norms or practices of the group or society to which the individual belongs. Conformity is an important concept for sociology, for without conformity social structures cannot be maintained. The sociological usage is to be distinguished from the everyday usage which defines conformity as the inability of the individual to make free choices for himself, but rather to be influenced by the opinions of others.

CULTURE. The pattern of behavior, transmitted by symbols, which forms the achievement of a group. Culture includes overt behavior, products of behavior, as well as traditional ideas and values which form the heritage of the group. Culture is not only current action, but a stimulus or condition for further action.

CRIME. An act prohibited by law. There are several levels at which a crime may be said to exist. It may be an act committed, but not known to the police. It may be known to the police, but the criminal may not be apprehended. The criminal may be apprehended, but not booked. The criminal may be tried or not tried, and finally he may be found guilty or not guilty. There is some question as to whether all of these situations should be classed as crime.

DEVIANCE. The obverse of conformity. It is the failure of individuals to pattern their behavior in accordance with the norms or practices of the group or society. Special subfields in the study of deviance include criminology, delinquency, narcotics addiction, etc. In social psychology the term deviance as the obverse of conformity does not exist. Here the obverse of conformity is independent judgment.

DIFFERENTIAL ASSOCIATION. A theory in criminology which explains the development of the criminal on the basis of association with criminal patterns of behavior more frequently and more significantly than is the case for noncriminals.

DIFFUSION. The process by which culture is transmitted from one group to another, usually spreading from one area to another. Diffusion takes place as a result of migrations, trade, exogamous marriage, and other instances where contact between two cultures occurs. The term comes from anthropology and has been used to describe the process by which cultural traits spread from one area to another, and as a possible explanation for observed cultural similarities in widespread areas.

EQUILIBRIUM. A state of balance or integration in which all the parts which comprise a society or smaller social unit are functioning together. In contemporary structural-functional theory, equilibrium is a central concept. From this theoretical perspective, social organization is directed toward the maintenance of equilibrium, the continued functioning of all of the structural parts of society, and it is on this basis that conformity is required.

ETHNIC GROUP. A social group identified by the national origin, religious affiliation, or race which all of its members share, and which demonstrates a pattern of identifiable cultural traits. Jews, Negroes, Italians, and Irish in the United States are some examples of ethnic groups.

ETHNOCENTRISM. A pattern of response to the behavior and values of others in which the criterion applied in evaluating the behavior of others is the behavior and values of one's own ethnic group.

FAMILY. A social unit composed of a man and woman who have a relationship sufficiently enduring to provide for procreation and upbringing of children. Family arrangements may vary considerably from one culture to another. Family may include multiple wives (polygyny), multiple husbands (polyandry). A family may be "nuclear," composed of a man, a woman, and their children, or it may be "extended," composed of the nuclear family as well as other defined blood relatives.

FOLK CULTURE. A term first used by Robert Redfield to refer to a form of social organization which describes the cultures of primitive people, peasants, and isolated groups. Folk culture is characterized by highly conventionalized behavior, the prominence of kinship as a unit of social organization and as an agent of informal social control, and by the importance of tradition transmitted orally. Folk cultures are relatively stable, so that there is a similarity of culture from generation to generation.

FOLKWAYS. The traditions and way of life of a group.

FUNCTIONALISM. A theory in which social processes or actions are viewed as having consequences for other social processes or social structures. These consequences hinge on the interrelationship of various parts of the social structure so that changes in one part affect other parts as well. See EQUILIBRIUM. In structural-functional theory, the conditions which are necessary to maintain the social unit are stated, and the contribution each makes to the maintenance of the system is called its function.

IDENTIFICATION. A process by which an individual internalizes a social role and adopts it as his own. Identification is part of the learning process and also part of socialization. The term identification is also used to refer to the process by which the individual internalizes and adopts an image of another person who then becomes a model for behavior.

IDEOLOGY. A set of ideas and beliefs characteristic of a society or group within society. Ideologies consist of normative and factual observations which, together, offer an explanation for complex social phenomena. An ideology consists of ideas about the group itself, its relation to larger social units, its history and its goals. Ideology may be used in the descriptive sense as when it defines the ideas, values, beliefs, and interpretations of a particular society or group. Ideology also refers to such a set of ideas, beliefs, and interpretations when they constitute a socio-political choice presented in order to influence the political behavior of a population or present a rationale for the behavior of the group.

INDUSTRIALIZATION. The process by which modern industry is introduced into a hitherto nonindustrial society. Industrialization includes the economic and structural changes that accompany this process as well as the changes in values.

INSTITUTION. An organized and integrated pattern of procedure by which activities of society are carried on. Institutions are complex and enduring. The activities around which they are organized are carried out by organizations, associations, groups, etc. Thus, for example, medicine is an institution whose work is carried out by hospitals, doctors, clinics, medical associations, laboratories, etc.

INTEGRATION. The promotion of ethnic, social, or religious assimilation; for example, in the U.S., the process of making public facilities, employment, etc., available equally to people of all ethnic origins. Compare SEGREGATION.

INTERACTION. A process in which the action of one person, group, or other social entity creates a response in another, and in which the action of either serves as a stimulus for further action for the other.

INTERNALIZATION. A learning process in which one acquires, in the course of interaction, a symbol or sign that represents the object or social process which is being learned. It is a form of "cognitive map" in which the symbol being learned has meaning to the individual. Thus the internalized image contains attitudes, emotions, and motivations. The object of internalization can be another person, an object, a role, or the self. In the case of internalization of the self, personality and identity are developed; in the case of internalization of roles, social behavior and norms are learned.

LEGITIMACY. The condition under which the authority or power of a government or leader is accepted by the governed. The basis of legitimacy is a law, principle, or other commonly recognized form of authorization. Max Weber, who first used the term extensively in sociology, distinguished three kinds of authority on the basis of their sources of legitimacy: traditional, rational-level, and charismatic. See AUTHORITY and POWER.

MOBILITY. Movement or change in position within the stratification system. Mobility can be horizontal or vertical. Change of role, particularly in occupation, without a change in class position, is called horizontal mobility. Thus a change from carpenter to plumber is an example of horizontal mobility. Vertical mobility is a change in social class position. Thus a change from carpenter to engineer would be an example of upward mobility, while a change from physician to salesman would be an example of downward mobility. See STRATIFICATION and CLASS.

MORES. Folkways or popular habits and traditions which are generally considered to be of crucial importance to the welfare of society. Violation of mores on the part of a member of society results in severe and formal punishment, whereas violation of folkways, being less crucial to the welfare of society, is punished informally by ostracism, avoidance, exclusion, etc.

MYTH. A traditional story, generally with a religious or magical content, which originates within a group and is passed down by the members. It very often is a story which either describes the activities of supernatural beings worshiped by the group, or provides an explanation of the origins of religious rites, natural phenomena, or of the group itself.

NORM. An abstract standard or criterion, accepted by members of a group, which defines those behavior patterns which are acceptable and those which are not. Deviation from norms results in punishment for the deviant.

NUCLEAR FAMILY. A social group composed of a man and a woman who have an enduring relationship, and their children. The nuclear family is of importance in sociology because it is within this social unit that much of the socialization of the child occurs.

OCCUPATION. The kind of work performed by an individual. The same kind of work may be performed by individuals who receive greater or lesser financial reward (a salesman in a small store and a salesman in a large insurance company). Occupation is not related to status; thus a research assistant and a department head, working in the field of book publishing, have different status but a similar occupation.

PEER GROUP. A group composed of individuals who are homogenous or "equals," generally in respect to age. Most frequently, the term is used to refer to children's groups. The concept enables sociologists to study social learning that occurs in the process of interaction among children rather than within the family, or between children and adults.

POWER. The capacity of an individual or group to produce intended effects over other individuals or groups; i.e., to influence them, on the basis of explicit or implicit use of force.

PRESTIGE. The esteem in which individuals or groups are held on the basis of some criterion such as quality of performance, occupational rank, achievement, etc.

REFERENCE GROUP. A group to which an individual either aspires to belong, with which he compares his own achievements, or whose goals and values he adopts. It is not a group to which he belongs as a member.

SANCTION. Punishment or reward, the purpose of which is to produce conformity with the norms of the group. Sanctions are techniques of socialization by which members of the group are taught that conforming behavior will lead to rewards (positive sanctions) and deviant behavior will lead to punishment (negative sanctions).

SEGREGATION. A process by which an ethnic minority group, occasionally by its own choosing but more generally through explicit or implicit coercion, comes to live in a delimited geographic area. This geographic or residential segregation leads to and is accompanied by discriminatory practices which further restrict the minority group members from opportunities to participate in the majority culture. Compare INTEGRATION.

SITUATION. Those social structures, processes, and persons relevant to the understanding of action which is being studied. The situational approach involves the analysis of behavior, not as an individual attribute or isolated event, but in the context of social processes and other individuals relevant to it.

SOCIAL CHANGE. The process by which social structures or patterns of behavior become modified. Theories of social change either try to seek a causal explanation for change, or attempt to predict the consequences of social change for the individual or group affected, or for other parts of the social structure.

SOCIAL CONTROL. The process by which a social group or society secures conformity from its members and either metes out punishment to deviants, or takes measures to restrict the effects of deviance on the entire social unit.

SOCIAL DISORGANIZATION. A disruption or disturbance in the social structure which creates a situation in which the ordinary functioning of the social institutions and of the agencies of social control is disrupted.

SOCIAL ORGANIZATION. A relatively stable pattern of relationships among the members of a group or among the parts of a social system. Social organization can be viewed as those patterns, relationships, and units of a social system which are necessary to meet the needs of the system.

SOCIAL SYSTEM. Refers to a social organization. The term has been used in the theory of Talcott Parsons to mean a system of interaction in which two or more persons are involved in a situation where each person must take the behavior of others into account, and where behavior is directed toward goals. Roles and constellations of roles are the basic units of analysis. The term social system is also used to refer to the total society as it is analyzed in terms of the organization and integration of its component parts.

SOCIALIZATION. The process by which members of a social group learn the appropriate norms and roles, i.e., the appropriate behavior to enable them to function in their social group. Socialization usually refers to the process by which children acquire this knowledge, but it also refers to adults who become members of a new group.

SOCIETY. A complex of social relationships among people. The term is also used to refer to such a complex of relationships in a particular, distinctive, self-perpetuating group. Another use of the term society defines it as the institutions and culture of such a distinctive, self-perpetuating group.

STATUS. A position occupied by an individual within a social system, by virtue of which the individual has certain rights and privileges. The position a person occupies also prescribes certain obligations, that is, certain expected behaviors. This aspect of social position is called role. Another usage of the term status refers to the individual's prestige or standing in society compared with that of other individuals.

STRATIFICATION. The process by which individuals are ranked differently within society, generally according to their social class, achievements, or access to the benefits of their society.

SUBCULTURE. The culture of a subgroup of a society. The subgroup may be based on ethnic, religious, regional, or other characteristics held in common. This common characteristic becomes the basis of a feeling of membership in the subculture, though its members do not necessarily interact with each other. It also forms the basis of an identifiable cultural pattern.

VALUE. A concept or standard by which things are judged to be desirable or undesirable. Values have a strong emotional connotation. They are general standards, not prescriptions for behavior. See NORMS.

VALUE-FREE. Objectivity in sociological analysis. It means that the sociologist as observer, researcher, theoretician, or analyst of social behavior attempts to use no value judgments so that he may observe or analyze without the intrusion of preconceived ideas.

CHAPTER 7

"A Heightened Imitation . . ."

The Language of Literature

MARTIN TUCKER

Words make and break literature. Unlike other areas of communication, however, literature does more than inform or persuade or argue. It fulfills an emotive and esthetic sense. It suggests a meaning, and conveys a tonal coloring. Thus a word in literature may mean more than it says, or say more than it means. While informative and reportorial prose is intended to be objective, to keep the fact squarely before the reader, literature has a multiple purpose. It has, to use a term current in literary criticism, an *affective* quality. It results in a host of reactions inferred and directly received from the language presented to the reader.

The task of understanding these reactions, of abstracting them for initiation into the mysteries and pleasures of the literary art, is the task of the critic, and the critic has his personal language as well as the universal language. Often he has a language common to a group, and that group may be fashionable or not fashionable in the barometer of public taste. The group known as the "New Critics" was revolutionary thirty years ago; today its guiding principle, that the text must be examined on its own merits and not by the standards of philosophical and historical evaluation, is accepted as a conventional approach.

For his task the critic has crafted many verbal tools. Most readers are acquainted with the classic division of literature into respective genres—prose and poetry and drama. Genres are further classified into discursive and nondiscursive prose, into the novel and the short story, the biography and autobiography, the essay, and the epic and the lyric, to name but a few examples. The word *genre* comes from the Latin verb *to beget;* the root is used in such English words as *generate, engender, genus,* and *gender.* Genre is then an example of how literature has taken an etymological root used mainly in biological de-scriptions to form its own distinctive word.

In general both the traditional and more newly coined terms of literature come from the Western languages—from Greek and Latin, in many cases using the same terms as Aristotle and Plato used; from French and Italian and German. Occasionally a critic will use an Eastern term—like *dharma* or *Zen Buddhism* or *haiku*—to describe a work or aspect of literature. Even more rarely an amateur critic will invent his own language or distort a commonly held one, as when a student described *kinesthetic* as "the art or esthetics of family life." Eccentricities of lan-guage are of course not rare in literature—the artist is, by a romantic definition at least, an eccentric, someone who sees the world in a new way and who uses language in a new light, as Shakespeare and Dante and Joyce have used it. Yet a fairly stable store of words exist which will not buck their meaning for some time to come. These are the words presented later in this chapter.

Although Latin and Greek provide the basis of most literary terms, the student and critic today use the Anglicized form, unless they wish to exude an air of pomposity. *Divine afflatus*, coming from the Latin meaning "to breathe upon" and today meaning "inspiration," is a descriptive term that inevitably characterizes the writer as balloon-like in his physical as well as esthetic constitution. *Magnum opus*—the literal Latin for "the great work"—is a term in as low repute now as "The Great American Novel"; a reference to it is like pinching a phantom. Even *malapropism* (from the French *mal à propos,* meaning something said or done awkwardly or at an inopportune time) and *obiter dicta* (literally a thing said by the way), somewhat sanctioned in their use, are used rarely. Words like *periphrasis* and *circumlocution* when used as technical terms are acceptable diction, but the literary critic avoids them.

Before examining the terms well-informed laymen and critics use, one should distinguish that evanescent line between the critic and the reviewer, and the language each uses. Often enough a reviewer of books is a critic of substance, and a critic makes a living by reviewing books. But the reviewer is less careful with his terms and more facile with his abstractions. Reviewing terms are familiar to the reader because they come from the general store of language, but once the season is over, they are marked down as a result of overhandling. Among such terms are the familiar "writer's vision," "illumination" (a currently fashionable key word), "enlightenment," "convincing," and "insight." "Camp" is another term everyone is spouting these days, but its definition is as changeable as a camp follower. Because the phenomenon of "camp" has created a new literary-sociological jargon, its verbal derivatives cannot be ignored. No one knows the origin of "camp" or its first utterance in its new guise somewhere on the banks of the Hudson or the heights of Madison

Avenue. It may be defined (keeping in mind that "camp" has as many meanings as a thermometer has degrees) as the presentation of status to extravagant nonsense. The most often quoted examples of "camp" are the craze (another "reviewing" term) for Bette Davis movies, Tiffany lamps, and Carol Channing vocal exercises. "Camp," from these examples, can be seen to involve a conscious defense of the excessive mannerism; an acceptance of the odd as the artistic. "Camp" is then another degree of baroque, another form of decadence.

Among the basic terms in literature are *connotation* and *denotation, abstract* and *concrete, rhetoric, diction, style, imagery, symbol, irony, point of view, ambiguity,* and *paradox.* These terms indicate the way art forms extend to reflect the intensity of the artist's experience.

Denotation refers to the literal meaning of a word or phrase. It is the act of naming an object or idea and thus identifying it. One denotes a house by calling it a house. *Connotation* means that to the primary meaning of a word, a secondary and implied meaning has been added. Thus, in calling a house a mansion or a shack, the object has not only been identified, it has had added to it a critical attitude. From this base has evolved the symbol which carries with it associations and implications beyond the primary expression. A symbol is at once something abstract and concrete: in representing something it is abstract. The Statue of Liberty is the symbol of the concept, Liberty, but it is also concrete. A symbol which has universal application may then be said to be a *concrete universal*—that is, it expresses the universal through the particular. Concrete terms, embodying universal symbolic value because of their power to create imagery and sensory experience through tangible objects and palpable experience, are thus the basic words of literature. Abstract terms, on the other hand, which transform the particular object or experience into a generalization, are the root words of science and philosophy.

Rhetoric is the organization of language for its most effective presentation. The question of whether rhetoric can be separated from content, or style from form, is an ancient quarrel. In Aristotle's time and in the eighteenth century, rhetoric was theorized into decoration—that is, the rhetorical flourishes were added to a body of writing to make it effective. In the twentieth century such an approach is unthinkable, for style in the modern writer's eyes cannot be separated from content: the statement of a writer is the way in which he presents his thoughts. *Style* then is the writer's technique, and his technique states his point of view or belief. James Joyce's *Ulysses* cannot be discussed without discussing the manner of its presentation; the view of life it presents is indivisible from the stream-of-consciousness technique controlling the novel.

Yet while style and rhetoric have a closer intimacy with form and content today than in the eighteenth century and classic times, such terms as *stylized* and *rhetorical* retain their historic trappings. A rhetorical question, for example, is one obviously designed for its oratoric effect, and the man who answers it is not likely to have much of any style. Parallel to this is *stylized*, a word that connotes, even when the treatment is successful, an artful, eccentric language that does not intend to imitate reality.

While rhetoric is the body of principles for effective use of language, and style is that language best suited to present a particular set of ideas, *diction* may be said to deal with the proper choice of individual words. Style combines words in the best manner; rhetoric combines the units of the entire piece of writing most effectively; while diction refers to the choice of the most apt words for a particular thought. A man with good diction may have an excellent vocabulary and know the precise shading of words, but he may have little style, nor does he necessarily practice well the principles of rhetoric.

A good reader will be aware that diction is a matter of taste and that the proper choice of words is often a matter for the particular occasion. Several levels of diction exist, but their applicability depends on the particular situation. What is slang to one man is biblical to another (Speak to any young "hipster" and listen to the devoutness of his tongue when he is uttering his own-world phrases). Among the levels of diction are the following: *Formal,* a level of usage found in serious, formal discourse and writing; in religious and government pamphlets and in graduate-student term papers. *Informal,* a level of usage found in casual but polite conversation of cultivated, educated people. *Colloquial,* the language used every day, with no conscious attempt to purify it; thus, the colloquial language of many people is unacceptable in the parlors of others. *Slang,* this level of usage is several steps lower than that of colloquial language, but its principle remains the same; it is the language used by people when they feel most natural; it involves the distortion of words to express an effect. *Low,* this is the lowest kind of language that is unacceptable at its highest level. *Poetic,* words chosen for particular poetic effect. The practice of poetic diction was more common in other centuries than the twentieth and led to what, in effect, was no more than labored, artificial language disguising itself under this bloodless label. Poetic diction, rightly or wrongly, is today considered effete. *Technical,* language used in various specific occupations with special meaning; for example, "fade out" as used by a movie or television cameraman.

Two other terms are so widely used in literature that

they represent an indispensable part of the critic's vocabulary. *Irony* may be defined as a figure of speech in which the words used are opposite to the intended meaning. Since irony is an attitude as well as a technique, it is difficult to find it pure. While *sarcasm* is easily recognizable and the sardonic wit reveals himself by his mocking smile, the ironist is quiet while he is loosening the anchor-holds of his readers' intellectual or religious or philosophic beliefs. Irony takes many forms, the most familiar of which are these: *Dramatic,* when the audience knows something which the protagonist or other actor in a drama does not know, and thus can interpret his words on several levels; and *Irony of Fate,* when the opposite of what is expected to happen occurs.

Closely allied to irony are such terms as *tension, ambiguity,* and *paradox.* Since the ironist means something other than what he literally states, his statement is capable of at least two meanings. The tension built up by these conflicting levels of meaning is used for artistic effect by the ironist, who often will employ a paradox to heighten the tension caused by his ironic point of view. A *paradox* is a seeming contradiction found to have validity in truth; it may be described as a situation or circumstance impossible to accept in the light of universal and/or conventional beliefs, and impossible to deny by the standards of reason or observation.

Irony may also be said to represent a point of view or attitude, but the term *point of view* when used by the literary critic has a specialized meaning. Point of view is the technique by which the writer tells his story. The writer may tell it through the eyes of one person who narrates the events in the first person; he may narrate it through the limited omniscient point of view, that is through the eyes of a person who relates it in the third person, and thus is restricted to what that character knows and to what events that character is a witness. Or he may choose to tell his story from the camera-eye or objective point of view, stating only the sensory effects observable on the surface—what is seen, heard, felt, touched and smelled—and never exploring, except by implication, the thoughts within his characters' minds. When the author moves freely into the mind of any character and does not restrict himself in time and place, he is said to be using the omniscient point of view.

Below are listed other basic terms in literature.

WORD LIST

ACHRONOLOGICAL. A method of presentation that does not follow strict chronology, or the forward movement of time. From the prefix indicating a negative and the Greek root meaning time.

ALEXANDRIANISM. An attitude characterized by a rational approach to literature. The Alexandrians, because of their superior resources in the library at Alexandria, Egypt, have become the butt and praise of modern critics, depending on one's own approach to literature.

ALLEGORY. A systematic collection of extended metaphors in a narrative whose surface action is a device for teaching a moral, religious, political, or social lesson. An allegory differs from a symbol or collection of symbols in that the structure of allegory demands that each metaphor be a part of a unified pattern. John Bunyan's *Pilgrim's Progress* is the most famous Christian allegory in prose, while George Orwell's *Animal Farm* is a well-known modern allegory about Communism as practiced in the Soviet Union. From the Greek prefix meaning other or otherwise and the root meaning to speak (*allos* plus *agoreus*).

ALLITERATION. The repetition of the same sound at the beginning of words. Old English verse is characterized by alliteration. Other words from the same root are obliterate, literate and illiterate. From the Latin prefix and root meaning a letter to, or letter with.

ALLUSION. A literary expression for reference. A critic alludes to a work or a writer makes allusions when his reference is indirect and subtle. From the Latin prefix and root meaning to play to.

AMBIGUITY. The quality of indeterminateness in meaning. When a work is ambiguous, its interpretation must remain uncertain, although the very suggestiveness of a work of high ambiguity provides richness and subtlety. The word comes from the Latin prefix, *amb*, and the root, *agere*, thus meaning to act in both or two ways.

ANALYTICAL CRITICISM. A synonym for New Criticism or the work pursued by the New Critics. Analytic criticism examines a work of art in terms of the "logic" of that work, although it may have recourse to historical conventions and traditions.

ANAPEST. The rhythmic pattern of an unstressed syllable followed by another unstressed syllable and then a stressed syllable. The words *intervene, pioneer,* are examples of anapestic rhythm.

ANTAGONIST. The character who opposes the central character and thus sets in motion the conflict necessary for a dramatic work. A **FOIL** differs from an antagonist in that the foil is used to contrast with the central character and to move the action forward, but he does not necessarily oppose the protagonist. Antagonist, literally, is the anti-actor.

ARCHETYPE. A term made popular by the psychology of Carl Jung. An archetype serves as an image of all human experience, reaching beyond the conscious historical past. Archetypes are found naturally in folklore and myth, where recurring images of prehistoric nature and what T. S. Eliot called "pre-logical mentality" evoke the profound sense of eternal human pattern. From the Greek prefix meaning chief, and the root meaning type or kind.

ARCHITECTONICS. A term borrowed from architecture (plus *onics*) used to express the sense of proportion of a work of literature—its unity of theme, its foundation in a proper structure. Architectonics stresses the total organization of a work and might be said to be the working plans of the organic theory.

ASSONANCE. The repetition of vowel sounds in words separated by different consonants. "Ships of the Spanish Main came to South America in search of great wealth" contains assonance in the words *Main* and *came*. From the Latin prefix and root meaning to sound to.

AUTOTELIC. A term denoting that a work, like beauty, creates its own excuse for being. Such a work needs no other justification. The opposite of *autotelic* is **DIDACTIC**: a didactic work has its justification in the teaching and spreading of a moral lesson derived from that work. From the Greek prefix meaning self, and the root meaning purpose.

BALLAD. A narrative poem meant for singing or recitation, and usually containing a highly dramatic episode; the style of a ballad is simple, even severe. Ballads may have originated in the communal dancing of early times. Folk ballads reflect the sentiments of semiliterate folk struggling against a hostile environment. An art ballad is a conscious imitation of a ballad by highly trained literary hands.

BALLAD QUATRAIN. A four-line ballad stanza, a typical form for the ballad. The rhyme scheme is usually abcb.

BAROQUE. A description for a work that attempts to achieve its artistic effect by startling movements of style and form. Baroque was first used to describe the architectural style of the Renaissance and its nervous thrusts of style. Baroque has been used to describe Donne's metaphysical poetry, Monk Lewis' Gothic fiction, and Edith Sitwell's poetry. French word meaning irregular, odd, grotesque; through association, it was applied to "irregular" harmonies and style. Derived ultimately from Portuguese and Spanish words meaning "rough pearl."

BILDUNGSROMAN. A coined word from the German, *bildung,* growth or formation, and the French, *roman,* applied to novels dealing with the growth of a young man to maturity. Thomas Mann's *Buddenbrooks* and D. H. Lawrence's *Sons and Lovers* are examples of *Bildungsroman.*

BLACK HUMOR. A further development of sick humor. More grotesque in its treatment of subject matter, it is, by its nature, a protest against what "black humorists" consider the complacent insanity of modern mores. Terry Southern and Joseph Heller are probably the best-known "black humorists" in America today.

BLANK VERSE. Unrhymed iambic pentameter. Shakespeare's plays are written in blank verse. See IAMB.

CACOPHONY. The unpleasant sound of words. From the Greek prefix for bad and the Greek root for sound.

CONNOTATION. Act of implying a secondary meaning or emotional attitude to the primary meaning. The opposite is **DENOTATION,** or the literal meaning of a word. From Latin, *con,* with, *notāre,* mark.

CONSONANCE. The sound of consonants repeated in words that are preceded by different vowels. "The *effect* of the *affable* temper is questionable" contains consonance and assonance. From the Latin prefix and root meaning to sound with.

CONVENTION. Any device, whether in style or technique or subject matter, which a writer uses to make his work effective. Shakespeare used the convention of blank verse for his plays; nineteenth-century French farces employed the convention of the maid with the feather-duster to open the play and tell the audience the necessary information. Other conventions employed in literature are the use of dactylic hexameter for the meter of a Homeric epic; and the use of soliloquies. (Off the stage, men do not talk out loud to themselves, at least not usually.) Conventions are accepted for a number of reasons, not necessarily because they remain close to "reality." For example, ghost stories may be "conventional" in the literary sense, and not at all probable. However, it would be true to say that a writer who tends to use conventions without adding to the tradition is a conventional writer, in the general meaning of the word.

DACTYL. The rhythmic pattern of a stressed syllable followed by two unstressed syllables. The words *travesty, yesterday,* are examples of dactylic rhythm.

DONNÉE. The French word for "something given." It is a term indulged in by Henry James who employed it as a synonym for the writer's "premises" or the material of the situations with which he is about to deal.

EPIC. Originally a long narrative poem in which a person of heroic stature fought many battles and engaged in many adventures, although the center of an epic is one single action of great magnitude. Epic comes from the Greek word, *épos*, meaning word, song, or poetry.

ESTABLISHMENT, THE. A reference to those writers entrenched at the top of the literary world. The anti-Establishment is always a younger, rebellious, "Out" group who wants "In" and usually becomes the Establishment in the next decade. Compare the rise to fame as a literary rebel of John Osborne, who now is accepted as the most "entrenched" playwright in England. The phrase originated in England to describe the established classes in government, and through association was applied to other professional fields.

EUPHONY. The pleasant sound of words. From the Greek prefix *eú*, meaning well, and the root, *phone*, from the Greek word for sound. Compare telephone (sound over a distance), dictaphone, phonograph (the writing of sound).

EUPHUISM. An artificially elegant style of speech or writing, characterized by flowery paraphrasing, strained similes, excessive use of alliteration and antithesis, and by similar affectations. It derives from *Euphues*, an Elizabethan prose work by John Lyly, who created a style in which qualifying words and balanced parenthetical expressions successfully prevented the expression of any bluntly honest opinion.

EXEGESIS. A literary term originally referring to the abstracting of meaning from Biblical stories. Today, exegesis refers to the process by which a critic explains the growth of a poem from its metaphoric and symbolic patterns. From the Greek prefix *ex*, meaning out of, and the root meaning to guide.

FABLE. An allegoric tale usually employing animals as its chief characters but occasionally using inanimate objects as well. Fables have been popular since Aesop's time. A fable with animal characters is known as a beast fable.

FIGURE OF SPEECH. A word or phrase not meant to be taken literally or on the normal level of usage. Among figures of speech are images, metaphors, and tropes. A trope is a word or "figure" in which a change of meaning has taken place from the literal meaning.

FLAT CHARACTER. A character not developed beyond the one or two traits assigned to him by the author; a character without individual distinction.

FOLK EPIC. An epic whose single authorship cannot be determined and which is believed to have been composed by a group of poets. See EPIC.

FOOT. A foot in poetry is the unit of rhythm. Poetic meter is determined by the number of feet and the kind of feet (or rhythmic pattern).

FRAME STORY. A convention by which the major narrative is initiated. In a frame story an introductory narrative device is used to provide a reason for the story or stories which follow. *The Canterbury Tales* is an example of a frame story: to while away the time on their journey to Canterbury, the pilgrims tell each other stories. A frame story is a story enclosed within a story, like a picture within a frame.

FREE VERSE. Verse that does not follow an easily recognized standard of rhythm. Free verse has its own rhythm, but its metrics are difficult to scan.

GOTHIC. A historic term first used to describe an aggressive tribe of people, then later to connote an air of incredible, tortured, romantic storytelling. A Gothic writer may be characterized as an author of grotesque and supernatural tales.

HAIKU. A poetic form deriving from the Japanese using seventeen syllables in three lines, and, traditionally, concerning the seasons.

HEXAMETER. Six feet or units of rhythm to a line of poetry.

HYPERBOLE. A figure of speech in which overstatement is used for effect. It derives from the Greek prefix for above and the root for throwing; its literal meaning is throwing beyond, or in excess. Compare PARABLE.

IAMB. The kind of foot or rhythm pattern composed of an unstressed syllable followed by a stressed syllable. The words *collect* and *contrive* are examples of iambic rhythm. See PENTAMETER.

IMAGERY. The collection of images within a literary work or the images singly. An image may be literal, with no extension of the meaning of the word, or it may be a figure of speech. An image differs from a symbol in that the image refers to the actual object it evokes (the image of a horse, or the countryside), whereas a symbol is an extension of meaning of the image (the horse evoking the sense of power to become a reference to that power, the countryside evoking the quality of calm, and these evocations leading to an abstraction of meaning). Many critics believe that a writer's most profound thoughts are revealed by the choice of imagery in his work.

KÜNSTLERROMAN. From the German, meaning a novel about an artist. A *Künstlerroman,* like the *Bildungsroman,* treats the growth of a character from an early age to maturity, but the hero is an artist. James Joyce's *Portrait of the Artist as a Young Man* is an excellent example of a *Künstlerroman.*

Litotes. A figure of speech in which understatement is used for effect. The word comes directly from Greek word meaning smooth, plain, or small.

Lyric. A short poem dealing with an emotional expression or experience. As an adjective, lyric means characterized by tenderness, sweetness, and brevity. From the Greek word for lyre; the characteristics of a lyric originally are those of the musical instrument by which the word is signified.

Mimesis. The Greek word for imitation, used by Aristotle. The mimetic art is a reproduction of the real world. Its emphasis is on capturing reality rather than reflecting its esthetic essence. The words mime and mimicry also come from the same root.

Monometer. One foot or unit of rhythm to a line of poetry.

Motif. A device or element used in literature to serve as the basis for suggestive expansion. The motif may be a situation or a device of language or recurrent symbols. Like the motif in music, it is a basic element repeated throughout the work.

Myth. A story usually from folklore or primitive belief employing a supernatural force or forces to interpret questions and circumstances of mortal nature.

Ode. A serious poem written in an elevated style; today no special conventions characterize the ode except that of a serious intent and style. The Greek root for song has also produced melody, threnody, prosody, and other words for poetic forms and descriptions.

Onomatopoeia. The quality of a word or phrase having a sound that suggests its meaning, as in the phrases, "hissing snake" and "drip, drip, drip." From the Greek word meaning the making of a name; the word was first used in England in 1860.

ORGANIC THEORY. A principle of criticism that holds the work must be judged as a whole. The organic theory would object to any separation of form and content, style and statement, even for purposes of abstraction.

PARABLE. A story that illustrates a moral or teaches a lesson. The most quoted parables in English are those found in the Bible. Hyperbole and parabola come from the same root, *ballo,* to place, put. From the Greek prefix meaning side by side and the root meaning to place.

PARADOX. A seeming contradiction that may be valid and true. "Preventive wars preserve peace" is a paradoxical statement whose validity will continue to be debated for some time to come. Paradox and orthodox both come from the Greek root *doxos,* meaning opinion; *ortho,* straight; *para,* contrary or side by side.

PARODY. An imitation of another writer's work, usually for the sake of burlesque. The convention is to take a serious work, and by parodying it, to mock it and its author. In recent times, parody has also been used—perhaps incorrectly—to refer to any conscious imitation of a writer's style. Compare MELODY, PROSODY, and ODE, all derivatives of the same root. From the Greek prefix meaning side by side and the root meaning word or song.

PASTICHE. A term implying some critical condescension, since a pastiche is one of the following: an imitation of another writer's style and technique, usually done for satirical or humorous purpose; or a collection of passages from many works by one or more authors. A pastiche in this sense is a medley or mock-anthology; *farrago,* a word connoting something unimportant and disorgan-

ized but busy, is another synonym for it. From *pasticcio,*
Italian for muddle, mess; ultimately derived from *pasta,*
paste.

PENTAMETER. Five feet or units of rhythm to a line of poetry. See IAMB.

PERSONA. A convention used to express a point of view.
The persona is a mask or attitude worn by a character
or the narrator. The persona may be the character himself or the attitude of the character. In one of Eugene
O'Neill's plays a persona may be recognized by the use
of an actual mask, but generally the persona is the
agent-narrator through which the writer's attitude is
given expression. The word comes exactly from the
Latin, *persona,* a mask used by a player or a character
acted in a play.

PERSONIFICATION. The quality of endowing inanimate life
with human qualities. It derives from the Latin, to
make a person of.

PROTAGONIST. The central character in a dramatic work.
The protagonist pushes the action forward. From the
Greek prefix meaning first or chief, and the root mean-
ing actor.

PUTATIVE AUTHOR. The fictional author of a work; a character assigned the authorship by the actual writer. The
putative author is almost always the narrator of a story
and pretends to have written it. Putative comes from the
Latin word, to think, and folk etymology suggests the
phrase arose because the narrator and his readers really
did think he wrote the book.

QUATRAIN. A four-line stanza. From the French *quatre,*
four.

ROMAN À CLEF. From the French, meaning a novel with a

key. A novel in which actual characters are portrayed in fictional guise and can be identified through extra-literary sources or a *clef*. Aldous Huxley's *Point Counterpoint* is a *roman à clef* in which many readers have been able to identify real people.

SENTIMENTALITY. The quality of imparting more emotion to a situation or experience than is inherent in that experience. The reader should be aware of the distinction between *sentiment,* which is a proper display of emotion, and *sentimentality,* which through the overrefinement of feeling has vitiated its emotional substance. Sentimentality and sentiment are derivatives from the Latin word, *sentire,* to feel.

SICK HUMOR. A term used first to describe the comedy of certain types of entertainment which points up contemporary evils by ridiculing those who engage in them or who accept them. Sick humor in literature is a form of satire, an exploitation of subject matter not usually painted on a comic or polite level. It is a protest against the absurdity of life.

SOLILOQUY. A speech by a character while he is alone which reveals his inner thoughts. Shakespeare's characters often engage in soliloquies. The word derives from Latin, *solus,* alone, and *loquor,* to speak. A **COLLOQUY** is a discussion between several people. Dramatic monologues and interior monologues are similar to soliloquies but differ in some respects. An **INTERIOR MONOLOGUE** is the revelation of a character's mind and deals with more than the conscious, verbal level; it is a term used mostly for fiction and the novel. A **DRAMATIC MONOLOGUE** is a term restricted to poetry in which a character speaks to the reader and reveals a significant aspect of himself.

SPONDEE. A foot or rhythmic pattern of two stressed syllables. Two monosyllabic words can make up a spondee as in *blue book* or *strong heart*.

STOCK CHARACTER. A typical character found in various forms of literature. A stock response is the response expected; a stock situation is the kind of situation customarily expected in the given set of circumstances.

STREAM OF CONSCIOUSNESS. The "stream" or uninterrupted flow of consciousness of a character. William James originated the phrase in his philosophic emphasis on sensations as a profound level of awareness. Writers can convey stream of consciousness in an ordered manner, as in Henry James; in the apparently disordered ramblings of a *Tristam Shandy;* or in the associational methods by which one word or image or response sets off another, as in William Faulkner and James Joyce. From Latin *conscius,* knowing.

TETRAMETER. Four feet or units of rhythm to a line of poetry.

TEXTUAL CRITICISM. An attempt by scholars to reconstruct the original manuscript and to criticize the work in terms of the original *text*.

TROCHEE. The rhythmic pattern of a stressed syllable followed by an unstressed syllable. The words *loving* and *random* are examples.

VERS DE SOCIÉTÉ. Light lyrical verse or verse for society. Characterized by sophistication and polish.

...
...

CHAPTER 8

Atom Particles at Work
The Language of Electronics
HAROLD A. RODGERS, JR.

The field of electronics has relatively simple modes for
the formation of new words, as do the closely related areas
of physics and chemistry. The most formal of these is the
combination of Greek and Latin roots into new forms.
Xerography, for example, is formed in this way (the word
means literally *dry writing,* an allusion to the fact that up
to now practically all copying machines have required the
use of a developing solution). In some cases words are
formed by adding combining forms that are derived from
Greek and Latin to common English words. *Multipath* is
an example of this sort of word. The use of standard prefixes, as *de-* in *descramble,* is very common, as is the use
of suffixes. (For some reason the prefix *de-* is strongly
preferred over *un-.*)

Acronyms and word fusion are two important modes.
From these have come such words as *radar* (*ra*dio *detec*-
*tion a*nd *r*anging), *laser* (*l*ight *a*mplification by *s*timulated
*e*mission of *r*adiation), and *alphanumeric* (*alpha*betic and
*numeric*al). Acronyms are often used even when unpro-

156

nounceable; in a case of this sort the letters are simply spelled out as in MTBF (*mean time between failures*).

Physical units are often named after people who have made significant contributions in the field. The *newton,* a unit of force, is named for Sir Isaac Newton; the *watt,* a unit of power, is named for James Watt.

Perhaps the most common mode of word formation in this field is the application of new meanings to already existing words, sometimes by a process of fairly logical extension but often in very witty and imaginative ways. That *noise* should expand from its common meaning to include static in a radio receiver, snow in a television picture, and finally any unwanted random disturbance is quite logical, as all these things have something physically in common. That *chirp,* the sound that would be produced if the frequencies involved were audible, should be used to designate a radar system in which the operating frequency is increased during the time a pulse is being transmitted, is obviously capricious. Of course precedents galore exist for this sort of thing in the history of language, and one should not be too surprised to find a good deal of it in a situation in which a fairly restricted group of people are called upon to expand a system of terminology at an ever increasing rate.

For completeness, one should also mention that, as elsewhere in English usage, many terms are really phrases of two or more words. The meanings of these terms are usually, but not always, apparent from the combined meanings of the individual words. *Negative feedback* and *white noise* are terms of this type.

A list of words follows, of which some are new to the field of electronics. Most of them, however, while rather old hat to the engineer or technician, are recent arrivals to the more general vocabulary. For the most part they are a selection of some of the words on which one trips when reading a news article about a space probe or in carrying on a conversation with the enthusiastic audiophile who lives next door. While many people will not find these words cherished parts of their vocabularies, almost everyone will find it useful to understand them.

WORD LIST

ABORT. To halt an operation or mission of an aircraft, guided missile, spacecraft, etc., short of its intended goal, usually because of some failure or malfunction of equipment. (A communications failure made it necessary to *abort* the mission.) The word sometimes means to fall short of the intended goal. (The mission *aborted* because of technical problems.) Both of these meanings are clearly derived from the common meaning of the word.

A-B TEST. A type of test common in high-fidelity showrooms in which various components (loud speakers, amplifiers, pickups, etc.) are switched in and out of a system in order to compare them with others of the same kind.

ALPHANUMERIC. Involving the letters of the alphabet and numerals. The readout of a computer may be alphanumeric.

ANALOG COMPUTER. A computer in which a problem is translated into a physical, usually electrical, analogy with the READOUT (q.v.) taking the form of a current, voltage, etc. For instance, in an aerodynamic problem, voltage might represent pressure, and current represent the flow of air, while the circuit elements are arranged to simulate the conditions of the problem. A problem treated in this way is said to be analogued. One might find it useful to compare this with a DIGITAL COMPUTER (q.v.).

ANODIZE. To treat a metal in an electrolytic process, in which it forms the anode, so that it forms a protective coating of oxide. Aluminum is very often anodized.

ATTENUATOR. A device for making a signal weaker without any other undesirable effects. A volume control is a simple kind of attenuator. This is another extended meaning. Attenuate, the verb, and attenuation, the noun, can also be used in this context.

AUDIOPHILE. A person who wishes to have his phonograph, radio, etc., reproduce music with a high degree of accuracy and who often invests in rather expensive high-fidelity equipment. Few audiophiles enjoy playing their equipment at less than concert-hall volume.

BACKUP. This word designates an item or component that is intended to take over the function of another device in case of failure. A set of manual brakes that could be used in case a set of power brakes failed would be a backup system.

BANDWIDTH. A continuous range of wave frequencies between two stated limits. The word is often used with respect to the distance between these two limits. An FM broadcast takes up more bandwidth than does an AM broadcast.

BINARY NUMBERS. Numbers which can be written with only the numerals 0 and 1. In the binary system 2, written 10, takes the position that 10 takes in the decimal system. That is to say that one does not count units, tens, hundreds, thousands, etc., in increasing places to the left, but units, twos, fours, eights, etc. For instance, 3 is equal to 2 plus 1 and is written 11, that is one 2 and one 1; 7 is written 111, that is one 4, one 2, and one 1, in the binary system. While this system may seem cumbersome, it is invaluable in the design and operation of digital computers.

BIT. The amount of information that is contained in the difference between a 0 and a 1, or a yes and a no, etc. It is considered to be the basic unit of information. Bit is a shortened form of *bi*nary dig*it*.

BOOLEAN ALGEBRA. A system of representing logical operations in mathematical notation, introduced by the English mathematician George Boole in 1847. Symbols are used to represent *and, or, not, then,* etc. Boolean algebra has important applications in the field of digital computers.

CANNIBALIZATION. The taking of parts from one machine or system for use in another. Taking the bulb from an infrequently used lamp as a replacement for the bulb of a frequently used lamp which has just burned out is a simple but common form of cannibalization. The verb cannibalize and its associated forms also occur in this context.

CAPTURE EFFECT. The ability of an FM receiver to completely suppress the weaker of two signals that arrive on the same or close to the same frequency. The minimum ratio of the strengths of the signals for which this is possible is called the **CAPTURE RATIO.** This ratio is usually given in the specifications of any high-quality FM receiver or tuner.

CHIRP RADAR. A radar system in which the operating frequency is increased during the time that a pulse is being sent out. This is done to improve efficiency and immunity to noise and jamming. This system is especially useful for airborne radars, in which weight limits the power supply installation. The name for the system apparently comes from the fact that an upward sweep in frequency would sound like a chirp if it were done at an audible frequency. Before the echo from such a signal can be displayed on a radar screen it must be DE-CHIRPED. The ratio of frequency change to time is called the CHIRP RATIO.

CHROMA. The distinctive quality, excluding brightness, that identifies any particular color. Chroma is entirely absent from black, white, and gray. CHROMINANCE is the difference between two different but equally bright colors.

COAXIAL CABLE. A cable in which one conductor completely surrounds the other and is separated from it by an insulating material. A cable of this kind is completely immune to the effects of external electric and magnetic fields. It is called coaxial because both conductors have the same longitudinal axis.

COHERENT. Having a constant and regular relationship between the phases of all its component waves. The light from a laser is said to be coherent.

COMPANDER. An amplifying device that amplifies weak signals more strongly than strong ones, thus reducing the range of signal strengths. It also reverses the process, at some later point, essentially restoring the original range. The word comes from *comp*ressor-ex*pander*.

COMPRESSOR. A device that performs the first function of a compander. These are often used in recording and broadcasting music, to insure that the loud passages will not overload the system and that the weak passages will override the noise in the system. For these advantages, a small reduction in intensity of the dynamic range is accepted.

CROSS-MODULATION. An effect in which an unwanted carrier wave enters a radio receiver and is picked up along with the one that is wanted, producing all kinds of spurious reception. This often happens by brute force, as in the case when the receiver is near a strong station. This one station may cross-modulate many of the others. The ability of a receiver to reject cross-modulation is an important index of its quality.

CROSSOVER NETWORK. A system of components that divides audio frequencies into groups and distributes them to the loud-speakers in which they are reproduced most efficiently. In the simplest case the high frequencies are sent to the tweeter and the low frequencies to the woofer; the frequency at which they are divided (although with some overlap) is called the **CROSSOVER FREQUENCY.** A crossover network is sometimes called a **DIVIDING NETWORK.**

CRYOGENICS. The branch of physics that deals with the production and study of very low temperatures and their effects on materials and systems. At temperatures approaching absolute zero (−459.7° F. or −273.16° C.) many strange phenomena occur, one of them being superconductivity in some metals.

DAMPING FACTOR. In high fidelity, a number that indicates the ability of an amplifier to stop a loudspeaker from vibrating at its own natural frequency in the absence of a driving signal. A value that exceeds 4 is considered acceptable, but some high-quality amplifiers have damping factors that are many times this.

DATA PROCESSING. The operation and procedures necessary for the handling and storing of information, especially when done by machines. A system of machines that perform these operations is called a data processing system.

DIGITAL COMPUTER. An electronic calculating machine that works with numbers, roughly the way an ordinary adding machine works but with far greater speed and flexibility of operation. The answer to a problem is presented in numerical form rather than as a measurement of some quantity as in an analog computer.

DISCRIMINATOR. A device that turns variation of frequency or phase into variations of amplitude, useful as an FM detector when preceded by one or more limiters. Most high-quality FM equipment has abandoned the discriminator in favor of the ratio detector, which is superior for multiplex reception.

DOPE. To add tiny amounts of impurities to germanium or silicon, producing a material that is a semiconductor. Pure germanium and silicon are very poor conductors of electricity. One should note, however, that even after these impurities have been deliberately added the total content of impurities is several times less than that allowed under conventional standards of purity.

DOPPLER EFFECT. A change in the frequency of a wave caused by a change in the effective distance between its source and point of observation. This effect was discovered by the nineteenth-century German physicist Christian Johann Doppler. In a **DOPPLER RADAR** the effect is used to determine the velocity of a moving object once it has been detected.

ELECTROACOUSTIC. Involving both sound and electricity, as a loudspeaker or microphone. The field that deals with the design, manufacture, and use of such devices is called electroacoustics.

ENVELOPE. The curve formed by connecting the peaks of the graph of a wave that varies in amplitude. In the case of an AM-modulated carrier wave this curve forms the modulating wave. In the field of electronic music, attempts to achieve musical starting tones or to synthesize the attacks of particular musical instruments require careful attention to the nature of the envelope.

FEEDBACK. The return of part of the output delivered to a system to the input of the system in order to modify or control its operation. Feedback is necessary to any systems that are designed to operate as oscillators. See POSITIVE FEEDBACK, NEGATIVE FEEDBACK.

FLASH TUBE. A tube filled with a rare gas that produces a short, high-intensity flash of light when a high-voltage pulse is applied to it. These tubes are used in electronic photoflash units.

FLUTTER. A rapid variation in the pitch of a musical tone produced by an electronic system. It is usually caused by some irregularity in the movement of a mechanical part. When present to any marked degree the effect is annoying in the extreme. High-quality music reproduction systems have very low figures for flutter. See Wow.

FRONT-TO-BACK RATIO. A number that indicates the efficiency of a directional antenna in transmitting or receiving signals in the direction for which it is designed as compared with its transmission or reception in the direction that is 180° removed.

GIGA-. A prefix meaning 10^9 or one billion, as in gigahertz, one billion cycles per second. See HERTZ.

HARMONIC. A wave frequency that is an integral multiple of some other wave frequency. For instance, 6,000 cycles per second and 9,000 cycles per second are both harmonics of 3,000 cycles per second. In music, harmonics are very important as they create the distinctive tone color or timbre of various instruments and voices. A music reproduction system that adds harmonics or increases them over what they were in the original is said to produce **HARMONIC DISTORTION**. A measure of the quality of such a system is its freedom from this effect.

HERTZ. This unit, recently adopted by the U.S. Bureau of Standards, has been in use in Europe for some time. One hertz is equal to one cycle per second. For higher frequencies, one kilohertz equals one kilocycle per second, one megahertz equals one megacycle per second, etc. The unit hertz is named for the German physicist Heinrich Rudolph Hertz (1857-94).

HUMAN ENGINEERING. The techniques of designing machines so that they are convenient for human beings to use.

HYBRID. Consisting of or using devices or techniques that are considered to be of two or more essentially different types. An electronic device containing both tubes and transistors would be a hybrid device.

IMPEDANCE MATCHING. The matching of two systems so that one is most easily able to receive the energy delivered by the other. For instance, in baseball (disregarding batting averages) it is a far more pleasant sensation for a batter to hit a ball well than to miss it. This is because when he hits the ball the energy he has given to the bat is smoothly transferred to the ball; when he misses, since the match between bat and air is not as good as that between bat and ball, much of the energy is returned or *reflected* back from the bat and the batter himself has to absorb it. Electrical systems act in quite an analogous way. Various devices can be connected between two systems to match their impedances and facilitate the transfer of energy.

INTEGRATED CIRCUIT. A circuit that is constructed in a

single tiny block of germanium or silicon by doping different areas in various ways and connecting them as necessary by minute conductors. Integrated circuits are far smaller than conventional circuits. They are sometimes called MONOLITHIC CIRCUITS.

INTERMODULATION. An effect produced in any system or device in which the input and output are not related in a linear fashion when two or more frequencies pass through it at the same time. Additional frequencies equal to the sum and difference of the original frequencies are produced, along with frequencies equal to the sums and differences of their harmonics, if any. The newly created frequencies interact with each other and with the original frequencies to form still more frequencies. When controlled the effect can be a boon, as in the converter stage of a radio receiver; when uncontrolled or unintentional, as in a high-fidelity system, the effect is called INTERMODULATION DISTORTION. When present to any great degree this distortion is very unpleasant, as it creates tones that are not musically related to the original.

LASER. A device that produces light which (unlike light from most sources) is exactly in the same phase of oscillation at any moment and precisely of the same wavelength. This is done by stimulating excited atoms or electrons to release energy in certain characteristic modes. The word is an acronym for *l*ight *a*mplification by *s*timulated *e*mission of *r*adiation. By back-formation, a device that produces light in this manner is said to lase.

LIMITER. A stage of an FM radio or tuner that removes any spurious amplitude modulation that has been collected by the carrier wave, thus suppressing any noise from this source.

MASER. A device that works like a laser but produces **MICROWAVES** (radio waves of very short wavelength). This word is also an acronym, that is, *m*icrowave *a*mplification by *s*timulated *e*mission of *r*adiation.

MODULE. A group of components or parts arranged to perform a single function and packaged together in such a way as to allow connection with other such groups to form a larger system. Sections of computers are often made in modules. Modular is the derived adjective form.

MULTIPATH SIGNALS. Signals that travel from one transmitter to the same receiver by different paths, usually because of reflections. Such signals are the cause of television ghosts and of a form of distortion in FM multiplex broadcasts.

MULTIPLEX. The transmission of two or more signals over the same communications channel at the same time. This is important in making efficient use of telephone channels. The left and right channels of a stereophonic signal may be broadcasted by multiplexing an FM signal.

NANO-. A prefix meaning 10^{-9} or one billionth, as in nanosecond, one billionth of a second.

NEGATIVE FEEDBACK. Feedback applied from the output to the input of a system in such a way as to decrease the total amount of energy delivered. While in an audio amplifier negative feedback decreases the available gain, it substantially lessens the amount of distortion produced. The manner in which a thermostat controls a heating system is an example of the use of negative feedback, that is, the tendency of the thermostat is always to turn the heater off as it produces more heat.

NOISE. Any random disturbance of a system, especially a communications system. Some noise is produced outside such a system (from lightning, auto ignition, etc.), while some is unavoidably produced in the equipment itself. The ratio of signal to noise is an important measure of the operation of an electronic system.

Pico-. A prefix meaning 10^{-12} or one-trillionth, as in pico-farad, one trillionth of a farad.

Pickup. A device that converts audio, visual, or other information into electrical form, especially the device that translates the information contained in the grooves of a phonograph into an electrical signal.

Piezoelectric. A term that refers to crystals that produce a voltage when subjected to mechanical pressure, or that produce a mechanical force when subjected to a voltage. Such crystals are widely used in phonograph pickups, microphones, and earphones. Because crystals of this type are very stable in maintaining their natural frequencies of oscillation, they are used as frequency standards when a good degree of precision is needed.

Plasma. A gas that has been divided completely or in part into positively and negatively charged particles, often by heat, an intense electric field, etc. A motor that uses electrical means to expel such a gas in a jet has been designed for propulsion of space vehicles. This *plasma jet* produces a small thrust, but one that can be maintained for long periods of time.

Positive Feedback. Feedback returned from the output to the input of a system in such a way as to increase the overall output. This is used in various types of radio amplifiers to improve their sensitivity. Positive feedback will, at a certain level, produce oscillation. The howl produced by a public address system when the microphone receives too much sound from the loudspeaker is an example of this. In general, oscillating systems use positive feedback to make up their inherent losses.

PRESENCE. The degree to which a sound reproduction system creates the illusion that the performers, etc., are actually present. Some people believe that this effect is produced mainly by a band of frequencies in the middle range of the audio spectrum. For this reason some high-fidelity equipment has provisions for artificially boosting these frequencies. All authorities, however, do not agree on the success of this method.

PROGRAM. A particular sequence of operations that a computer must perform in order to handle a certain problem. In general, some person must program the computer, that is to say, instruct it as to the nature of these operations and their proper sequence. This person is called a **PROGRAMER.**

PULSE. A quick burst of electrical energy or, sometimes, electromagnetic energy. Pulses are applied to various circuits in order to convey information, as in a digital computer.

PUMPING. The process of supplying energy to a laser or maser to excite the system that will be stimulated to emit the characteristic coherent radiation. In the case of a laser this energy is often provided in the form of light from a flash tube.

RATIO DETECTOR. A form of FM detector that tolerates a very wide signal bandwidth and acts as a limiter to some degree. It is almost universally used in FM multiplex reception equipment.

READOUT. The form in which a computer delivers information to the user. This is sometimes in written form (a **PRINTOUT**), but it may also be in the form of readings on meters, patterns on an oscilloscope, collections of punched cards, or the like.

REDUNDANCY. The extent to which a signal gives the same information more than once. This is useful in exposing errors in transmission or reception but may also be wasteful in that it reduces the information capacity of the channel. Communications systems are designed so as to keep redundancy at an optimum value. The recognition of redundancy depends heavily on the theory of probability. Note that the statement, "It will be hot tomorrow" is far more redundant when made in July than when made in December, as in the summer there is far more reason to expect such a statement. Redundancy also means the practice of having several devices perform the same function in a system in order to improve reliability.

REPEATER. A device that receives a signal, amplifies it, and retransmits it. Repeaters are used in telephone circuits to make up losses incurred in long transmission lines. The Telstar satellite is a highly sophisticated form of repeater.

SCRAMBLE. To alter (a signal) so that normal receiving apparatus cannot restore it to usable form without special additional devices. *Scramblers* are used to insure secrecy of communication and were at one time considered for use in conjunction with pay television. The special receiving apparatus is said to *descramble* the signal.

SEMICONDUCTOR. Any of various devices, as transistors and certain rectifiers, diodes, etc., that are made from specially treated or doped crystals of germanium or silicon.

SINK. Any device into which energy, generally excess energy, is or can be drained. A heat sink is a device for disposing of excess heat.

SQUELCH. To keep (a radio receiver) silent between communications or when it is tuned between stations. This is done mainly to avoid aural or mental fatigue on the part of the operator, who would otherwise hear constant noise or chatter from other stations. On many receivers this function is performed automatically.

STROBOSCOPE. An instrument that allows motion of some kind to be observed at certain discrete intervals by illuminating it with short, timed flashes. If the moving object moves in a periodic way and its period matches that of the flashing light, the object will be always at the same point when illuminated and will appear to stand still.

SUPERCONDUCTIVITY. A property observed in certain metals when they are cooled to within a few degrees of absolute zero, by which the metals lose all electrical resistance. That is, once an electric current begins to flow in a loop in such a material, it will flow indefinitely with no further voltage applied.

TELEMETRY. The practice or techniques of measuring various quantities at a remote point and transmitting the data back to a local observation point. To perform this function is to telemeter the data. Telemetry is, of course, very important in space research.

TERA-. A prefix meaning 10^{12} or one trillion, as in teraton, one trillion tons.

TRANSDUCER. A device that transmits energy from one system to another. Although they work, usually, in opposite directions, microphones and loudspeakers are both electroacoustic transducers.

TRANSISTOR. This by now is an old friend. For the sake of completeness however, it is a semiconductor device having three terminals called the emitter, collector, and base. The current flowing between the emitter and base controls the larger current flowing between the emitter and collector. The transistor can be connected so as to behave in a way that is analogous to the action of a vacuum tube and can replace it in many applications. The transistor has the advantages of small size and decreased consumption of power. The name comes from *trans*fer re*sistor*.

TWEETER. A loudspeaker designed to reproduce high frequency sounds.

VIDEO. This word mainly refers to the visible portion of a television broadcast. Since the signals involved in this occupy a bandwidth on the order of 4.5 megahertz, video has come to mean also very wide bandwidth. A video amplifier is one that has an even response from about 15 hertz to about 5 megahertz. See HERTZ.

WHITE NOISE. Random noise that is made up of an infinite number of components distributed evenly throughout the entire frequency spectrum in random phase relation. White noise is analogous to white light.

WOOFER. A loudspeaker that is designed to reproduce low-frequency sounds. A woofer is generally larger than a tweeter.

WOW. An effect similar to flutter in which some irregular mechanical movement in the reproducing system causes a sound to vary in pitch, but in this case at a very slow rate. The effect is annoying in the extreme. Try slowing down a turntable with a finger while a record is playing sometime; this will cause wow, which sounds just the way it is spelled.

XEROGRAPHY. The technique of copying documents, etc., by converting an image into a pattern of electrostatic charges which are used to attract a pigmented powder into positions on a paper that duplicate the original image. The powder is then fused to the paper by heat. This principle is used in office copying machines.

CHAPTER 9

"Speak the Speech, I Prithee. . . ."

The Language of the Theater

HENRY POPKIN

The theater, like every other business, profession, or art, has its own special language. In fact, it has many special languages. First, in no particular order, there is the vocabulary of the critic, the historian, and the academician. Such individuals as these derive some of their jargon from Aristotle, but they have adapted to modern times, too, and so they can jabber on about *well-made plays, expressionism,* and *epic theater.* Next, we must take note of the technical language of the stage itself. Stage technicians handle complicated equipment, and they must possess comparably complex terms to describe it. In addition, actors have their own curious language, much of which has entered the day-to-day conversation of nonprofessionals, and the language of actors tends to be special, even when they are not talking about the stage. Tallulah Bankhead made "Darling!" a byword. By now, surely everyone knows that, in the speech of actors, *darling* means "casual acquaintance whose name I do not remember." To these three categories we must add a qualification that turns them into six: American and British usages differ. Sometimes the same

173

terms are used; sometimes the terms differ; and, once in a while, the terms not only differ but have exactly the opposite meaning, as with *bomb*, which, in America, is a colloquial word for a failure, and, in Britain, is a colloquial word for a success.

The special terms of the stage come from everywhere, and the origins of some of them are lost in time. Some merely combine words (like *agit-prop*, from *agit*ation and *prop*aganda), others translate foreign words (like *well-made play*), but still others have strange histories of their own. At one time, the words *System* and *Method* were used interchangeably with reference to Stanislavski's acting technique (and they are defined accordingly in the authoritative *Theatre Language*, by Walter Parker Bowman and Robert Hamilton Ball, published 1961), but it has become increasingly clear that we need a new word for the technique which the American director Lee Strasberg has derived from Stanislavski's teaching. Accordingly, we hear now of Stanislavski's System and Strasberg's Method. Free tickets are called *Annie Oakleys*, but we may be a little uncertain as to just what is the association with the celebrated American sharpshooter who was the heroine of the stage musical *Annie Get Your Gun*. It is well known that a *turkey* is a failure, but the explanation that is generally given seems wildly improbable. *Turkey* is said to be named for an old association of bad shows with Thanksgiving Day; the authorities agree on this matter, therefore one must suspend disbelief. Still, we must be cautious in examining tall stories about the history of a word—especially in show business. As an incentive to caution, one remembers a British film critic who found one of Clifford Odets' plays to be, he thought, marvelously influential. Although *Waiting for Lefty* was seen by a comparatively small audience in a short period of time, for years, after it was staged, characters bearing the name Lefty would turn up in films. So, nothing is easier than to deceive oneself.

In approximately one hundred entries, it is impossible to pretend to anything like completeness. Those who want completeness are referred to *Theatre Language,* by Bowman and Ball, and to *The Theatre Dictionary* (1952), a curious, unpredictable, idiosyncratic British volume by Wilfred Granville. But many words have been included, such as "subtext" and "thrust stage," which do not appear in these books. The selected entries primarily include words of some popular interest, and often omit some of the more exclusively technical terms.

WORD LIST

ABSURD. Used in reference to "the theater of the absurd," a school of playwriting that emphasizes absurd, illogical, ridiculous aspects of human experience, generally illuminating them by exhibiting them in highly stylized form. The term is especially associated with the plays of Eugène Ionesco and also with the plays of Samuel Beckett, *The American Dream* by Edward Albee, and other works. (The question is whether to emphasize similarities in the theater of the absurd or to discriminate differences among the various absurd or absurdist dramatists.) The term probably derives from the "philosophy of the absurd" of Albert Camus and was given its widest currency in Martin Esslin's *The Theatre of the Absurd* (1961).

AD LIB. To speak words or to perform actions which are not in the play being acted. (On radio, Fred Allen would frequently ad lib; that is, he was a celebrated ad-lib artist.) From the Latin *ad libitum,* at will.

AFFECTIVE MEMORY. The recollection of personal emotions which an actor can use in interpreting a role. (He called upon his affective memory in playing the lover at a moment of exultation.) Invented by the Russian director Konstantin Stanislavski and in use among his disciples.

AGIT-PROP. Conveying social protest in an extreme and emphatic fashion; used in reference to plays. (Agit-prop dramas were widely performed in the 1930's.) From a combination of the words *agit*ation and *prop*aganda.

ALIENATION EFFECT. The effect of keeping the audience from identifying with the actors and the situations on the stage. (The actor applied the alienation effect by addressing his love speech alternately to the audience and to his girl friend.) From the term *Verfremdungseffekt*, coined and used by the German dramatist Bertolt Brecht. Also translated *estrangement*.

ANNIE OAKLEY. A free pass for admission to a theater. (He had a pair of Annie Oakleys for the first night.) From the name of Annie Oakley, nineteenth-century American sharpshooter, either because she was generous in giving out passes, or because holes punched in passes resemble bullet holes.

ANTICLIMAX. A period of falling interest in a play, following the climax, or high point of interest. Usually the term is pejorative, but it may be merely descriptive. (After the climactic theft of the jewels, there followed an anticlimax, in which the repentant thief returned them.) Derived from the Greek words *anti* and *climax*, meaning literally "reversing the ascent."

APRON. A section of the stage jutting out into the audience. Also called a THRUST STAGE (q.v.). Used with reference to stages built on the Elizabethan model, such as those at Stratford, Ontario; Chichester, England; and Minneapolis. (Hamlet stepped forward to the apron to deliver his soliloquy.) Derived from the shape of the common article of household apparel.

ASIDE. A speech reflecting a character's private thoughts, and so, according to the convention, not heard by other characters on stage, although perfectly audible to the audience. This convention prevailed among the Elizabethans and at other periods in the history of drama. (He promised fidelity but added, in an aside, that he would break his promise at the first opportunity.)

AUDITION. A demonstration, more or less in the form of a sample performance, by an actor seeking a role. Can be used as a noun or a verb. (The producer scheduled auditions for the role of Osric.)

BACKDROP. A painted curtain or screen at the rear of the stage. (He stood alone against a backdrop which represented the blue ocean beyond.)

BANANA. A comedian in American burlesque. (Phil Silvers became celebrated in the show called *Top Banana*.) Derived from a burlesque sketch involving the sharing of bananas.

BELOW. Downstage; in front of. (He passed below her, diverting the audience's attention.)

BILLING. An advertisement for a play. Also, the relative prominence of actors' names in such an advertisement. (The contract guaranteed top billing to Zero Mostel.)

BLACKOUT. The sudden darkening of the stage, especially to mark the end of a comic sketch in a revue. (A blackout followed the comedian's discovery that he had been fondling a man-eating tiger.)

BLOCK or (less commonly) **BLOCK OUT.** To plan the movements of the actors as a first step in directing a play. (The director spent the day blocking the play.)

BOFF, BOFFO, or **BOFFOLA.** Hearty laugh. (This show has plenty of boffolas in it.) Apparently derived from box office.

BOMB. In American slang, a failure. In British slang, a success. (American: The play was a bomb; the whole audience walked out. British: The play went like a bomb; the cheers could be heard all the way down the street.)

BREAK-EVEN. The minimum weekly sum for which a theater can profitably be operated. (In view of the expense of the production, it was very difficult to reach the break-even point at the Winter Garden Theater.)

BREAK UP. To cause a fellow actor to be unable to continue, generally because of tears or laughter. Also, the actor who cannot continue is said to break up. (Every night, Bert Lahr used to break up one of his supporting players by reducing him to hopeless laughter.)

BURLESQUE. An American form of entertainment, featuring earthy humor, girls undressing, and music. (Mayor La-Guardia banished burlesque shows from New York.) Ultimately derived from the Italian *burla,* a jest.

CATCH FLIES. To attract attention on stage by pantomime while other stage action is going on. (The clown was catching flies as the lovers plighted their troth.) Derived from a practice of clowns in the Italian *commedia dell' arte.*

CATHARSIS. The purgation that, according to Aristotle's *Poetics,* is effected by a tragedy. (He experienced an emotional catharsis at *Oedipus Rex.*) *Catharsis* is the Greek word for purgation.

CLIMAX. The high point of interest in a play, usually the turning point of the plot. (At the climax, the duke revealed his true identity.) *Climax* is the Greek word for ladder.

COMMEDIA DELL' ARTE. Popular improvised Italian comedy, flourishing especially in the seventeenth century, making use of stock comic characters who wore masks. (Gozzi made a last effort to continue the tradition of the *commedia dell' arte.*) In Italian, the term means comedy of art, or of skill.

COUNT THE HOUSE. To look at the audience from the stage, even when acting. (While expressing grief for his brother's death, Claudius counted the house.)

CURTAIN CALL. The assembling of actors at the front of the stage after the performance is over, for the purpose of acknowledging applause. (Mr. Barrymore took his curtain call with great confidence.)

CYCLORAMA. A concave backdrop at the rear of the stage. (Behind the outline of the Lomans' house was a cyclorama.) Derived from the Greek *cyclos*, circle, and *horama*, view.

DEAD PAN. A blank, emotionless face. (Ned Sparks was a dead-pan comedian.)

DECORUM. Propriety, according to classical critical principles, especially in reference to character. (The clown's slapping the king was a grievous lapse of decorum.) Latin neuter of *decorus*, proper.

DÉNOUEMENT. The resolution or completion of the play following the climax. (After most of the characters died, the play moved swiftly to its dénouement.) Derived from the French *dénouement*, untying of the knot.

DEUS EX MACHINA. A surprising but convenient turn of

events in a play. (Rollo's unexpected arrival with money to pay all of Esmeralda's debts was a veritable deus ex machina.) Derived from the Latin words meaning "god from the machine," an allusion to the occasional intervention of a deity, raised high by a machine, at the end of a Greek tragedy.

DIRECTOR. The person who guides the actors' interpretation of a play. In the British theater, called the *producer*. (The director assembled his cast.)

DOUBLE. To undertake two roles in one play. (He doubled as Marcellus and Osric.)

DOUBLE TAKE. A comedian's belated recognition of someone or something, delayed for comic effect. (He perfunctorily noticed that his wife was walking on the ceiling, but, a second later, he did a double take.)

END MAN. The comedian seated at either end of a row of performers in a blackface minstrel show. (The two end men were Mr. Tambo and Mr. Bones.)

ENSEMBLE. The whole company of a play or of a theater, especially with reference to the unified, cooperative effect of their performance. (The ensemble effect of the Moscow Art Theater's production of *Uncle Vanya* was widely admired.) Derived from the French word *ensemble*, meaning "together."

EPIC THEATER. A kind of theater stressing episodic structure, social comment, and an objective attitude toward the action on the part of the audience. Associated with the work of the German dramatist Bertolt Brecht. (Brecht's *Galileo* is an example of epic theater.) The word epic is used to indicate an analogy with the narrative techniques of epic poetry.

EXPOSITION. That early portion of a play which tells what has gone before and introduces the characters. (We learn in the exposition of *Ghosts* that Oswald has been away from home for some time.)

EXPRESSIONISM. A school of theatrical writing that distorts objective reality in order to express a personal, often dreamlike vision. Traced to such early examples as the Swedish August Strindberg's *Dream Play* (1902) but generally thought to have flourished from 1910 (especially in Germany) to 1930. (Arthur Miller's *Death of a Salesman* is a belated example of expressionism.) Probably originates from an analogy to the expressionistic school of painting.

FARCE. A broad comedy based on swift action and surprising situations. (Georges Feydeau was a notable author of farce.) From the French *farcier*, to stuff, from the practice of stuffing or completing a theatrical program with a brief farce.

FLASHBACK. A scene that shows a previous event. (A flashback explained how the murder had been committed.)

FLAT. A piece of scenery, usually consisting of canvas stretched over a frame. (The rear wall of the room was indicated by a painted flat.)

FLIES. The area over the stage, generally out of the audience's sight. (The flies are a convenient place to keep a set that is not being used.)

FOLK DRAMA. 1. A play of popular, traditional origin, like the mediaeval St. George plays. 2. A play about simple people leading a rather traditional sort of life, like Lorca's *Blood Wedding*. (Contemporary folk drama tends to be unpretentious.)

FORESHADOW. To prepare the audience for a subsequent turn of the action. (The discovery that Engstrand is careless with matches foreshadows the fire at the orphanage in *Ghosts*.)

FOURTH WALL. The missing wall, through which the audience looks into a room, in a realistic set. (The actor stared out at the audience, admiring a painting that was hung on the fourth wall.)

GATE. The box-office returns. (The gate doubled in the second week of the play's run.)

GO UP. To forget one's part during a performance. (He went up in his part during the graveyard scene.)

GRAND GUIGNOL. Short, violent, sensational plays—or the sensational method of staging them. (The use of the dead man's hand in *The Duchess of Malfi* might be called an example of Grand Guignol.) Derived from the name of the theater in Paris where, until recently, such plays were performed.

GREEN ROOM. A room in the theater where actors may meet one another or entertain their friends. (Wait for your actor-friends in the green room at the Tyrone Guthrie Theater.)

GRID. A network of metal bars above the stage, from which lights and scenery may be suspended. (The set was lowered from the grid.) From the longer form, *gridiron.*

HAMARTIA. A flaw or error in a tragic character, according to Aristotle's *Poetics.* (His hamartia was his excessive trust.) A Greek word meaning "missing the mark."

HEAVY. A villain in a play. (Basil Rathbone played the heavy.)

HIGH COMEDY. Genteel, articulate comedy of wit, manners, and social relations. (Like many other plays of the Restoration, *Love for Love* is regarded as a high comedy.)

ICE. An illegal commission paid by a ticket broker to a theater box-office employee. (The Attorney General has investigated the payment of ice in the Broadway theater.) Possibly derived from an analogy with *icing*, an extra ingredient on a cake.

INGÉNUE. The role of an innocent young girl. (Miss Carruthers specialized in ingénue parts.) From the feminine form of a French adjective meaning frank or artless.

INTERLUDE. A short, generally comic play of a kind popular in England in the sixteenth century. (*Fulgens and Lucrece* is a typical interlude.) From the Latin words *inter*, between, and *ludus,* play.

JUVENILE. The role of a young man. (Casper Odsnap is getting to be known as a perennial juvenile.)

KABUKI. Kind of Japanese drama combining music, dance, and spectacle. (Mr. Ito is a star of kabuki drama.)

LAY AN EGG. To fail hopelessly. (Famous *Variety* headline referring to the Stock Market crash of 1929: Wall Street Lays an Egg.)

LIGHTING PLOT. Plan of the lighting effects for a stage production. (The director examined the lighting plot.)

LIMELIGHT. The most prominent, best-lighted place on stage. Now especially used figuratively, with reference to the general, off-stage prominence of an actor. (Miss Bancroft enjoys the limelight.) From *limelight*, a bright light making use of calcium oxide, otherwise known as *lime*.

LIVING NEWSPAPER. A play which dramatizes recent news events and indicates some social comment. It flourished in the Federal Theater of the United States, 1935-1939. *Triple A Plowed Under* was a living newspaper dramatizing the fate of the AAA.

MASQUE. An elaborately produced allegorical entertainment of the Renaissance. (Milton's *Comus* is a late example of a masque.)

MELODRAMA. A swiftly moving, sensational play which pays minimal attention to plausibility and characterization. (Not all of the heroines of melodrama are necessarily tied to the railroad tracks.) From the Greek *melos*, song, and *drama*, play. Originally, a melodrama was a musical play, but that usage has died out.

METHOD. A system of acting evolved by the American director Lee Strasberg from the teachings of the Russian director Konstantin Stanislavski. (Marlon Brando is a Method actor.)

MINSTREL SHOW. A comic entertainment performed by white actors in blackface. Now dying out in the United States but still popular in England. (He was the interlocutor at a minstrel show.)

MIRACLE PLAY. A play representing the life of a saint or a biblical theme. A genre, frequently comic, popular during the Middle Ages. (*The Conversion of St. Paul* is one of the few English miracle plays.)

MORALITY PLAY. An allegorical play, with characters who represent and bear the names of abstractions. A genre popular during the Middle Ages. (*Everyman* is by far the best-known morality play.)

MULTIPLE SET. A setting showing several different places for action. (*Hogan's Goat* is played on a multiple set.)

MYSTERY PLAY. A play dramatizing a story out of the Bible. A genre popular during the Middle Ages. (Mystery plays were performed at Wakefield.) The reference is to the sacred mysteries of religion, presumably expounded in these plays.

NUT. The weekly cost of operating a show. (The play had gone over its nut, and it was losing money.)

OBLIGATORY SCENE. A scene which must be included because it is eagerly anticipated. (In the obligatory scene, Gabriella revealed her scarlet past to Gaston.)

OFF-BROADWAY. Collective term for those professional theaters in New York which are (for the most part) not in the Times Square area, play to smaller audiences, charge lower prices, and pay their employees less. (*The Blacks* was an off-Broadway play.) Broadway has always been the center of professional theatrical activity in New York. New York's large professional theaters are located between Fortieth and Fifty-fourth Streets, near Broadway.

PANORAMA. A moving cyclorama. (At the back of the stage was a huge panorama.)

PANTOMIME. Silent acting that conveys its effect by gesture alone. In British practice, an extravagant musical entertainment, usually intended for children and performed at Christmas time. (Marcel Marceau is a master of pantomime.) From the Greek *pantos,* derived from *pas,* all, and *mimos,* mimic.

PAPER THE HOUSE. To fill a theater by giving out many free tickets. (The producer papered the house and thereby created the impression that his play was doing well.)

PASSION PLAY. A religious play about the last days of Christ. (A passion play is performed at Oberammergau.)

PERIPETEIA. A striking reversal in the action of a play. (Oedipus' discovery of his true identity constituted the peripeteia.) The word is Greek and has the same meaning in that language.

PERMANENT SETTING. A stage set which remains substantially unchanged in the course of a play. (*The Member of the Wedding* has a permanent setting.)

PICTURE-FRAME STAGE. A stage framed like a picture, with no part jutting out into the audience. (Most Broadway theaters have picture-frame stages.)

PLAY DOCTOR. Someone hired to revise a play; frequently, he does not get official credit. (Abe Burrows is a celebrated play doctor.)

PRODUCER. The person who makes necessary arrangements for production of a play. In British usage, *manager.* (David Merrick is a leading Broadway producer.)

PROPERTY. Anything used on the stage in the course of a play. (He was in charge of the stage properties.)

PROSCENIUM. The front part of the stage, marked off at the top by the *Proscenium Arch.* (Most spectators see the actors through the proscenium, not through the rear of the stage.) From the Greek, *pro,* before, and *skene,* stage, tent.

PUNCH LINE. An emphatic line spoken in a play. (He caught his breath before speaking the punch line.)

RAKED STAGE. A stage that is slanted, higher at the rear, lower at the footlights. (The actor almost lost his balance on the raked stage.)

REPERTORY. A number of plays which a given company of actors is ready to perform. (They decided to include *Hamlet* in their repertory.) From the Latin *repertorium,* inventory.

ROAD, THE. Provincial towns; in the United States, towns other than New York. (After its success in New York, the play went on the road.)

RUNWAY. A narrow path extending from the stage into the

audience. In use mostly in burlesque. (The comedian stepped onto the runway to address his audience more directly.)

SCRIM. A curtain that may be transparent, or opaque, depending on how it is lighted. (In Zeffirelli's production, all of *The Lady of the Camellias* was played behind a scrim.) From Old High German *scherm,* screen.

SHOW-STOPPER. An actor, scene, or song that draws continuing applause, thus temporarily stopping the show. (Miss Brice discovered that "My Man" was a show-stopper.)

SIDES. Sheets containing the lines of a single part in a play, with accompanying stage directions and cues. (Mr. O'Brien requested the sides for his role.)

SIGHT LINE. The angle of vision from a seat in the audience to the stage. (The sight lines help to determine the placing of the action.)

SOLILOQUY. A monologue spoken by an actor when he is alone on stage. (Hamlet has several opportunities to deliver a soliloquy.) From the Latin *solus,* alone, and *loqui,* speak.

SOUBRETTE. A frivolous girl character, often a lady's maid. Familiar in both light opera and comedy. From the Provençal *soubretto,* affected, sly.

STAGE BUSINESS. Physical activity by an actor on the stage. (He fumbled his way through a great deal of stage business before speaking his next line.)

STICHOMYTHIA. Dialogue consisting of the exchange of single lines, especially in classical drama. (There ensued a particularly pointed stichomythia between Jason and Medea.) From the Greek *stichos,* line, and *mythos,* speech.

SUBTEXT. A pattern of meaning in a play that is not directly expressed in its words and should be made evident in a production. (The subtext of the play is the characters' striving for respectability.) Formed by adding the prefix *sub*, under, to the word *text*.

SYMPHONIC DRAMA. A historical pageant play, presented with music and considerable spectacle. (Paul Green's symphonic drama, *The Lost Colony*, is performed annually in North Carolina.) Although dramas of this kind were acted early in the century in St. Louis and in certain British communities, Paul Green was, in the 1930's, apparently the first to apply this name.

SYSTEM. The acting technique conceived and taught by the Russian actor-director Konstantin Stanislavsky, stressing realistic acting and the actor's identification with his role. (Did Stanislavsky apply the system in his own acting?)

TABLEAU. The stage picture created by motionless actors, normally at the end of a scene. (The curtain fell on a tableau.) From the French *tableau*, picture.

THEATER-IN-THE-ROUND. A theater that sets up its stage in the middle of the audience. (Margo Jones ran a celebrated theater-in-the-round in Dallas.)

THEATER PARTY. A group of people, generally belonging to the same organization, who buy theater tickets in concert for the same evening. (The theater party was for the benefit of the International Grandmothers League.)

THROW AWAY. To underplay some lines or business on the stage. (Miss Hepburn threw away "The quality of mercy is not strained" by speaking the words rapidly.)

THRUST STAGE. Apron stage. (Sir Laurence Olivier set up a thrust stage at Chichester.) See APRON.

TIN PAN ALLEY. The business of writing and selling songs, originally applied to Twenty-eighth Street between Broadway and Fifth Avenue in New York City. (Tin Pan Alley replied to World War I by turning out patriotic songs.) *Tin Pan* is a reference to the tinny sounds created by pianos in Tin Pan Alley.

TONY. Prize award given by the American Theater Wing. (Zero Mostel wins a Tony almost every year.) In memory of *Antoinette Perry,* an actress-producer, in whose honor the awards are given.

TOTAL THEATER. Theatrical efforts that make use of drama, spectacle, music, dance, and perhaps other theatrical elements. (Was *Oklahoma!* an example of total theater?)

TREADMILL. A moving belt on the stage, on which actors may give the impression of walking but remain in the same place. (Mother Courage's wagon was set on the treadmill, and so, without leaving the spot, the actors gave the impression that they were going a great distance.)

TURKEY. A bad show that fails. (*Grandma's Diary* was a turkey.) From the practice of giving such a show on Thanksgiving, when turkey has been eaten and the audience is possibly lethargic.

TWOFER. Two tickets for the price of one—a policy often in effect at Broadway theaters after a drop in box-office sales. This policy is usually effected by distributing pasteboards, called Twofers, resembling theater tickets, exchangeable for tickets at the box office. (The management put the show on twofers.) From the expression, "two for one."

VARIETY. British term for the American vaudeville. A program of entertainment acts of various kinds. (Charlie Chaplin made his start in Variety.)

Vaudeville. American term for a program of entertainment acts of different kinds. (Are those the jokes that killed vaudeville?) From *Vau-de-Vire*, a place in Normandy famous for its light songs.

Well-Made Play. A carefully manufactured play of entertainment, with more attention given to plot than to characters or ideas. Associated with the nineteenth-century French dramatists Eugène Scribe and Victorien Sardou. (Ibsen adapted the structure of the well-made play.) A literal translation of the French, *pièce bien faite.*

CHAPTER 10

Structures of Man

The Language of Architecture

Eugene Raskin

The special words or terms used by architects and people concerned with architecture fall generally into three categories: those dealing with questions of structure or technical building problems; those which name elements of building that are stylistic rather than structural, such as columns, cornices, friezes, etc.; and those which are applied to matters of esthetics, such as symmetry, monumentality, proportion, functionalism, etc.

By and large the first group, words dealing with structure or building technique, derive from local usage. They are the words that carpenters and masons use in their trade; hence, since local building customs differ from one region to another, expressions such as "ridge pole" or "bargeboard" will be common in one place and quite unknown in another.

The words that name stylistic elements, on the other hand, frequently are descended from Latin or Greek originals, just as are the architectural parts which they describe. This is particularly true in classical or traditional architecture, much of which of course has roots in the deep past.

The third category, words dealing with matters of esthetics, comes from a great variety of sources, of which perhaps the largest is French, for the simple reason that for at least two hundred years (up until the beginning of the twentieth century) the only important school of architecture was in Paris. Most architects got their training there, or were apprentices in the offices of Paris-trained masters.

The number of specialized architectural terms is very large—a recent estimate puts the sum at 2,200. The following list is illustrative rather than comprehensive.

WORD LIST

Abacus. The uppermost part of a column or capital. Not to be confused with the Chinese counting instrument.

Abutment. A pier or wall that receives an outward or sideways strain, as from an arch or vault. The syllable *but* is the same as the one that appears in the word *buttress*.

Aggregate. Any coarse material, such as gravel or broken stone, which, when mixed with cement, sand, and water, becomes concrete. An aggregate may be said to be "gregarious," in that it mixes well with others, as one might say of socially minded people.

Aisle. The side division of a church or its wings. The term comes from the French, from which we get the same root that appears in the word **Aileron,** or wing edge.

Arabesque. An ornament, either painted, carved, or inlaid, in a fanciful mixture of plant forms, sometimes with entwined figures of men and animals. Although named for an Arab origin, the ornament appears mainly in Roman or Renaissance work.

ARCUATED. Any system of structure or decoration which is made up of series of arches. For example, the Coliseum in Rome.

ASHLAR. Term describing square-cut stone laid in horizontal levels or beds, as opposed to rough or "rubble" masonry.

BARGEBOARD. A carpenters' term, meaning the finished board or strip covering the exposed edge of a gable roof. The bargeboard in much nineteenth-century American work was carved and pierced in the style called *Carpenter Gothic.*

BAROQUE. A French term originally applied to a style of ornate architecture of the eighteenth century. Now by extension, any exuberant twisting or curving of architectural forms.

BASILICA. A building of rectangular plan of the type used by the Romans as courts of justice. Since the early Christian churches used the same form (sometimes the same buildings), the term was extended and is now often applied to churches, particularly Roman Catholic ones.

BATTER. To build a wall so that it slopes inward as it rises, as the walls of wharves or fortifications. Such walls are spoken of as being "battered." (Not to be confused with the word meaning broken or beaten.)

BATTLEMENT. A parapet for a fortress, notched or indented along its top to provide protection for the defenders. Battlements are of great antiquity, but the word as we use it is from the same root as our own battle or the French *bataille.*

BAY. The space between major supports in any regular structural framing system. Thus the expression "bay window" usually means a fairly large window filling a whole bay and sometimes, but not necessarily, projecting outward.

BELT COURSE. A course or layer of brick or stone projecting forward from the main face of a wall.

BOND. The overlapping of brick in alternate courses to hold a wall together. Various bonding patterns are known as Common, Flemish, English, etc.

BUTTRESS. An extra projection or thickness in a wall to create greater strength. When the extra projection, or buttress, is partly separated from the wall it is helping to strengthen, it is called, as in Gothic architecture, a **FLYING BUTTRESS.** The term also is used as a verb, to buttress.

CAMPANILE. An Italian word meaning bell tower. The campanile may be attached to a church or be separate from it. In much modern church architecture the campanile survives as a symbolic form only, the bells themselves being usually electronic.

CANTILEVER. Any structure that projects out beyond its supporting wall or column.

CAPITAL. The top of a column or pilaster, usually decorative in nature. The root, *cap*, means head or top, or even hat.

CLERESTORY. A row of windows at a high level, above the lower part of a building, as the windows above the aisles of a church. With a modification of the spelling one can see that the term comes from "clear of the story."

COLUMN. A vertical structural element. In classical architecture the column consisted of three parts—base, shaft, and capital. In modern usage it means any steel, concrete, or wood post bearing a vertical load.

COMPLEX. A group of buildings arranged to function together, as for example the Lincoln Center for Performing Arts, which consists of two theaters, a concert hall, and an opera house. These, together with a projected school of music and dance, can aptly be spoken of as a complex.

CORBEL. Projection from a wall to carry a weight above, as bracketing for a balcony, wide window sills or the like. Such supported construction is said to be corbeled out as distinct from cantilevered.

CUSP. The point formed by the meeting of two curves, as in the tracery of Gothic windows. Sometimes the point is decorated with floral or other carved forms. The word comes from the Latin *cuspis* meaning point; it is often misused by people who use it in reference to the curve itself rather than its pointed end.

DADO. Panels or moldings around the lower part of a room, forming a continuous base along the wall.

DENTILS. An ornamental row in classical architecture, the elements resembling teeth, from which the name is derived.

DOME. A round, vaulted roof. Originally the term comes from the Italian *Duomo,* meaning cathedral, in turn from Latin *domus* [Dei], the house of God, but since in the Renaissance most cathedrals were domed, the word is now applied to the cupola or roof itself.

DORMER. A window piercing a sloping roof, usually in a top story or attic. Since bedrooms are most frequently found in upper stories, the word derives directly from the French *dormir* (to sleep), as does our English word dormitory.

ENTABLATURE. The horizontal crowning element that crosses above the columns in classical architecture. The entablature consists of three parts: the lowest is the **ARCHITRAVE,** the middle one, sometimes decorated with sculpture, is the **FRIEZE,** while the topmost one is the **CORNICE.**

ENTASIS. The gentle inward curve of the shaft of a column to give greater delicacy to its proportions. By extension, the term is sometimes used to describe other subtle variations of dimension for esthetic effect.

FAÇADE. From the French, the exterior front or face of a building. By extension the term is sometimes used to imply a false screen applied over a structure.

FENESTRATION. The scheme or pattern of windows in the design of a building. From the Latin *fenestra,* window.

FLUTINGS or **FLUTES.** Vertical depressions or channels cut in columns or pilasters for decorative purposes. Using the word as an adjective one might say that a column is fluted as distinguished from plain. The derivation of the word is unknown, but it has been suggested that a row of flutings resembles a set of reed flutes such as shepherds play.

FOILS. The curved spaces between cusps in the tracery of Gothic arches. The number of foils per arch is usually given by a prefix, as **TREFOIL, QUATREFOIL,** etc. The derivation is from the French *feuille* meaning leaf, since the foil has a leaf-like form.

FRIEZE. The middle horizontal portion of an entablature, but the term when used by itself more often than not means a decorative band of sculpture or painting.

FUNCTIONALISM. An esthetic theory based on the principle that architectural form should derive from a study of a building's contemporary uses, as opposed to design deriving from tradition. The slogan of the functionalist school is "Form Follows Function."

GEODESIC. Term invented by R. Buckminster Fuller to describe his system of constructing domes and vaults by combining short struts by means of bolts.

GIRDER. A main beam which supports crossbeams or joists.

GROIN. The edge formed by the meeting of curved surfaces. Vaulted ceilings having groins are called **GROINED VAULTS.**

GROUT. Thin mortar poured into the joints of masonry or tilework. The word comes from the Old English *grūt* or *grўt,* meaning coarse meal.

INTRADOS. The inner or under side of an arch, as opposed to the **EXTRADOS,** or outer side. See **SOFFIT.**

KEYSTONE. The central stone or **VOUSSOIR** (q.v.) at the top of a masonry arch; the last to be placed in position and the one which holds the whole arch together.

LINTEL. A horizontal member such as a timber, stone, or steel beam, placed across a doorway, window, or other opening to carry the load of the structure above. Latin in derivation, the word has the same origin as the word *limit,* or boundary—in this case the boundary of the opening.

LOUVRE. Originally a turret or small lantern to allow for the escape of smoke or for general ventilation. Now applied to the sloping narrow boards with which the sides of the turrets were covered to exclude rain. Present-day louvres can be found in everything from shutters to clerestories.

MASONRY. Stonework. Originally the term excluded brick, but now includes not only brick but concrete as well. From the Old French *masson*.

MEMBRANE. The outer "skin" of modern buildings, such as glass and steel panels attached to the structural frame, and supporting no load in themselves.

MODULE. A unit of structure or measure, applied to buildings which are composed of many exactly measured similar parts such as window-wall panels, etc. The expression "modular design" is used to describe this kind of architectural approach.

MULLION. Slender vertical member separating window sections in paired or continuous fenestration. In much modern membrane architecture the mullions are also the structural frame. Looking at a new office building one can use the phrase "millions of mullions."

MULTI-STORY. Expression used to describe buildings in which the basic floor plan is substantially repeated for each story with the exception of the ground or lobby floor.

NAVE. The main part of a church west of the choir. By extension, any main axial volume in a large building such as a railway terminal.

OCULUS. A round window, so-called because of its fancied resemblance to the human eye. The word oculist comes from the same Latin root.

ORDER. One of the five classical systems of architecture: Tuscan, Doric, Ionic, Corinthian, and Composite.

ORGANIC. Word much used by Frank Lloyd Wright describing architecture whose parts have a natural relationship to one another, as the branches and trunks of trees.

PARTI. The basic scheme for the plan of a building, without regard for the particulars of style or treatment. From the French.

PERISTYLE. A colonnade or row of piers surrounding a building or courtyard. From the roots *peri*, meaning around, as in perimeter, and *stylos*, the Greek word for pillar.

PIER or **PILASTER** or **PILLAR.** Variations meaning vertical sections of masonry furnishing support to structure above, as in piers of a bridge or pillars of a church. Pilasters are more often decorative rather than structural.

PLINTH. The square base of a column or pedestal, or the projection at the bottom of a wall where it meets the ground.

PORTICO. A row of posts, piers, or columns forming a sheltered entrance to a building. From the root *port*, meaning door or entry.

QUOINS. From the French *coin*, meaning corner, and referring to the external corner of a masonry building. Decorative stones at the corner are called **QUOINING.**

REVEAL. The vertical side of an opening in a wall made for a window or door, as distinct from the exterior trim. So-called because it exposes, or reveals the edge of the wall construction.

RIB. A decorative molding dividing panels of a ceiling or the intersecting surfaces of vaulting. See **GROIN.**

RUBBLE. Rough masonry work built of irregular stones as they come from the quarry, with minimal shaping, as opposed to ashlar masonry.

SOFFIT. The underside of minor parts of a building, such as stairways, archways, cornices, etc., as distinct from main undersurfaces such as ceilings.

SPANDREL. Originally the triangular space between the side of an arch and its rectangular frame, if any; in modern buildings, the panels which separate the bands of windows of successive stories. The spandrel also serves to cover the structural beam which spans the bay.

SPRING. The point at which an arch joins its support, or impost. The lowest stone or VOUSSOIR (q.v.) of an arch is sometimes called spring or springer.

TRACERY. The pattern of separation of glazing parts in decorative fenestration such as stained-glass windows in Gothic work.

TRUSS. An arrangement of struts or relatively short elements to form a principal support for a wide span in a building.

VAULT. Curved roof form; a vault may be said to leap or jump from its spring across a span to a corresponding support at the other side, thus vaulting the space.

VOUSSOIR. An individual wedge-shaped stone used in making up an arch or vault. From the French.

WAINSCOT. Panels of wood or stone around the lower part of the wall of a room. Like a *dado,* but rarely decorated.

CHAPTER **11**

"Heard Melodies Are Sweet. . . ."

The Language of Music

CARYL DALY FRIEND

Western music is a composite art with roots in many cultures. Therefore, its vocabulary has a variety of origins. Music, as we know it, began in the shelter of the church, so to trace its vocabulary, we must also look briefly at church history. The early Christian church was a mixture of Judaic, Greek, and Middle Eastern traditions. Because of the desire for uniformity of worship, the new liturgy was gradually organized. As this organization took place, technical terms were needed to explain music and how it was to be used, and early theorists of the church turned to even earlier times for some of their terminology.

In ancient Greece the studies of mathematics and music were considered to have much in common. Pythagoras, in particular, wrote about acoustical discoveries and also about the technicalities of the art of music. The word which had meant scale structures was translated into Latin by Christian theorists as *modus*. The order of intervals—the distance between tones—and the limitations of the new church modes, as we call them in English, were different. The names for the church modes were still Greek: *Dorian, Lydian, Phrygian,* etc.

Since it was within the church for many hundreds of years that the growth and sophistication of music took place, a wide range of technical terms are Latin. Direct translation of some of these gives a clear picture of their character. *Counterpoint* was originally three words: *punctus contra punctus,* note against note. This comes to mean melody against melody, or simultaneous independent melodic lines. It is shortened to *contrapunctus* or *counterpoint. Cantus firmus,* a term familiar to all students of counterpoint, means literally *firm song.* This firm song was the chant or borrowed tune used as the foundation for contrapuntal (counterpoint) composition. The cantus firmus itself was familiar, something firm to hear and recognize, while the added counterpoint was fresh. *Hocket,* or *hoketus,* probably comes from the same root as *hiccup* (French *hoquet*). Hocket is the breaking up of an essentially simple melody between two voices, each singing only one or two notes at a time. When put together the whole melody can be heard, but the breaks between first one voice and then the other, as they take turns, create a breathy quality, almost as if the performer had the hiccups.

As musicians eventually became more and more active outside the church, they turned to the vernacular for their terminology. The wealth of Italian terms is common knowledge. These came into use during the seventeenth and eighteenth centuries when Italy and its performers were especially influential throughout Europe. There are indications of tempo (speed): *adagio, allegro;* there are names of forms: *opera, cantata, sonata;* and there are instructions for performance: *legato, staccato, marcato.* Most of these reflected an increasing interest in how the music was to be performed and what effect it was intended to achieve.

During the nineteenth century we find a composer using his own language to name compositional devices and score indications. Sometimes we have words from different languages meaning closely related ideas: *Leitmotif, Idée Fixe, Motive.* Playing instructions in all languages were used by composers who were eager to achieve an exact quality from the performer: *cédez, ungeduldig, con molta forza,* etc.

The composer and performer now find themselves in the twentieth century with a rich heritage of terms to which they have added according to their needs. Reflecting the tendency toward complexity of texture, the prefix *poly* (many) is often in use: *polychord, polyrhythm, polytonal, polyphonic, polymeter.* These are used to mean vertical combinations of the word after the prefix *poly.* Therefore, a polychord is two or more chords used simultaneously. Some words have also come into the vocabulary to describe new compositional approaches. One of these is *aleatory,* which means dependent on the "throw of a die." This is the name of an improvised kind of music in which certain limitations are established—of pitch, pattern and/or rhythm— but the exact result in performance is different each time. This is true because the performers are given certain freedoms about order of materials, repetitions, speeds, etc. The performance is like a musical Happening. There are other new words for music structure to be found in the word list below.

This brief group of definitions does not include words related to instruments or performing directions. Rather, it contains terms in music which might be used in reviews of concerts and records, or in books discussing musical style. Familiarity with these words should help one become better acquainted with the language of music.

WORD LIST

ACCIDENTAL. A sign used to alter a single note chromatically—a sharp, flat, or natural. This comes from one use of the word *accidental,* when it means incidental.

ANHEMITONIC. Used to describe a scale or melody which consists entirely of intervals of a whole tone. (Debussy has written many anhemitonic melodies.) From the Greek, without semitones.

ANTIPHONAL. Voices singing alternately, choir answered by choir. (Because of the structure of St. Mark's Church in Venice, the choirs often perform antiphonal music.) From the Greek, to sound in reply.

ARIA. Part of an opera, oratorio, etc., where action is stopped and the characters sing their reaction to the dramatic situation. The music is usually metered and the form is clear with a full support from the accompanying instruments. A common form for the aria is the *aria da capo,* A A B A. See DA CAPO. (The mezzo-soprano performed her aria in the second act with great perception.) The term is Italian and means song, air.

ATONAL. The absence of tonality; no emphasis on or gravitation toward one note. Many twentieth-century composers write atonal music. From the Greek, not tonal.

AUGMENTATION. Restatement of previously heard material in proportionally longer note values, usually double the original note value. (The third time the subject was used it appeared in augmentation.) From the Latin *augmentum,* increase.

BASSO CONTINUO. Also called *figured bass* or *thorough bass.* The baroque practice of using Arabic numbers beneath a bass line as a shorthand to indicate harmonic progression. It served as a guide to the keyboard player, who improvised within the indicated harmonic pattern. This improvisation is called a realization. (Mr. Kirkpatrick realized the basso continuo at the harpsichord.) The term is Italian and means thorough bass or continued bass.

BEL CANTO. A vocal technique which emphasizes the quality of sound rather than emotion. It also stresses virtuoso singing. This is a style found in Italian and Mozart opera. The term is Italian and means beautiful singing.

BLUE NOTE. Varied inflections of the third and/or seventh notes of a diatonic scale, found in jazz. Called "blue" because of its use in the *Blues.*

CADENCE. A point of rest or conclusion, accomplished by rhythm, harmony, and melodic line. In tonal music the most complete cadence is that arriving at the tonic of the key. (The cadence had a most gratifying effect.) From the Latin *cadere,* to fall. See TONALITY.

CADENZA. An extended cadence; a pause is made at the suspenseful part of a cadence while the soloist either improvises or plays a composed virtuosic display, thus delaying the arrival of the restful part of the cadence. A common place to find a cadenza is just before the end of the first movement of a concerto. (He played the cadenza with much fire and brilliance.) The term is Italian and means cadence.

CANON. A polyphonic piece in which the voices enter successively with the same material. A *round* is a form of canon. The adjective *canonic* is often used a little more freely to describe a piece or section of a piece in which the voices imitate each other but not exactly. (The middle section was an extended canon.) From the Greek word meaning rule.

CANCRIZANS. In crab-like motion. Using a melody or whole section of a piece in reverse, in retrograde. From the Latin *cancer,* crab.

CANTATA. A baroque multimovement form, like a small oratorio or opera consisting of recitatives, arias, and choruses. (Johann Sebastian Bach wrote many cantatas during his years in Leipzig.) From the Italian *cantare,* to sing.

CHORALE. Hymn tune of the German Protestant Church. Sometimes used as the basis for instrumental variation or development forms, such as chorale prelude or chorale fantasy. From the German *Choralgesang,* derived from the Latin *cantus choralis.* Chorale is also now used as a name for a singing group.

CHROMATIC. Designates tones outside the diatonic scale. Also describes a progression of semitones such as C C♯ D D♯ E. The chromatic scale consists of the 12 semitones within an octave. From the Greek meaning color.

CONCERTO. This word was first used to mean music played by a group of instruments. Later it meant a composition for solo instrument or solo group of instruments and orchestra. From the Latin *concertare,* to fight side by side.

CONCERTO GROSSO. A baroque multimovement instrumental form. Its most outstanding characteristic is the contrast between a small solo group (*concertino*) and the full orchestra being used (*ripieno*). The literal translation from Italian is large concerto.

CONSONANCE. A harmonious or agreeable relationship between two or more pitches. Certain intervals are particularly consonant because they are natural intervals.

Consonance is a relative term, since in different historical periods different sounds are pleasing to the ear. From the Latin *cum,* with, and *sonare,* to sound.

CYCLIC. A compositional approach which uses a recurrent thematic idea throughout a work for unity. From the Greek, meaning circle.

DA CAPO. Repeat from the beginning. An aria da capo is a form which states material—A; repeats it—A; departs from it—B; then returns to the first A. The term is Italian and means from the head or beginning.

DEVELOPMENT. 1. A compositional device. Previous thematic material grows, is transformed, is fragmented, is stated in new keys, new instruments, etc. Features economy of material. 2. The name of the middle section of a sonata-allegro form. (He varied the second theme in the development.) From the French *développer,* to unfold.

DIATONIC. A scale pattern made up of whole and half steps. This word is used to imply limiting the material to the scale, rather than using CHROMATIC (q.v.) tones. (The thematic material was diatonic.) From the Greek words meaning at the interval of, and tone.

DIMINUTION. A rhythm device which restates material in proportionally smaller note values, usually half as long. (The tenor voice states the subject in diminution.) Compare AUGMENTATION. From the Latin *deminutio,* a lessening.

DISSONANCE. The opposite of CONSONANCE (q.v.). A tense or displeasing relationship between two or more pitches. Dissonance is also a relative term, changing in different musical styles. From the Latin *dis,* against, and *sonare,* to sound.

DODECAPHONIC. See SERIAL.

ELECTRONIC MUSIC. Music composed for instruments which create their sound by electrical or electronic means. Experimentation in this area has been a part of twentieth-century musical activity.

ENHARMONIC. Used to identify pitches a quarter tone apart which sound the same on a piano, such as D-sharp and E-flat. (D-sharp and E-flat are called enharmonic equivalents.) From the Greek, denoting the scale which includes quarter tones.

FUGUE. A polyphonic form consisting of a number of imitative explorations of the theme, or subject, separated by episodes. In most fugues the use of related keys is very important to the form. From the Latin *fuga*, flight.

HARMONY. Any simultaneous combination of sounds; a chord. From the Greek word with the same meaning.

HARMONIC RHYTHM. The speed of the harmonic change. This does not usually coincide with the melodic rhythm.

HOMOPHONIC. The opposite of POLYPHONIC (q.v.). Music in which there are a melody and an accompanying voice or voices. These work together to make a single effect. (Most music from the classical period was homophonic.) From the Greek, meaning same sound.

IDÉE FIXE. The name used by Berlioz to identify the subject which is restated, in transformations, throughout a multimovement work. This is a French term meaning fixed idea.

INTERVAL. The difference in pitch between two notes. This is measured numerically. For example, the interval of a third, D–F, includes three notes, D, E, and F. These numerical indications may also be qualified by various modifiers—major, minor, etc., which define the distance more exactly. D–F is a minor third, or three semitones. D–F-sharp is a major third, or four semitones. From the Latin *intervallum,* the space between ramparts.

ISOMELOS. A compositional technique which uses the repetition of a melody to create unity, and rhythm changes for variety. From the Greek term meaning same melody.

ISORHYTHM. A compositional technique which uses the repetition of a rhythm pattern to create unity, and melodic changes for variety. Note that this is the reverse of ISOMELOS (q.v.). From the Greek term meaning same rhythm.

LIBRETTO. The words or text for an opera, oratorio, etc. This is Italian and means little book.

LIED. Originally this was the name of a secular German song. In the nineteenth century it meant a sectional song, in German, often grouped together in a song cycle. A sensitive musical treatment of the text is an important characteristic of the form. There are many examples by Schubert, Schumann, Brahms, Wolf, and others. This word is German and means song.

LEITMOTIF. A motive or theme which has a specific dramatic association, with a character, place, idea, etc. The term was first coined to describe Wagner's use of motive. A hunting-horn motive is a simple example. This word is German and means leading motive.

MADRIGAL. An early poetic form with a pastoral theme (fourteenth century). In the sixteenth century it was a sectional, secular polyphonic vocal form in which the sections were often imitative. It is historically important because madrigal composers were concerned with a dramatic treatment of the text, and it became a forerunner of opera. From the Greek *metra,* womb.

MELISMA. A florid melody with free rhythm structure. It may be used as an adjective. (A recitative is often melismatic.) From the Greek expression for song or chant.

METER. The regular grouping of pulses (beats) through the use of quantitative and/or qualitative accent. Meter is indicated by a time signature, which tells how many pulses are to be in each group and what kind of note gets one pulse. From the Greek word meaning measure.

MODULATION. Changing or shifting from one key to another by a transitional device. This is usually made comfortable to the ear by smooth voice lines. From the Latin *modulari,* to regulate.

MONOPHONIC. Music having one melody and no accompaniment. From the Greek term meaning one sound.

MOTET. An early contrapuntal form in which the voices were independent, not only in melody and rhythm, but also in text. In the sixteenth century it was an imitative, sectional, sacred polyphonic form. From the French *mot,* word.

MOTIVE. A short, distinctive, self-contained musical idea used as the germ for development. A well-known example is the first four notes of the Fifth Symphony of Beethoven. From the Italian *motivo,* motive, something causing movement.

MOTOR RHYTHM. An insistent repeated rhythm, usually of even notes, which pushes the music forward. The Latin root for motor means something that imparts motion.

NEOCLASSIC. This is used to describe twentieth-century music which returns to earlier compositional techniques or esthetic principles. (Many works of Hindemith are neoclassic.) The prefix *neo* means new. Classic is used to mean standard in an earlier period; therefore, we have a new use of standard techniques.

NONHARMONIC TONE. A nonharmonic tone is a note which is outside the prevailing harmony. When a nonharmonic tone appears on a weak beat or part of a beat, and is approached and left smoothly, it seems to embellish. When it appears on a strong beat or part of a beat, or is skipped to, it becomes a dramatic moment in the melodic line.

OPERA. A sung drama, with orchestral accompaniment, made up of recitatives, arias, and choruses. This form first appeared in the late Renaissance and continues to be an important form of musical expression. The term is Italian and means works, the plural of Latin *opus*, work.

ORATORIO. A large multisectional form which is really an unstaged sacred opera. The text is usually scripture, and the sections are recitatives, arias, and choruses, with orchestral accompaniment. It evolved from the older mystery plays and liturgical dramas which dramatized Biblical stories to make them more accessible to the congregation. From the Latin *oratorium*, oratory.

ORGANUM. The earliest form of **POLYPHONY** (q.v.). Voices were added to a chant by moving in parallel motion, and later in oblique or contrary motion, note for note with the chant. A variant of this was **MELISMATIC ORGANUM**, which added a melismatic line to a slower moving chant. From the Greek word for organ.

OSTINATO. A repeated melodic pattern whose insistence becomes a characteristic of the piece. The term is Italian and means obstinate.

PANDIATONIC. This is a twentieth-century harmonic approach which considers any notes of the diatonic scale consonant when combined with any others. It combines the Greek prefix meaning all, with "diatonic."

PASSACAGLIA. A formal structure based on a repeated bass pattern in triple meter. Variety is achieved in the repetitions by changing the voices added to the bass pattern. This form is closely related to the form called *chaconne*. It is thought to be derived from the Spanish *pasacalle*, meaning street song.

PENTATONIC. A five-note scale. The usual five-note pattern consists of the sound heard when the black notes on the piano are played scalewise. From two Greek roots meaning five and tone.

PLAINSONG. This is also sometimes called Gregorian chant. It is the melodic intonation of the liturgy, having a limited range, and an unmetered speech rhythm. From the Latin *cantus planus*, flat song.

POLYMETER. The simultaneous use of two or more meters. This word was coined in the twentieth century, but is based on two Greek roots—much or many, and meter.

POLYPHONY. The simultaneous combination of two or more independent melodies. Synonym: COUNTERPOINT (q.v.). From the Greek, combining many and sound.

POLYRHYTHM. A contrapuntal device which stresses an independent rhythmic personality for each of several voices. The result is a texture of cross-accents and cross-phrasing. From the Greek, many and rhythm.

POLYTONALITY. Writing in two or more keys at the same time. Each key defines itself in one voice and when these voices are combined polyphonically we have simultaneous keys or polytonality. From the Greek, many and tone.

PROSODY. The art of setting a text to music. The composer shows his interpretation of the words through the use of melody, rhythm, pitch, and harmony. From the Greek *prosodos,* an approach.

QUARTAL HARMONY. Chords structured in intervals of a fourth. From the Latin *quartus,* fourth.

QUODLIBET. A form consisting of quotations of known melodies placed together in seemingly incongruous order. The term is Latin and means "what you will."

RECITATIVE. The part of an opera, cantata, or oratorio, etc., where the story is musically recited. The melody is declamatory and the rhythm is asymmetric. Usually accompanied by sparse chords. From the Italian *recitativo.*

RETROGRADE. A compositional device in which previously heard material is used in reverse. Synonym: **CANCRIZANS** (q.v.). From two Latin roots, *retro,* backwards, and *gradus,* step.

RHAPSODY. A free form, ballad-like or epic in character, for instruments or voice. As an adjective, *rhapsodic,* the word may be used to mean free in quality. The Greeks used this word to mean portions of an epic or a free grouping of these portions. (There followed a rhapsodic section played by the cellos.) From the Greek terms meaning stitch together, song.

RHYTHM. The division of time into various lengths of sound and silence. It is usually related to a consistent pulse or meter and has some kind of recognizable organization. From the Latin *rhythmus;* Greek *rhythmos.*

RONDO. The form whose distinctive characteristic is a returning theme. An example would be A B A C A B A. (The last movement of a symphony is frequently in rondo form.) From the Old French *rondel,* round or circular.

SEMITONE. The pitch distance between two adjacent notes on the piano. From the Latin prefix *semi*, half, and tone.

SERIAL. This is from the word *series*. It is a compositional technique which establishes an order of pitches (row or series) and uses this row as the basis for all further development. The row is usually made up of all twelve chromatic notes (hence the name twelve-tone or dodecaphonic). These notes in the series are ordered in such a way as to avoid any diatonic or tonal implication. The row may be used horizontally, vertically, polyphonically, in different directions, transposed, inverted, etc. In strict serial writing, no note may be used which does not take its place in some statement of the row. Because of the recurrence of the row, this is a kind of variation technique. The sounds of disjunct melody and atonality associated with serial music are an important twentieth-century musical development. From the Latin *sero*, to join or connect.

SONATA. This word was first used simply to mean sound-piece or piece intended to sound on instruments, as opposed to voices. Later, in the last part of the eighteenth century, it was used to mean a three- or four-movement work for solo instrument, sometimes with piano accompaniment. The first movement is usually in *sonata allegro* form. (Beethoven wrote thirty-two piano sonatas.) From the Latin *sonare*, to sound.

SONATA ALLEGRO. This is a form which is employed extensively in first movements. It consists of an exposition, which states the thematic materials of the movement, and changes key; a development, which explores many keys and usually develops some of the material presented in the exposition; and a recapitulation, which returns to the key of the piece and restates the material.

This form was a favorite in the classical period but continues to be used. The changes in the use of the form have come from changing compositional attitudes. The term is Italian, *allegro*, fast.

SPRECHSTIMME. A combination of speaking and singing which only approximates pitch. Exact rhythm is written in the score but there is a certain amount of freedom left to the performer about pitch intonation. This is an extremely dramatic style of declamation. From the German *sprechen*, to speak, and *Stimme*, voice.

STIMMTAUSCH. The practice of exchanging material. Voice A sings melody X while voice B sings melody Y, then they exchange parts. *Stimmtausch* is a forerunner of canon. The term is German; *Stimme*, voice, and *Tausch*, exchange.

STRETTO. A contrapuntal rhythmic device which pushes two or more voices closer together in time than they had been previously. This could mean that two voices in canon, the second voice having begun four beats after the first, is now only two beats late. It adds urgency and excitement. The term is Italian and means narrow.

SYNCOPATION. A rhythmic device which deliberately disturbs or confuses the normal pulse by shifting accent, delaying accent, or avoiding accent. From two Greek roots meaning with and strike.

TERTIAN HARMONY. Chords structured in thirds. The harmony our ear knows best is tertian harmony. From the Latin *tertius*, third, and harmony.

THEME. Subject material for a composition or movement of a composition. From the Greek, meaning to lay down.

THROUGH-COMPOSED. This is a formal structure in which there is new thematic material for each new section of music. It is particularly appropriate in songs to show the changing drama of the words. From the German *durch-komponiert*, through-composed.

TIMBRE. Timbre is the unique quality of sound produced by a particular instrument or voice. From the French *timbre*, bell.

TONALITY. The gravitation of music toward one note, called a tonic. Tonality often means, more specifically, the use of triads, such as C E G within a key to create the feeling of pull to the tonic note. From the Latin *tonalis*, pertaining to a tone.

TONE CLUSTER. A chord consisting of adjacent seconds, such as C D E. It is so called because of the appearance of the seconds on a score. They seem to be clustered. This chord is a twentieth-century sound.

TRANSPOSE. This means to change the pitch location of a whole pattern or piece. In tonal music it means to change to another tonality or key. From the Latin prefix *trans*, over, and French *poser*, to place.

TRIAD. A three-note chord made up of two adjoining thirds. The quality of chords built this way changes depending on the quality of the component intervals. From the Greek word meaning a group of three.

VARIATION. A compositional technique which repeats material in its entirety, changing the quality in each new repetition. The changing quality may be achieved in any number of ways: added notes, added ornaments, changing register or instruments or rhythm. The change usually affects the whole repetition. Each repetition is called a variation. Theme and Variations is the name of the form which consists of a theme and any number of variations. From the Latin *variare*, to vary.

WHOLE TONE. An interval made up of two half steps, or half tones.

CHAPTER 12

A Tool for Every Job

The Language of the Construction Trades

Frank W. Stubbs, Jr.

Construction is one of mankind's earliest activities. Some of the words included in the abbreviated list of construction terms have come from other languages. But more commonly they come from job operations or job machines and graphically depict that particular operation or machine. Some words have regional meanings, although this seems to be changing due to the mobility of construction workers. We can only guess when some words came into use, especially those arising from a chance remark. A few examples will indicate how certain terms may have come into being: *skyhook* is the term applied to any imaginary support when none exists. *Gofer* or *gopher*, while not in the following list, is the term applied to a plumber's or steamfitter's helper. It seems to come from an order to "go for" a pipe or wrench. This has been shortened to "gofer" and refers to an individual rather than an operation. *Cat's eye* is a glass ball set in a pavement to reflect light and thus delineate the boundaries of traffic lanes. It is useful on curves. The shining of the glass ball is not unlike the reflection of a light beam striking the eyes of a cat alongside the road. *Cherrypicker* probably first came into use as applying to a small hoist mounted on an arm to reach out and pick up a car to be transferred into loading position in tunnel work. The reaching out or stretching to pick the load resembles the reaching in picking cherries from a tree. It stems from a chance remark. *Mudcapping* certainly gets its name from the act of covering an explosive charge with mud to direct the force downward against the rock to be broken. Similarly, *snake holing* applies to the act of placing a small charge of explosive in a small diameter hole beneath the rock. The hole is small and usually made by forcing a stick or metal rod underneath the boulder. Snake hole generally connotes a hole of smaller diameter than a prairie-dog hole. A *coyote shot,* on the other hand, indicates a larger size, and the tunnels and drifts for placing the explosives may be likened to a coyote's den. This probably arose in construction of western railroads.

Muck in agriculture may be defined as decayed peat or black swamp earth and is of Scandinavian origin. However, in construction and especially in tunnels, the term applies to the broken stone and earth resulting from blasting. It is a catchall term for designating all material to be removed. In early ore mines in Colorado the waste materials dumped outside the mine made a muck pile. And, too, we have *muck cars, muck trains, mucking machines,* and just *mucker.* The last term applies also to the laborer using a pick and shovel in a mine, as opposed to one who operates machinery. *Scalper* is the first in a series of screens and takes off the top fraction, probably coming from the old Indian custom of taking off the top hair and skin from the head of an enemy. Some laborer, seeing the long tube with a hopper at the top, likened it to the head and trunk of an elephant, so we call the device an *elephant trunk*. This is more likely to be applied to the black rubber spout but may be applied to metal spouts as well. However, when the metal spout and hopper are used to place concrete under water, they become a *tremie*.

WORD LIST

AIR-LEG DRILL. A lightweight one-man pneumatic drill mounted on an extensible leg or air ram which supports the weight of the drill and helps the miner in pushing the drill into the hole. Its maximum working height is about 6 feet. It is generally used for drilling into a vertical face.

BACKHOE. A type of front-end operating equipment mounted on a power excavator which enables the excavator to dig several feet below the level of the machine. The *hoe dipper* is attached to the end of the *hoe arm* which in turn is connected to the end of the *hoe boom*. The hoe arm is pulled toward the boom in loading and the entire assembly raised to dump the dipper. It is commonly used for digging trenches. Similar devices are mounted on tractors and operated by pneumatic pistons from a central control. Frequently it is referred to as *hoe*.

BLASTING CAP. A small metal tube closed at one end and loaded with a highly sensitive explosive, used to detonate explosive charges. One type of cap is ignited by a safety fuse and the other by an electric current. The electric blasting cap is more commonly used.

BLASTING MACHINE. A source of power for firing electric blasting caps. One type derives its power from an internal direct current generator actuated by a quick twist of the handle or by a strong push on a rack bar. The other type is a condenser-discharge machine which uses batteries or a generator to charge the condenser. The size of the machine is designated by the number of electric blasting caps which can be fired at one time. The internal generator type rates 10, 30, or 50 caps. The condenser-discharge machines may fire 1,200 electric blasting caps.

Boom. The frame or arm on which the dipper stick of a shovel is mounted, or on which the boom point sheaves of cranes are mounted. The line from the hoisting drum to the load passes over the boom point sheaves.

Boom Stop. A device to prevent the boom of a crane from being raised beyond the vertical so as to fall backward across the top of the machine.

Bottom Dump. A type of tractor-drawn hauling unit with longitudinal doors along the bottom which when opened dump the material in a windrow immediately below the unit. They are frequently called bottom dump wagons, and are manufactured in a variety of sizes up to 100 tons capacity. Bottom dumps are not self-loading.

Buckerup. The member of a riveting crew who holds the dolly against the manufactured head of a rivet while the field head is formed by the driving hammer.

Bulldozer. A large steel blade mounted on the front of a tractor for pushing soil forward or drifting it sidewise (angledozer). The term *dozer* is sometimes used to designate both the tractor and the blade. The dozer may be used for removing stumps, clearing land, digging out large boulders, push-loading scrapers, or for general cleanup around a power shovel. The blades may be straight, angling or U types. The capacity of U blades for large tractors may exceed 12 cubic yards of loose material. The blades may be operated by cable or hydraulic controls and may be mounted on a crawler or wheel-type tractor. If there is a basic machine for earthmoving, it may well be the bulldozer.

BULL PIN. A tapered pin with button head on one end used in aligning structural steel members during erection. The rivet or bolt holes are forced into place, so the erection bolts may be inserted to draw the connected members tightly together.

BULLWHEEL. A large diameter wheel at the base of mast and boom of a stiffleg or guy derrick and used to rotate them for placement of hoisted load. A bullwheel with clamping dogs is used at the head end of tram for reversing the direction of the traction cable and to hold it against slipping.

BUNTON. Horizontal members, in a shaft used to support the vertical guides, to hold the cage or skip in proper alignment while being raised or lowered. The bunton may be a steel-H section or timber.

BURN CUT. Moderate-sized rock tunnels are usually drilled full face with holes spaced somewhat concentrically about the face center. Four holes near the center are slanted toward the center line to form a pyramid. These are fired before the other holes to remove the rock, so subsequent charges will blow the material toward the center. A larger diameter hole centered on the four forming the pyramid is drilled about three-fourths of the depth of the others. The group provides a burn cut.

BUTTON LINE. The line (cable) provided in a Lidgerwood reeve cableway to support the load-line between the head tower and the carriage. As the carriage moves away from the head tower, fall-rope carriers to support the load-line are dropped off at appropriate spaces as set by the location of the buttons on the button line. A traveling cableway generally has two movable towers running on parallel tracks so the cableway spans the construction site. The operating equipment is located on the head tower. The tail tower provides an anchor for the track cable and supports the sheaves needed for other cables.

CAISSON. A box-like structure used in the construction of deep piers in water. The bottoms of the walls taper to a relatively thin section and thus provide a cutting edge. This part is usually made of steel. The box is arranged so that it will float. When at the site, the walls are extended, and the box sinks until the cutting edge is in the soil. The undesirable soil is removed by dredging, and the walls are extended farther until the caisson is founded on the appropriate material. The bottom is sealed with concrete and additional work completed. The caisson becomes a part of the pier. In a way, a caisson is really a method of placing piers. The type described above is sometimes called an open caisson. Under certain conditions, the space surrounded by the cutting edge is so arranged that it can be sealed and placed under compressed air. The undesirable soil is hand-loaded into buckets which are hoisted through a lock device to maintain the air pressure which is sufficient to exclude the entrance of water. The second arrangement is a pneumatic caisson and is probably the most expensive method of placing piers. Here too the space is sealed with concrete when proper foundation material is reached. The walls are extended as the caisson sinks.

CALIFORNIA SWITCH. A short section of double track, with a diamond switch and climber points at each end, which lies on top of the muck track in a tunnel. It is used for changing empty and loaded muck cars at the mucking machine in tunnel excavation. The section of double track is long enough to accommodate an entire muck train on either side. An empty car is pulled into loading position by an air hoist on the mucking machine and when loaded is removed to the loaded train by the locomotive on the other track. The time consumed in changing cars is one of the critical elements in the mucking operation.

Car Passer. A short section of track, usually one car in length, overriding the muck track with a dolly which permits an empty car to be moved sideways. When a loaded car is removed from the mucking machine, the empty one is moved back into the line of the muck track and pushed forward to the mucking machine by the locomotive. A car passer may be used in place of California switch or cherry picker for changing cars in tunnel excavation.

Cage. An enclosed platform for raising or lowering workmen in construction shafts operations for tunnels, dams, suspension bridge towers, etc. It is usually covered overhead to provide protection against falling objects. Such a cage operating on the near-vertical face of canyon walls at a damsite is called a **Monkey Slide.**

Cherry Picker. A hoist attached to a jumbo or mucking machine for transferring muck cars from one track to another or for lifting other equipment.

Chocker. A single wire rope sling with an eye spliced at each end. When one sling is used to lift a piece of steel by passing the sling around the piece and pulling one eye through the other eye and attaching it to a hoist hook, it is called a single sling chocker. When two slings are used and one eye of each is attached to the hoisting hook or clevis, the arrangement is called a bridle sling.

CLAMSHELL BUCKET. A type of material-handling bucket consisting of two jaws, each attached at one end to a common shaft and having the other end hinged to a bracket, which in turn is attached to a second shaft. The clamshell is operated by two lines, one for holding the bucket at the proper height and the other for closing or opening the bucket. It is used for hoisting materials in overhead bins and for excavation.

COFFERDAM. A temporary enclosure built in the water and pumped dry to permit work on bridge piers and the like.

COME-ALONG. A small hoist used for pulling steel members into position for bolting. It may be air-operated. If it is a lever-operated chain hoist, it is known as a **COFFING HOIST.**

COMPACTOR. A machine for increasing the density of soil in embankments, subgrades and bases for highways, earth dams, and backfill of trenches and around buildings. Some are hand operated, some must be towed by a tractor, some are vibratory, some are steel rollers with plain or toothed surfaces, and some are rubber-tired.

COMPRESSOR. A machine for putting air under pressure for use in construction or other operations. Three types used in construction are reciprocating, rotary, and centrifugal. The reciprocating is probably the most commonly used type.

COYOTE BLASTING. A method of placing large explosive charges to produce a large volume of stone. A tunnel is driven perpendicular to the face to a depth of about one-half to two-thirds of the face height. Here cross-cuts are driven to either side of the tunnel and at right angles to it. The length of the cross-cuts will approximate that of the tunnel. Large amounts of explosive are placed at appropriate places with the proper amount of inert material (stemming) to hold the charges in place. The tunnel is also charged. More than one tunnel, with associated cross-cuts, may be used for exceptionally large blasts. Two or more cross-cuts may be used for each tunnel for very high faces. This method has been used where the height above the tunnel exceeds 450 feet.

CRAWLER TRACTOR. A tractor mounted on self-laying endless tracks. The tracks are composed of a number of pads or shoes which are linked together and supported by idlers and actuated by a drive sprocket.

CREEPER TRAVELER. A stiffleg derrick mounted on a frame which is supported by the structure being erected. For erection of truss bridges, the creeper on rails is supported by the top chord of the trusses. The creeper frame is attached to one face of the towers for a suspension bridge. Raising the derrick from one position to the next is called "jumping the derrick."

CRIB. An open-wall box constructed of members at right angles to each other and in alternate rows. The box is filled with stone or earth and is used as a dam or retaining wall. The material for the box-like frames may be timber, reinforced concrete, or steel. If used in a dam, it is usually of a temporary nature for diverting the stream during the construction of a permanent dam.

CRUSHER. A machine for reducing the size of quarry or natural stone to usable sizes. Crushers are classed as primary or secondary, depending on the position in the production line. There are several types including jaw, gyratory, cone, roll, impact, hammermill, and ball mill.

CYCLE. A series of operations usually done in sequence and

repeated over and over. In tunneling, the cycles are called rounds and include the drilling operation, mucking, and timbering. The usual sequence of operations in the cycle for excavating with scrapers is load, haul, dump, turn, return, and turn.

DERRICK. A hoisting apparatus, supporting block-and-falls, for lifting loads. Two essential elements are the mast, which is usually vertical, and the boom, which can be raised or lowered to vary its reach. The mast may be held in place by rope guys or by struts. Derrick is also applied to the rectangular tower frame used for raising and lowering the tools in drilling deep wells.

DERRICK CAR. A long railroad car with a derrick mounted on one end and power unit on the other. It is usually provided with extensible side shores which provide greater lateral stability.

DEWATERING. The removal of water from a construction site. It may be accomplished by use of a number of wellpoints or by sump pumps. Dewatering permits work to be done in the dry. It may provide stability to banks in excavation area and reduce upward pressures.

DIPPER STICK. The part of a power shovel which mounts the dipper at one end. The dipper stick may be moved forward and backward and up and down. The dipper is loaded by crowding it into the bank face and hoisting it through the material.

DOLLY. A tool with a concave cup at one end to hold rivets in place while the field head is being formed by the driving hammer. There are numerous handle shapes for special purposes. The term dolly may also be applied to a small truck with one, two, or four wheels used for moving heavy objects.

DOUBLE CLUTCHING. Disengaging and engaging the clutch

twice during a single shift. This permits synchronizing gears and higher engine speeds.

DRAWBAR PULL. The power available to do work after the tractor has moved over level ground. It is the power available at the drawbar and is measured in pounds or as a percent of the gross vehicle weight (GVW).

DREDGE. An excavator mounted on a barge and capable of digging below the water surface. Three common types are dipper, ladder, and suction. The **DIPPER** is essentially a shovel with a long boom and dipper stick. A **LADDER DREDGE** is used to raise the excavated material by a series of buckets attached to moving chains, a bucket conveyor. The **SUCTION DREDGE** moves the material in suspension in water by pumping and usually discharges it through a pipe to the point of deposit. Dredging may also mean removing material below a caisson by a clamshell bucket operated by a crane or floating derrick.

ELEPHANT TRUNK. A large rubber pipe with a hopper on the top end which is used to place concrete in deep forms. The trunk length can be varied by adding or removing sections. Its use tends to prevent segregation of material. For narrow walls the pipes may be made of metal and rectangular in plan.

FAIRLEAD. A device mounted near the foot of a boom to guide the drag cable to the drum and thus avoid its fouling on other parts of the machine. It is commonly used on dragline excavators.

FORK WRENCH. An open wrench with a long tapered handle used in structural steel erections. The head is offset from the handle to permit its use on large flat surfaces, as in bolting up gusset plates for bridges. The tapered handle also serves as a pin for aligning rivet holes.

FRONT-END LOADER. A tractor with a bucket attached to

the front end by a mechanism which permits raising, lowering, and tilting the bucket. It is used for excavating and for loading hauling units or for charging low aggregate bins. Bucket sizes vary from about one-half to ten cubic yards.

FUSE. A black powder train, enclosed in a flexible waterproof sheath, used for igniting blasting caps. Two speeds of burning are common, 120 seconds per yard and 90 seconds per yard. This is known as a safety fuse.

GANTRY. A mobile frame operating on widely spaced rails and supporting a revolving crane. The haul road or track passes between the legs of the gantry. It is used in placing concrete in long masonry dams where a span of cableway would be too great. The gantry is supported on a trestle which is embedded as the concrete is placed. Gantry also applies to the frame mounted on the revolving superstructure of a shovel or crane to provide a more favorable angle for the boom hoist cables when the boom is at a small angle to the horizontal.

GINNYWINK. A derrick with an A-frame for a mast which is supported by a single strut. The boom of the ginnywink can operate through 180 degrees.

GIN POLE. A type of lifting device, having only a mast, to which a LOAD FALL (q.v.) is attached. The mast is held in place by guys, and the only movement possible is a slight tilting by slacking off the guys on one side. A gin pole may be used for light loads when it is inappropriate to move in a crane or derrick.

GRADE RESISTANCE. The resistance to movement of equipment up an incline over and above that due to rolling resistance. For grades up to 15-20 percent, it amounts to about 20 pounds per ton per percent of grade.

GRIZZLY. A gridded or slotted opening to separate out

oversize material before loading hauling units or belt conveyors. In some cases the grizzly is tiltable and thus self-cleaning; in others a dozer may be used to remove the oversize from the grizzly.

GUY DERRICK. The type of derrick whose mast is held in position by a number of rope guys. This type is commonly used for the erection of structural steel in a tier-type building (Empire State Building).

HAMMER HEAD. A type of derrick with a vertical mast supporting a horizontal boom which revolves about a vertical axis. The boom may be counterweighted; the mast is frequently erected and supported in an elevator shaft, and the whole assembly is raised as the construction progresses upward.

HAULROAD. The off-highway roads about a construction site over which construction equipment operates. The roads need to be substantial because the wheel loads of construction equipment are generally much larger than in over-the-highway type of equipment.

HEADACHE BALL. The term applied to a heavy, round, or pear-shaped metal ball used in demolishing buildings, pavements, or other structures. It is suspended by a crane boom and is raised and dropped or swung against a vertical wall. It is called a **SKULL CRACKER** in some areas.

HEADFRAME. A structural frame erected over a vertical or inclined shaft on which the head sheave (pulley) is mounted so as to provide space to dump the car into bins or hauling units. The headframe may be constructed of structural steel or timber and may be semi-portable in nature.

HEAD PULLEY. The top sheave over which the hoist line runs, or the pulley at the discharge end of a belt conveyor. The sheaves at the head end of a boom are also called **BOOM POINT SHEAVES**.

HEAD TOWER. The tower of a movable cableway on which the operating equipment is located and which supports one end of the track cable.

HITCH. The connection of the hoisting line to the member to be lifted. It is specially designed for heavy loads.

IDLERS. Non-powered wheels (pulleys) used to support the belt of a conveyor. They may be arranged to cause the belt to run flat, as in the return run, or they may be arranged to trough the belt to increase its capacity. Troughing idlers may consist of three pulleys, the center one rotating about a horizontal axis and the ones on either side rotating about an axis inclined about 20 degrees to the horizontal.

IMPACT WRENCH. A compressed air-operated wrench for tightening nuts on high-strength bolts used to connect structural steel members. The wrench is calibrated to tighten the nut so that proper tension is induced in the bolt. Connecting with high-strength bolts causes much less noise and nuisance than connecting with rivets. There are two men in a bolting crew and four men in a riveting crew.

JACKHAMMER. A one-man air-operated machine used to power a wide variety of tools including rock drills, cutting spades, sheeting drivers, and others for special purposes. The hammer is held in position by holding two handles at its top. A throttle for opening the air valve is located at one handle. Usually the tool is operated in a downward direction thus taking advantage of the weight of the hammer to force the tool into the material.

JETTING. The term applied to forcing water alongside a pile or caisson or other object to reduce the friction while driving or sinking. It may also be applied to forcing grout into crevices in foundation material. The latter operation may be called *grouting* in some areas.

JIB. An extension at the outer end of a crane or derrick boom to increase its reach. The jib may be in line with the boom or at a small angle. A sheave at the outer end handles the line for light loads. This line is called the **RUNNER LINE.**

JUMBO. A mobile working platform used to mount drills at different levels for drilling operations in tunnel construction. The working platforms may be hinged so they can be lowered to provide space for hauling units to pass through. Jumbos may be mounted on rails or on rubber tires so they can be moved back from the working face when the explosive is detonated and during the mucking operations. When necessary they are used for placing timbering to support tunnel roof and walls. The jumbo could also provide the working platform for placing reinforcing steel as in the inclined tunnels of the spillway structure at Glen Canyon Dam.

LAGGING. Members placed between timbering frames and the soil or rock to prevent its inward movement. Lagging is usually horizontal in tunnels and vertical in shafts. It is also the members placed between soldier beams used to support vertical faces of open cuts under appropriate conditions. Too, lagging is the term applied to the rubber-like coating placed on the drive pulley of a belt conveyor to increase the friction between the belt and the pulley.

LOAD FALLS. The combination of blocks suspended from the end of a boom of a derrick and attached to the load to be lifted.

LOAD LINE. The cable running from the boom point sheaves or head blocks to the hoisting drum.

MAST. The vertical member which supports the outer end of the boom of a derrick. The mast is held in position by guy cables or struts.

MILLISECOND-DELAY BLASTING. The detonation of a series of explosive charges in sequence by electric blasting caps which have closely controlled timing built in. The delays vary from zero milliseconds (one-one thousandth of a second) to about 550 milliseconds. Ordinary electric blasting caps have a predeterminated firing sequence of about one half to one second intervals. The use of millisecond-delay electric blasting caps permits the detonation of the several charges at the most effective time. Their use tends to control throw, reduce air blast and vibration, improve public relations and produce better fragmentation of the stone.

MISFIRE. An explosive charge which fails to detonate when fired. The misfire may be caused by an overloaded circuit, a faulty circuit, or a break in the powder train of a blasting fuse. A misfired shot is extremely dangerous and must be cleared only by experienced personnel.

MIXER. A revolving drum with fixed inside vanes used for mixing concrete or other materials. The cement, sand, stone, and water are tumbled together as the rotation causes the vanes to lift the materials up and drop them as the vanes move overhead. Those mounted on a truck chassis are called **TRANSIT-MIXERS** if the mixing operation takes place en route to the site and **AGITATORS** if the materials are premixed.

MOTOR GRADER. A machine consisting of a frame supported on three axles, a power plant mounted over the two rear axles and carrying a blade suspended between the front and rear axles. The front wheels may be tilted in or out. The blade may be revolved, tilted up and down and swung in a near vertical position outside the frame. The grader is used in road maintenance, digging ditches and contour furrows, and mixing in place bituminous surfacing materials. Sometimes a V-plow is attached in front of the grader during the winter to provide a machine for snow removal.

Muck Car. A car used for hauling excavated material from a tunnel. It operates on a track of 18, 24, or 36-inch gauge. It is dumped by tilting sideways. The size varies from one to six cubic yards. The gauge depends largely on the size of the bore, for the cars must be so sized that two can pass in the tunnel.

Mucking Machine. A machine for loading muck (shot rock) at a tunnel heading. The bucket of the mucker is forced into the muck pile by moving the machine forward; when loaded the machine retracts a short distance, then the bucket is tilted backward for dumping. The bucket of a small air-operated mucker dumps directly into an attached muck car. Larger muckers are electrically driven, and the bucket dumps onto a conveyor which enables the mucker to load long cars of large capacity. The cars mentioned above are for track haulage. In wide tunnels or under other conditions the haulage may be by rubber-tired trucks, and these can be loaded by a tractor-mounted overshot loader. The bucket is forced into the muck pile and dumped by raising it up over the tractor and throwing the rock into a truck. The tractor moves forward and backward. Close coupled wide trucks are desirable because of the limited throw of this type of mucker. The machine is generally powered by a diesel engine equipped with scrubber to remove noxious gases.

MUD-CAPPING. A scheme used for breaking large boulders or individual pieces of stone by explosives without drilling holes into the stone. The explosive charge is placed on the stone over a crack or seam. It is covered with mud and the charge detonated. The mud reduces the noise and air blast and tends to direct the force of the explosion downward into the stone. The mud must be free of small stones to avoid throwing them great distances. Mud-capping requires about twice as much explosive as when the charge is placed in a hole under the stone (snake-holing) and about eight to ten times as much as when placed in a drilled hole in the rock.

NIPPER. The term applied to the workman who delivers sharpened drill steel and picks up the used drills in mining operations. In large operations there may be a considerable number of drills operating at widely spaced areas.

OFF-HIGHWAY HAULING. The transportation of materials about a construction site. The hauling units, especially those for hauling earth, may be very large when compared to conventional trucks, and they have high axle loads. These are usually way beyond those tolerated on state highways. Some single axle loads may exceed 120,000 lbs., about twice that of heavy steam locomotives used in the past.

OUTRIGGER. An arm which is extended sideways from the chassis of a crane to provide lateral stability when lifting heavy loads. Early models were extended and blocked by hand, and frequently this operation consumed more time than making the lift. The outriggers on modern machines are power-extended and their footings are controlled from the operator's cab. Outriggers on truck cranes serve the same purpose as side shores on derrick cars.

PILE. A long slender structural member driven into the ground to provide suitable foundation support for a structure. Piles carry their load by point bearing or by skin friction along their sides or by a combination of the two. Piles may be made of timber, steel, concrete, or a combination of these materials. Most types are driven, but some consist of a driven shell which is subsequently filled with concrete. Some are solid; some are hollow pipe sections. There is hardly a limit to the length that may be placed.

PILE DRIVER. A machine for driving piles. It consists of a chassis, power plant, leads, and a hammer. The machine may be mounted on skids, rubber-tired wheels, crawler tracks, or a barge. The boom supports the leads and hammer and raises the pile into the leads which hold the pile and hammer in position for driving. The leads on some machines may be tilted so the piles can be driven at a batter to enable them to resist horizontal forces.

PILE HAMMER. The instrument which applies the force to drive a pile into the ground. Early models were simply a heavy weight which was raised in a frame and dropped on the head of the pile, hence the term "drop hammer." The next in line was a weighted piston which was raised by steam pressure and dropped. The height through which the hammer dropped is much shorter than in the first case, but many more blows per minute could be applied. This is a single-acting hammer. Probably the next generation was the double-acting hammer in which pressure was applied to both the upward and downward strokes, double-acting hammers. Early models of both types were powered with steam but some place along the line compressed air was introduced in place of steam. Two recent additions to the pile-driving hammer family are the diesel hammer and the vibrating hammer. In the first a diesel engine provides the power for the ram; in the second an eccentric mechanism sets up controlled vibration which aids the weight in forcing the pile down into granular materials.

POWDER MONKEY. The term applied to the workman who prepares explosive charges and delivers them to the working face for loading into drill holes. Here too, in mining operations there may be several widely spaced faces working at the same time.

PRESPLITTING. Inducing a crack in rock excavation to control overbreak and underbreak. This is accomplished by drilling closely spaced holes along both sides of the cut and firing light charges spaced up and down in each hole. These explosions induce waves which combine to cause tensile forces which in turn crack the rock on a line between the holes. This is done before drilling and blasting for the main excavation.

PUSHER. The term applied to the tractor or tractors used to push a scraper while loading and thus reduce the load time. Of course the pusher tractor could be used to help a hauling unit up a steep grade or through a muddy section of the excavation area or the haul road. The term is also applied to the foreman of a steel erection crew.

REEVE. The arrangement of rope (wire or manila) through the sheaves of a set of blocks. It also applies to the arrangement of the cables through sheaves and around drums in a cableway.

RIPPER. A tool consisting of one or more teeth mounted in a cross frame and attached to the rear of a tractor or, if separately mounted, towed by a tractor. Rippers are used for loosening earth or rock for scraper loading. It is sometimes called a ROOTER.

ROLLING RESISTANCE. The resistance to moving equipment over level ground. It is composed of the friction of moving parts, the flexing of the sidewalls of the tires, and the compaction and displacement of the ground under the tire or crawler track. It may be measured in pounds per ton or as a percent of the gross vehicle weight. On construction haul roads the magnitude starts at about 40 pounds per ton and increases about 30 pounds per ton per inch of penetration. This is one of the important elements affecting the travel speed of a hauling unit.

ROUNDS. The cycle of operations in driving tunnels in rock. The major elements are drilling operation, mucking operation, and timbering operation. The drilling operation includes setting up drill jumbo, drilling, loading holes, shooting, and ventilating. The mucking operation includes scaling the roof (sometimes called picking down the roof) and mucking which consists of loading and hauling the blasted material. Timbering includes setting steel ribs and lagging or setting roof bolts.

ROOF BOLT. A bolt used to support the roof of a rock tunnel. The bolt, with an expansion device at one end, is inserted in a drilled hole and the expansion device set. A large washer and nut at the outside end are pulled up tight. The bolts are usually spaced on about four-foot centers in both directions and fasten the exposed surface rock to more solid material inside the formation. The roof bolts may be applied to a vertical surface. Roof bolting may replace timbering under certain conditions.

SAND HOG. The term applied to a workman who works in

compressed air, especially in a pneumatic caisson. State laws generally control the maximum pressure and time men can work under compressed air.

SAND ISLAND. A method used in sinking a caisson in a stream where high velocities may cause excessive scour under the cutting edge. A large diameter sheet pile COF-FERDAM (q.v.) is built at the site with the sheets penetrating well into the river bottom. The cofferdam is filled with sand and the cutting edge and first sections of the caisson walls erected on the sand island. The sand is excavated and walls built up as in ordinary caisson construction. The operation is continued until the caisson is founded on suitable material.

SCALING. The removal of loose rock from roofs of tunnels or from faces of walls of deep cuts. Scaling is an exceedingly dangerous operation. At Glen Canyon Dam, wall scalers were suspended hundreds of feet in the air by ropes attached at the top of the canyon wall. These scalers used a pry bar to break out loose rock.

SCALPER. The first in a series of screens used to remove oversized material. This may be used to remove pieces too large to enter the crusher or to scalp off stones which are to pass through the primary crusher. The smaller material which does not need primary stage crushing thus by-passes the primary and thereby reduces the load on that crusher.

SCARIFIER. An attachment for a tractor or motor grader consisting of a number of teeth and used for shallow breaking of compacted materials. The surface may be loosened for removal, or it may be lightly roughened to accept an additional lift as in earth dam construction.

SCOW. A scow is a hull designed for construction operations and may be specially fitted to be used in specific operations. For hauling excavated materials, the scow may be side dump or bottom dump. In some cases a strong deck may be provided for mounting derricks, revolving cranes, piledrivers, or other equipment. The terms *scow* and *barge* are interchangeable. A scow is a barge on the inland waterways, and barges are scows on the Great Lakes, the Gulf, and the coastal waterways.

SCRAPER. An excavating machine, sometimes called a *pan,* which is able to self-load, haul, and dump. It consists essentially of a rectangular pan, open at the front, fitted with a cutting edge and capable of being raised or lowered. The soil is held in the pan by lowering the front apron to the cutting edge. The pan is loaded by lowering the cutting edge, and as the scraper is pulled forward soil is forced into the bowl. It is emptied by raising the front apron and forcing the soil out by a powered tail gate or by raising the hinged bowl bottom. The scraper is mounted on rubber tires and is powered by a crawler or wheeled tractor. Sizes range from six or seven to fifty-four cubic yards.

SCREED. A straight edge set to proper grade and used to determine the strike-off of concrete floors. It may be a straight piece of pipe or lumber; in either case it must be properly supported. The term may also apply to the member of a paving train to strike-off the material at the proper height. As it moves forward it oscillates back and forth across the pavement. On some construction jobs vibrating roller screeds have been used, especially on highway bridge decks.

SHEEPSFOOT ROLLER. A steel drum roller whose face is studded with projections six to eight inches long and of varying shapes. It is usually towed by a tractor and used to compact cohesive soils in embankments for highways and dams. Some self-propelled models are on the market. The compaction is attained by repeated passes of the roller over an area. The name comes from the kneading action resembling that resulting from the passing of a herd of sheep.

SHEET PILE. A rolled steel member with edges designed to interlock with adjacent sheets. These members are driven into the ground to form a COFFERDAM (q.v.) around a construction area to prevent the collapse of the sides as the excavation advances downward. In general the sheets must be appropriately braced whether forming an enclosure or driven in a single line to support a bank. Sheet piles are manufactured in various shapes and in a number of weights.

SHIPPER SHAFT. The shaft on which the shipper drum is mounted on the boom of a power shovel. The drum actuates the dipper stick in and out.

SHOO-FLY. A short section of railroad track built to pass around some temporary obstruction.

SIDE BOOM. A short boom mounted on the side of a tractor and used in laying steel pipe lines for gas and oil products.

SKIP. A bucket operating in a vertical frame used for hoisting material from one level to another. A skip could be used in a mine shaft for hoisting ore or waste. Usually the bucket and its guides are designed to make the bucket self-dumping.

SKIRT BOARD. Members mounted on both sides of a belt conveyor at a transfer point to direct the material to the belt and avoid spillage.

SKY HOOK. A vertical support when circumstances make it difficult or impossible to attain such support.

SLUSHER. A small drag scraper without a bottom used to pull material from difficult locations. The scraper is pulled with a wire rope powered by a two or three drum air hoist. The rope passes through a SNATCH BLOCK (q.v.) anchored beyond the material to be pulled.

SNAKE HOLING. A method of blasting boulders by placing the explosive charge in a hole below the boulder. This is more effective than mudcapping but less efficient than placing the charge in drilled holes.

SNATCH BLOCK. A single sheave (pulley) mounted in a wood or steel block which has a hook or clevis for attachment to an anchor or to the object to be moved.

SPIDER. Steel plate at the top of the mast of a guy derrick to which the rope guys are attached. The mast can revolve under the spider.

STEAM HAMMER. The type of pile-driving hammer in which the ram is actuated by steam. The hammer may be single or double acting, i.e., steam pressure is applied in one direction in the single acting and in both directions in the double acting.

STEMMING. The inert material placed over a charge of explosives in a bore hole to confine the power of the explosion and to take up space not needed for the explosive. In stratified materials stemming would be placed across the weak plane between the strata. The hole is topped out with stemming to avoid the vertical release of the explosive force.

STIFFLEG DERRICK. The type of derrick in which the mast is held in position by two struts (legs) about 60 to 90 degrees apart. The legs are attached to the top of the mast and to horizontal sills which are in turn attached to the base of the mast.

STOPER. A type of air drill used for drilling holes in the roof of a tunnel in a mine.

TAG LINE. A line used to control the swing of an object when it is lifted by a crane. Such a line is attached to a clamshell bucket to prevent its whirling and the consequent twisting of the closing and holding lines. Such a line is kept under reasonable tension by the tag line winder mounted on the crane boom.

TAIL TOWER. The tower which anchors the opposite end of the track cable from the head tower in a movable cableway. As with the head tower, the tail tower must be designed to hold the pull from the cable and ropes and provide height for suitable operation. Certain sheaves necessary for operation are mounted on the tail tower.

TIDE GATE. A device in a COFFERDAM (q.v.) in tidal waters to equalize water height inside and outside the enclosure as the tide goes out. Without such provision the tide "hangs up" in the cofferdam and causes an unbalanced outward pressure for which most cofferdams are not designed. The gate is provided by cutting one sheet pile at the low water line and leaving the upper section standing high. When dewatering is started the high end is dropped into place and tightly welded to the lower section.

TOPPING LIFT. The set of blocks and tackle used for raising or lowering the boom of a derrick or crane.

TRACK CABLE. The fixed cable of a cableway or an aerial tram over which the carriage wheels travel. The track cable is usually of the lock-coil type which has a smooth surface. One of the largest lock-coil cables manufactured was for the two 12 cu.yd. cableways at Glen Canyon Dam. Each had a rated capacity of about 50 tons.

TRACTION. The force developed parallel to the travel surface by a tire or crawler track. This usually determines the total force which can be applied to a load. The ratio of this force to the load on the tire is called the **COEFFICIENT OF TRACTION.**

TRACTIVE EFFORT. The power available to do work after taking the loss through the gear train but before the tractor has moved over level ground. It is sometimes called **RIMPULL.**

TRAM. A long aerial ropeway supported on several towers and used to transport materials and people over rough terrain. One type is composed of a stationary or track cable on which the dollies supporting the carriages or buckets ride and a moving or traction cable which provides controlled movement of the carriages. In addition to the cables there are other necessary appurtenances such as bullwheel, motor, and brakes. This type is used for transporting ore or aggregates where it is not practical to build a haul road. Ore buckets are attached to the traction cable by a clamping device which can be released for dumping. Another type of tram consists of a single cable and other gear. The carriers are attached to this rope and ride over the pulley supported on the arm of the tower. Ski lifts are of this type as are the trams used in spinning cables of a suspension bridge. A tram may be called a tramway or a ropeway.

TRANSIT MIXER. See **MIXER.**

TREMIE. A long circular steel pipe, with a hopper at one end, which is used to place concrete under water so as to avoid loss of cement due to water motion. The tremie is supported, hopper end up, by a derrick boom or other means. A sack of straw or a basketball is inserted in the pipe and the hopper filled with concrete which forces the plug and water ahead of it. The lower end is on the foundation material. Concrete is added to the hopper and the tremie raised a short distance to permit the concrete to flow out, but care must be used to keep the lower end submerged in the live concrete. The use of a tremie is probably the most satisfactory way of placing underwater concrete.

TREMIE SEAL. The block of concrete placed at the bottom of a cofferdam by the tremie method. It forms the base for the foundation of the structure. The seals are placed in a continuous pour.

TRENCHER. A specific type of excavator designed to excavate long, narrow, moderately deep trenches for pipe lines. There are two common types. The **WHEEL TRENCHER** mounts a number of buckets on a rotating wheel which can be raised and lowered. The buckets dump onto a short section of a transverse belt conveyor which discharges the soil in a windrow parallel to the trench. The second common type is the **LADDER TRENCHER** which consists of a number of buckets attached to two endless chains held in place by a frame, the ladder. The frame can be raised and lowered, and the buckets discharge onto a short transverse conveyor discharging soil in a pile parallel to the trench. The soil from both types may be discharged directly into a truck, if it is to be removed from the site. The trencher may be powered with a gas or diesel engine. A trencher is also called a ditcher. The ladder type is similar to a *ladder dredge*. See DREDGE.

WAGON DRILL. A frame and a mast, mounted on wheels or crawlers, used to support an air drill. The drill is mounted on a slide which can be moved up and down the mast by a roller chain operated by an air motor. The units are highly portable, which permits their use in very rough terrain. Heavier drills can be used than when they are hand held.

WALKING DRAGLINE. A dragline excavator mounted on a large diameter circular base. It is moved forward by placing its shoes on the ground and lifting the entire machine and setting it ahead. It is used in larger sizes (four or five cubic yards and up) where volume of material to be moved is large, where long booms are needed, and where low soil pressure may be required. Its maximum moving speed is about one-fourth mile per hour. It must be substantially dismantled for transfer from job to job.

WELLPOINT METHOD. A method of dewatering a construction site by the installation of a system of wellpoints. A wellpoint is about three feet long and has an outside screen diameter of about two and one half inches. One end is pointed for driving or jetting, and the other end is attached to a riser pipe. The riser pipes are connected to a header manifold by swing joints. The header is connected to the pump which discharges into an outfall pipe leading the water away from the area. The water table may be lowered 15 to 20 feet by a single stage of wellpoints.

CHAPTER 13

Homo Sapiens, Our Brother

The Language of Anthropology

HERBERT S. CAMENSON

Contrary to continental European usage, in the United States and Britain anthropology, the science or study of man, has a split-personality vocabulary, encompassing both physical anthropology, the bio-history of man, and cultural anthropology, the study of human cultures and comparative sociology. On the continent physical anthropology alone constitutes the field of study. As a consequence, in most of the English-speaking world the language of the science includes biological and social phenomena in a seemingly incongruous juxtaposition. If, however, anthropology is viewed as the scientific-humanistic blending which looks at man as a physical-intellectual entity, the reasons for the emergence of the unified Anglo-American discipline become understandable.

Anthropology is a growing science, the practitioners of which have a jargon which expands informally and unevenly but nevertheless continuously. New words must be coined to explain the new concepts, and old words must be redefined to meet the new challenges. Since many terms

defy absolutely precise definition and are used on the basis
of a tacit agreement on their meaning, standard dictionaries often differ and glossaries often reflect the biases of
their authors. In spite of these apparent disagreements
there is in reality a general consensus about the meanings
of practically all words in the terminology, and the creation of new words tends to follow a prescribed pattern.

From paleoanthropology we get the coined *Zinjan-
thropus* to explain and name a newly found fossil. The
anthropus ending is regularly employed to designate hu-
manoid fossils. *Zinj*, the Arabic for Ethiopia and by extension East Africa, where the fossil was discovered, indicates
the area of the find. Since it has been common practice to
name fossil men after their places of discovery—for example, *Sinanthropus pekinensis*, *sin*, from the Greek *sinai*,
China, and *pekin*, from the Chinese capital city, the site of
the find—this process of word formation will undoubtedly
continue.

From linguistics we adopt native words such as the
Eskimo *Adlet*, a mythical group of monsters produced by a
cross between men and dogs, or the Philippine Mandaya
Bagani, those who have killed six persons. As new customs
are observed and new cultures are studied, words from
those cultures will gain currency. The languages of the
various peoples of the world are thus continually enriching
the vocabularies of anthropologists, of scientists, and of
people in general.

WORD LIST

ACCULTURATION. The process and result of adopting
through continuous firsthand contact the culture traits
and patterns of another group. (To a great extent Japan
received its culture from China through acculturation,

by acquiring such items as writing, coined money, and Buddhism.) Derived from Latin *ad*, preposition "to," "toward," and *cultus*, from *colere*, to till.

ADAPTATION. (1) In sociology, a slow, usually unconscious change in behavior to adjust to or conform to changed or changing cultural patterns. (2) In biology, an alteration in the structure, function, or form of organisms that produces better survival adjustments to fit a changed environment. The human animal, by its adaptation to the urban environment, has changed its pattern of existence and probably improved its chances of leaving descendants. From the French *adapter* and Latin *adaptare*, to fit.

AGE. A long or short geological period of the history of the earth. The term *age* is a confusing one because the divisions into Paleolithic (Old Stone), Neolithic (New Stone), Chalcolithic (Copper), Bronze, and Iron Ages are not clear-cut divisions. From Old French *aage* from Latin *aetas* from *aevitas* from *aevum*, lifetime.

AMOK or **AMUCK.** A manic and homicidal condition originally noted among the Malays but now found to be common among many peoples. It follows a state of depression and usually occurs among men who have left home and who are overwhelmed by their new environments. Used only in the phrase *to run amok*. From Malay *amoq*, furious.

ANIMISM. Primarily the belief that natural phenomena and objects such as wind, trees, and rocks have souls and spirits. A belief in such demons or spirits. Animism probably originated in the Paleolithic Age as an answer to man's need to explain the unknown. From the Latin *anima*, air, soul.

ARTIFACT. Any object made by human work with a view to

subsequent use. Weapons, tools, pottery, and sculptured
and engraved objects are the artifacts most commonly
found in ancient grave sites. From Latin *arti-* (combining form of *ars,* art) and *factum,* the past participle of
facere, to make.

AUSTRALOID. A member of the subspecies *Homo sapiens
australoideus,* a white race with some survivors still in
Australia. One of the four major races, the Australoid
appears to be anatomically the most archaic of human
stocks now alive. Darker-skinned relatives may be found
in Melanesia and southern India. The Australoid was
hirsute, of medium height, with heavy supraorbital
ridges, feeble chin, and a short, broad face. From the
Latin *australis,* southern, and the Greek *o-eides,* form or
shape, and in English used to denote resemblance.

BRACHYCEPHALIC. See CEPHALIC INDEX.

CAUCASOID. A member of the subspecies *Homo sapiens
caucasoideus,* a white race with populations in many
areas of the world. There is great variation in this group
and a number of subgroups have been hypothesized in
an attempt to systematize the differences. One of the
four major races, Caucasoids are characterized by relatively light skin, medium to tall height, narrow to
medium-broad face, relatively high-bridge nose to high-
bridged, fine-textured straight or wavy hair ranging
from blond to dark brown, considerable body hair, and
eyes ranging from light blue to dark brown. From the
Caucasus region, the supposed ancestral home of the
subspecies.

CEPHALIC INDEX. A measure representing the ratio be-
tween head breadth and head length. C.I. $= \frac{\text{HB}}{\text{HL}} \times 100$.
If an individual's cephalic index is 80 or more, he is
short-headed (brachycephalic); if less than 76, he is

long-headed (dolichocephalic); if between 76 and 80 he is intermediate (mesocephalic). The great majority of fossil men are dolichocephalic, indicating that this may be an earlier form. From the Latin *cephalicus* and Greek *kephalikos* derived from *kephale*, head, plus index, from the Latin *indicare*, to point out.

CICATRIZATION. Contracted fibrous scar tissue produced by making incisions in the skin. In many groups this is often done in patterns for purposes of ornamentation. In some parts of Australia cicatrization is part of the initiatory rites for boys. The patterns of lines on the chest and back are absolutely necessary for the achievement of manhood. From the Latin *cicatrix*, scar.

CLAN. A kinship group usually living in one locality, with common interests, who claim common descent from an original ancestor who may have existed only in the mythological past. The members of the Scottish clan maintained the fiction of a common genetic descent from their legendary ancestor. From Gaelic *clann*, offspring, children, tribe, originally derived from Latin *planta*, offshoot.

COUVADE. A custom in many American-Indian tribes in which the father goes to bed and simulates childbirth, to prevent his regular daily exertions from harming the newborn infant. The *couvade* is probably a form of magical assistance in the establishment of the newborn in the everyday world, and a symbolic assertion of identification of the father and child. From French *couver*, to hatch, Old French *covee*, a brood, from Old French *cover*, to sit on, hatch, from Latin *cubare*, to lie down.

CULT. A group of followers who maintain an exclusive sacred ideology and an order and series of rites which are centered around their sacred symbols. The cult member believes that ritual activities promote the well-being and growth of men and gods in the carrying out of their daily activities. From Latin *cultus,* care, worship, the past participle of *colere,* to till.

CULTURE. The sum of the skills, arts, habits, instruments, concepts, institutions, ways of living, which are transmitted from generation to generation. Culture only exists where there is human life. The lower animals do not have the ability to perpetuate enough of their learning to transmit it socially. For etymology see CULT.

DIVISION OF LABOR, SEXUAL. The way by which societies divide men's work from women's. Most anthropologists take the position that the sexual division of labor is biologically based but subject to many cultural modifications.

DOLICHOCEPHALIC. See CEPHALIC INDEX.

ECOLOGY. The science concerned with the relationships between the distribution of human groups, their material resources, and the consequent cultural patterns and interdependency that result. In biology it is the study of the relationships between organisms and their physical environments. Some authorities on ecology have shown that primitive groups often share the uncertain yields of wild-seed crops so that good harvests will not spoil and bad harvests will not mean starvation. From the Greek *oikos,* house.

ENDOGAMY. The compulsory custom of marrying only within one's own group; inbreeding. The royal family of Egypt practiced extreme endogamy by allowing only brother-sister marriages. From Greek *endon,* within, and *gamia* derived from *gamos,* marriage.

ENVIRONMENT. The totality of the external conditions, circumstances, and influences surrounding and affecting man's development. Environment is important in shaping man's culture but most anthropologists feel that it is oversimplification to think of it as the only significant factor. Derived from Old French *en*, in, and *viron*, a circuit, derived from *virer*, to turn or to turn around.

EVOLUTION. The never-ending process of change by which organisms develop from simple to complex forms. In physical anthropology it is used to trace the development of *Homo sapiens*. Cultural anthropologists sometimes try to apply the concepts of evolution to the development of human institutions from the simple to the more complex. Derived from the past participle of the Latin *evolvere*, to roll out or to roll forth.

EXOGAMY. The compulsory custom of marrying only outside of one's own group; outbreeding. Usually found in clans and moieties. The practice of exogamy may serve to ally two separate social units and strengthen the position of each. From Greek *ex*, outside, and *gamia*, derived from *gamos*, marriage.

FETISH or **FETICH.** An inanimate object worshiped as having magical powers; originally an amulet or enchantment used by natives of the Guinea coast. The Portuguese explorers regarded the fetish as a work of art. From French *fetiche* and Portuguese *feitiço*, a charm, sorcery, derived from the Latin *facticius, factitius*, the past participle of *facere*, to make.

FEUD. A bitter, deadly, continuous quarrel marked by overt acts of hostility between families or clans usually lasting through several generations. Sometimes called a blood feud. From Middle English *fede, feide*, Old French *faide* probably derived from Middle High German *vede, vehede* derived from Old High German *fehida*, revenge.

GENE. The living biochemical components within the

chromosomes which are in all probability the ultimate carriers of the specific hereditary characteristics. It has been estimated that all humans have about 90 percent of the genes in common while only 10 percent of the genes account for the sexual and various racial differences. From the French *gene;* Greek *genes* derived from *gignesthai,* to be born, become.

GENE FLOW. The movement of genes from one group to another due to the migration or interbreeding of individuals. The melting-pot theory is an oversimplification of the gene flow theory. For etymology see GENE.

GENETIC DRIFT. The nonselective random distribution, the unpredictable changes due to mutation or aberration, the extinction or fixation of genes, usually in a small population. With geographic isolation, genetic drift may lead to distinct variation in type and form. For etymology see GENE.

HABITAT. The geographic region in which a person or group carries on the basic activities of living. The African Pygmy lives in and rules his habitat, the tropical rain forest of the Congo. From the Latin *habitat,* it or he inhabits.

HANDICRAFTS. Occupations and arts that require skillful use of the hands, weaving, potting (pottery), basket-making, carving, tool-making, etc. For most of humanity the age of handicrafts is dying because handicraft production cannot compete in the industrial society. From Middle English *handcrafte* from Anglo-Saxon *hand-craeft,* probably a variant of the Gothic *hinthan,* to seize, and Middle English *crafte* from Anglo-Saxon *craeft* from Germanic *kraft,* strength, force, and ultimately in English usage, skill.

HOMINIDAE. The family name for all the species of that

primate order of which only man survives. From Latin *homo, hominis,* man.

HOMO ERECTUS. Extinct form of man of Middle Pleistocene age, sometimes referred to as **PITHECANTHROPUS** or **JAVA MAN.** The probable ancestor of modern man, *Homo erectus* was an intermediate form who walked upright although his skull cap was apelike and his cranial capacity below that of *Homo sapiens.* In all probability he was descended from **DRYOPITHECINES,** a type of tree-dwelling ape. See **HOMINIDAE.**

HOMO SAPIENS. The only living species of the genus *Homo* and fossil men not designated *Homo erectus.* Most anthropologists now include Neanderthal man in the species *Homo sapiens.* From Latin *sapiens* from *sapere* to taste, know; thus wise, sagacious, full of knowledge, discerning.

HUSBANDRY. In agriculture primarily the exploitation of domesticated animals for consumption of their meat and blood, use of their hides, use of wool or hair for weaving or felting, milking and dairying, load-carrying or pulling, riding. Primitive animal husbandry represents adjustments to physical environments that are not suited to gardening. From Middle English *husbonde,* householder, Old English *husbonda* from Old Norse *husbondi, hus,* house and *bondi,* freeholder, derived from *bua,* to dwell.

INCEST. Sexual or marital relations between persons so closely related that society prohibits their marrying. The horror of incest exists in most human societies. Almost all prohibit marriage between father and daughter and mother and son. Brother-sister marriages are rare but do exist. Derived from Latin *incestum,* not chaste.

INDEPENDENT INVENTION. Relatively few of the total ideas and things possessed and shared by the peoples of the world have been invented more than once. When this has happened, it was occasioned by separate parallel discovery in divergent cultures. The independent invention of the concept of the zero by the Mayas and Hindus is an outstanding example of separate parallel discovery by divergent cultures.

INSTITUTION. A fairly permanent cluster of culturally imposed behavior patterns, established custom, law, religion, practice, system, etc. Those complexes of social living that are concerned with subsistence activities and the production and distribution of commodities and services are called economic institutions. From Latin *institutus,* the past participle of *instituere,* to set up, erect, construct.

ISOLATION. The process by which one population is cut off from its neighbors to the extent that interbreeding is stopped. In isolation the gene pool of the isolated group is slowly but steadily changed through mutation, and in time the isolated group will come to differ from the parent and other daughter stocks. Derived from Italian *isolato,* the past participle derived from *isolare,* to isolate, derived from *isola,* derived from Latin *insula,* island.

LEVIRATE. A custom of the ancient Hebrews by which a dead man's younger brother was obligated or permitted to marry the widow, especially if there were no sons. Children of a levirate marriage were considered to be descendants of the deceased brother. From Latin *levir,* husband's brother, brother-in-law, probably from hypothetical Indo-European *daiwer.*

LINEAGE. Direct descent from a common progenitor. One's ancestors collectively; ancestry, pedigree, family. From

Middle English *linage,* Old French *lignage* derived from *ligne,* line, derived from Latin *linea,* linen thread, derived from *linum,* flax.

MANA. An impersonal supernatural force to which some Polynesian and Melanesian groups attribute good fortune or magical powers. From the Polynesian.

MATRIARCHATE. A society or culture dominated by the female. From the Latin *mater, matris,* mother, and *patriarchate.* See PATRIARCHATE.

MESOCEPHALIC. See CEPHALIC INDEX.

MOIETY. One of two usually exogamous subdivisions in some tribes or clans. (The moiety system which may be patrilineal or matrilineal helps to promote mutual economic benefits. From Middle English *moite* taken from Old French *moitiet* going back to Latin *medietas,* half derived from *medius,* middle.

MONOTHEISM. A belief or doctrine that there is only one God. (Most anthropologists now maintain that the idea of a Supreme Being or High God antedates Hebraic monotheism and is indigenous to many primitive societies.) From Greek *monos,* single, alone, and *theos,* god. See POLYTHEISM.

MONGOLOID. A member of the subspecies *Homo sapiens mongoloideus,* one of the four major races. A relatively light-skinned people whose homeland seems to have been China. They have expanded so far and so wide that they are the most numerous of all the subspecies. Mongoloids are characterized by light to yellow-brown skin, medium-short to medium-tall height, broad to very broad face, low to medium nose bridge, brown to brown-black coarse-texture, straight head hair, sparse body hair, and brown eyes that have total internal epicanthic folds. Probably from a Mongol term, *mong,* brave.

MUTATION. A spontaneous change in the genes, creating new hereditary effects. It is thought that evolution arises from the possible rate of one mutation per 100,000 organisms. For the most part mutations are monkey wrenches thrown into the complex machinery of life, but on rare occasions they may increase the survival characteristics of a particular individual. From Latin *mutatio* derived from *mutare*, to change.

MYTH. A traditional story of unknown authorship that recounts purportedly historical events to explain natural phenomena, the origin of man, his customs, institutions, religious rites, etc. In myth the major protagonists are usually deities or supermen. In primitive societies, belief in myth is more than self-deception; it is in reality a form of social reassurance, a device of culture maintenance, a technique of education. From Greek *mythos*, a word, speech, story, legend.

NATURAL SELECTION. The process or tendency through which organisms possessing adaptively valuable genic variations, which allow them to adjust better to their environment than those lacking the variations, are able to leave a larger number of offspring. The theory of natural selection explains how individual variation within a species brings about long-range changes in a species as a whole.

NEANDERTHAL. An early form of *Homo sapiens* characterized by heavy thick bones, robust teeth, large brains, and massive faces and noses. Lived in western Eurasia during the Upper Pleistocene. Neanderthal man was originally described as having a stooped posture with the head carried far forward because the original skeleton found was that of a senile man who suffered from arthritis. Later finds indicated an upright posture for

the race. From German *neander,* after the writer Jo-
achim Neander, and *thal,* valley, a valley near Düssel-
dorf where the earliest Neanderthal fossils were discovered.

NEGROID. A member of the subspecies *Homo sapiens ne-
groideus,* a dark-skinned race that may be further fragmented into Congoids and Capoids in some anthropological analyses. One of the four major races, Negroids
are characterized by light-brown to brown-black skin,
very short to very tall height, narrow to medium-broad
face, generally low-bridged nose, black head hair ranging from a light curl to woolly, slight body hair, brown
to brown-black eyes, and everted lips. From Portuguese and Spanish *negro,* black, black person, derived
from Latin *niger,* black.

NEOTENY. The developmental retention in the adult of
traits which are juvenile or fetal in closely related species. Neoteny in man, according to the Dutch anthro-
pologist Louis Bolk, takes the form of ape fetalization
because man exihibits many characteristics which resemble those of fetal apes: long neck, flatness of face, retarded closure of cranial sutures, large volume of brain,
small face and large brain case, small teeth, thinness of
skull bones, and relative hairlessness of the body. From
Greek *neos,* new, and *teinein,* extend.

NOMADISM. The state of living of groups of people according to a regular seasonal or cyclical pattern in which
they move about in search of food and pasture, ordinarily without fixed homes. Nomads who hunt and nomads who collect food, as well as pastoral or even
agricultural nomads, indicate the diverse cultural patterns that nomadism may show. From Greek *nomados,*

living on pasturage, derived from *nemein*, to distribute, feed, pasture.

ONTOGENY. The natural history or changes in the life cycle of an individual beginning with the fertilized egg. The growth and development of the individual. It has been suggested by some anthropologists that human ontogeny recapitulates all the stages through which the species passed in the evolutionary process. From Greek *onto-*, combining form of *on*, being, existence, and *geny*, derived from *geneia*, manner of origin, production, development.

PATRIARCHATE. A society or culture which is dominated by the male. Ordinarily it is characterized by descent, inheritance, and succession derived through the male line, residence with the father, and the subordination of women and children. The patriarchate is a much more common form than the matriarchate which even when it exists exhibits only limited authority. Derived ultimately from Greek *patriarches*, derived from *patria*, family, derived from *pater*, father, and *archein*, to rule.

PATRILINEAL. Pertaining to descent through the father. Determining the transmission of kinship ties, name, property, or authority through the male line. Occasionally patriarchates such as that of the Hebrews practice matrilineal rather than patrilineal descent. Derived ultimately from Greek *pater*, father, and Latin *linea*, linen thread, derived from *linum*, flax.

PATRILOCAL. Referring to the practice whereby married couples live in the husband's community or with the husband's family; synonymous with *virilocal* residence. If anything, the American society in which females attempt to arrange residence tends to be more matrilocal than patrilocal. Derived from *patria* and Latin *locus*, a place.

PHRATRY. A grouping of clans or other social units within a tribe, usually based on supposed or mythical kinship. The phratry was a subdivision of an ancient Greek phyle or tribe. The phratry linked several clans in bonds of unity against clans joined in other phratries within the society. Taken from the Greek *phratria*, derived from *phrater*, brother, akin to Latin *frater*.

PITHECANTHROPUS. See HOMO ERECTUS.

POLYANDRY. The simultaneous marriage of two or more men to one woman. In fraternal polyandry several brothers marry one woman. Ordinarily found in economically depressed societies, the purpose of this arrangement is to prevent the family wealth from dissolving. Derived from Greek *poly*, many, and *aner, andros*, man.

POLYGAMY. Any multiple marriage. There are three basic kinds of polygamy, each having variations: polyandry, polygyny, and group marriage. Derived from Greek *poly*, many, and *gamia*, derived from *gamos*, marriage.

POLYGYNY. The simultaneous marriage of two or more women to one man. Polygyny occurs in societies that are characterized by surpluses of nubile women due to the loss of men through warfare and other hazardous occupations. Derived from Greek *poly*, many, and *gyne*, woman.

POLYTHEISM. The worship of or belief in many gods. A system of religion recognizing multiple gods. Opposed to MONOTHEISM (q.v.). Derived from Greek *poly*, many, and *theos*, god.

POPULATION. A group of individuals who propagate in a single interbreeding community. A population qualifies as an anthropological unit if its members display the same genetic drift and changes, such as mutation and selection concurrently, within a set geographic area. Derived ultimately from Latin *populus,* the people.

POTLATCH. A northwest American-Indian winter ceremonial, often competitive, of giving away or destroying property to enhance status. Often slaves were clubbed to death to show their owner's disregard for property. At a potlatch, very often the guests had to accept the gifts that were offered. Ultimately they were expected to return the gift, with 100 percent interest, to the family of the donor, or admit their inferiority. Derived from Chinook *patshatl,* a gift.

PRIMOGENITURE. The right of the oldest heir, usually a son, to inherit the family estate. The primogeniture rule was so strong among the Maoris of New Zealand that on occasion the first-born daughter would take a man's name and the status of a first-born son. Derived from Latin *primus,* first, and *genitura,* a begetting, derived from *gignere,* to beget.

RACE. A major biological division of mankind that exhibits particular distinguishing physical characteristics of hair color and texture, skin and eye color, stature, cephalic index, cranial capacity, other bodily proportions and attributes, etc.; primarily concerned with the four main divisions: AUSTRALOID, CAUCASOID, MONGOLOID, NEGROID (q.q.v.). In the anthropological sense the word *race* is reserved for groups of mankind which possess well-developed and primarily heritable differences from other groups. Taken from Italian *razza* which may be a vulgarization or corruption derived from Latin *generatio,* a begetting.

RANK. A social division that refers to institutionalized, hierarchical status that sets the position of individuals higher or lower according to their relationships to other statuses. The formal system of status gradation. From Middle English *renk* derived from Old French *ranc, renc, rank,* derived from Old High German *hring,* ring.

RITE or RITUAL. A prescribed or formal set or series of traditional magic or religious acts that usually reflect the daily lives of a people. The regular life cycle of peoples gives rise to rite and ritual so that the passing stages of life may be more readily accepted. The *rites de passage* mark key periods such as birth, puberty, marriage, and death, and there are fertility, agriculture, purification, and other rites to assure continued well-being. Taken from Latin *ritus,* ceremony.

ROLE. The part a person plays in putting his rights and duties, in his society, into effect; the dynamic aspect of a person's status. Taken from French *rôle,* originally the roll of paper containing the actor's part.

SHAMAN. A medicine man, a priest, one who controls spirits, often exhibits epileptoid seizure; originally applied to Siberian mystics, but now by extension any medicine man. Taken from the Greek modification of the Russian modification of Tungusic *saman* derived from Prakrit *samana,* a Buddhist monk, derived from Sanskrit śramana, ascetic derived from *śram,* to exhaust, fatigue.

SIBLING. A brother or a sister. A comember of a *sib,* a term synonymous with clan. From Middle and Old English *sib,* kinship, cognate with German *sippe.*

SORORATE. A custom by which a dead woman's sister (usually younger) was obligated or permitted to marry the widower. The sororate is the complement of the LEVI-RATE (q.v.), and its practice is widely distributed throughout the world. Derived from Latin *soror, sororis,* sister.

SPECIALIZATION. The development of an organism strongly in one evolutionary direction with special adaptations to particular habitats and modes of life. Specialization usually leads to evolutionary dead ends, but brain-enlargement specialization helped the apes to outwit their faster, stronger, but less intelligent natural enemies. Derived from Old French *especial* and Latin *specialis,* derived from *species,* kind or sort.

STATUS. The social condition or position of individuals or groups with differential reference to the other members of their society. In every society the members differentiate among themselves in terms of their individual attributes and abilities, their similarities and their differences. The grouping into recognized social categories creates the various status systems. Middle English *stat;* Old French *estat;* Latin *status,* state, position, standing, derived from *stare,* to stand.

STEATOPYGIA. The condition of having large deposits of fat on the buttocks, as in Hottentot and Bushmen women. The stylized steatopygia of an Upper Paleolithic statuette found in southern Europe indicates the possibility that this present-day Capoid specialty may have been commoner in Caucasoids at this early period. Derived from Greek *stear, steatos,* fat, and *pyge,* buttocks.

TABOO or **TABU.** The forbidden and the sacred; a sacred prohibition which if violated leads to an automatic penalty. Taken from Tongan *tabu.* Found in several forms (*tapu, tambu, kapu*) throughout Polynesia.

TEKNONYMY. The practice of designating or naming an adult after the name of its child. In the practice of teknonymy among primitive people and in some instances among the more civilized, *X* is known as *X* until he has a child *Y;* thereafter he is called "Father of *Y.*" From Greek *teknon,* child, and Aeolic Greek, *onyma,* name.

TOTEM. An object, usually an animal, plant, or mineral, toward which individuals and social or kinship groups have a special mystical relationship. Most peoples who use totems observe totemic taboos. In Ruanda, for example, the Buffalo people will not eat their totem animal. Often, natives explain their abstinence by inferring that they are descended from the animal for which they are named. **TOTEMIC NAMES** include the Latin *Lupus, Leo, Ursus;* Germanic *Eberhard,* "strong as a boar," *Wolfgang,* "wolf step." Taken from Algonquian (Chippewa or Ojibway) *ototeman* or (Cree) *ototema,* "his relations" or possibly *aoutem,* hereditary emblem, the initial *t-* then would be a supposed final sound of a possessive pronoun.

TRIBE. A social group, usually living within a definite area, that speaks a distinctive language or dialect, that has a distinctive culture which sets it apart from other tribes. It may include subgroups, such as sibs or villages. A tribe usually has a leader and may have a common mythical ancestor as well as its own special god or gods. Its members are linked through social, economic, political, religious, or family ties. From Middle English *trybe, tribu,* from the Latin *tribus,* which is derived from *tres, tria* (three) and refers to the three original groups into which the Romans were divided.

ULTIMOGENITURE. Inheritance or succession by the youngest son or daughter. Among certain peoples, what is left over at the father's death is given to the youngest because he is least likely to be well set up. Derived from Latin *ultimus,* last, and *genitura.* See PRIMOGENITURE.

VIRILOCAL. See PATRILOCAL.

VODUN, sometimes VOODOO. A complex polytheistic system of religious belief and practice with elements taken from African cults (especially Dahomean) and Roman Catholicism developed by Caribbean Negroes. The use of magic and spells is merely incidental to the larger complex of the system. The word vodun (voodoo) came to the United States with Haitian Negroes who were brought to Louisiana in the early nineteenth century. From a Creole-French corruption of the West African (Dahomey) *vodu.*

CHAPTER **14**

Terms of Tension

The Language of Political Science

EARL L. PACKER

Any space-restricted compilation of new terms which have recently entered into use in a particular field of knowledge or study is likely to omit pet terms favored by some persons well informed in that field who may yield to a temptation to criticize the omission. Both critic and compiler have to live with this situation as best they can, at least temporarily. Eventually the appearance of new or revised compilations—or the mere passage of time—may serve to soothe outraged feelings.

Any attempt to include in a compilation old terms or words which have acquired new meanings inevitably produces a similar situation. Traditional meanings for such terms or words are, as in the present instance, usually allowed quietly to repose between the covers of standard dictionaries.

In this compilation, which pertains to the field of political science, special, perhaps undue, emphasis has been placed on words and terms frequently encountered in the current phase of the cold war between communist-controlled states and the states of the free world. The nature and stakes of the cold war may justify the emphasis.

Examination of the material included under such terms as *Cold War, Communism, Deviation, Dogmatism, Peaceful Coexistence, People's Democracy, Reformism, Revisionism, Sectarianism, Socialism,* and *Wars, Kinds of* may offer more than a momentary reward to the reader of the daily and periodical press or the auditor or auditor-viewer of broadcasting programs—where they are all too apt to take too much space or time.

The material furnished under the term *Positions of Strength* is of more than passing interest. The compiler has not noted elsewhere the point brought out that the term appears to be the result of a process of double translation—from English into Russian and back into English—of another term.

A secondary emphasis has been allotted to current terms used in the civil rights movement in the United States, for reasons somewhat analogous to those mentioned above with reference to cold war terms. Some of the civil rights movement terms—*Kneel-in, Lie-in, Ride-out, Sit-in,* and *Teach-in*—have a very special form and flavor. Other terms in this general area are also very expressive: *Frontlash, Freedom Rider, Negro Revolution,* and *Backlash, White.*

A third category—each consisting of an abbreviation—relates to international affairs, particularly to *Regional Security Arrangements.* These include *ANZUS, CENTO, NATO, OAS,* and *SEATO.* Others pertain to international economic affairs, such as *Comecon, Common Market, European Economic Community, European Free Trade Association, GATT, OECD, Outer Seven,* and *Inner Six.*

Most of the other terms included in the compilation can be classified in one of the above-mentioned categories or under the very broad category of miscellaneous. Especially industrious readers may be impelled to try their own hands at a further breakdown.

WORD LIST

AEROSPACE. The earth's atmosphere and outer space.

AESOPIAN LANGUAGE. The obscure, indirect, sometimes code-like phraseology used by Lenin and other Bolshevik leaders to deceive the Tsarist censorship. A survival, or revival, of the practice is to be found in present-day communist propaganda which deceives the uninitiated and gullible by the use of such words as DEMOCRACY, LIBERAL, LIBERATION, PEACE, PEACEFUL COEXISTENCE, PEACE-LOVING, PEOPLE'S DEMOCRACY, PROGRESSIVE, REACTIONARY, SOCIALISM (q.q.v.), etc.

ANZUS. A security, or collective defense, treaty which was signed at San Francisco on September 1, 1951, by representatives of Australia, New Zealand, and the United States.

AQUANAUT. A person who, for scientific purposes, stays submerged in an underwater vehicle for a lengthy period to study underwater life and formations.

ARAB DEFENSE TREATY. The treaty of joint defense and economic cooperation between the states of the Arab League of June 17, 1950. The signatory states were Egypt, Iraq, Jordan, Lebanon, Saudi Arabia, Syria, and Yemen. The agreement entered into force on August 22, 1952. See REGIONAL SECURITY ARRANGEMENTS.

ASTRONAUT. A space traveler; literally, a star traveler. The Western equivalent of the Russian term, COSMONAUT (q.v.). According to unofficial estimates, American astronauts have penetrated into space a distance of 219 miles above the surface of the earth.

BACKLASH, WHITE. The negative reaction of certain white Americans to what they consider excesses of the civil rights movement.

BAMBOO CURTAIN. The Asian communist counterpart of the IRON CURTAIN (q.v.) in Europe; generally considered less solid, more easily penetrable than the Iron Curtain.

BERLIN WALL. The wall, construction of which was begun on August 13, 1961, by the communist East German regime, to prevent the escape into West Berlin of increasing numbers of East Germans seeking a freer, more abundant life in the West. See IRON CURTAIN.

BIPOLAR. Consisting of two poles, in a political sense they comprise the United States and the Soviet Union. While the world, insofar as nuclear power is concerned, is still bipolar in character, the political world can no longer be considered to consist of these two polar powers, each with its own group of adhering or subservient countries. An important third bloc or group of so-called nonaligned or neutralist states now exists; they are often courted by each of the two more powerful groups. This bloc consists of most of the newly independent states of Asia and Africa. Some Latin American countries appear at times to be oriented toward this bloc.

BIRCHER. A member of the John Birch Society, a right-wing organization in the United States.

BLACK MUSLIMS. A Negro religious sect, based on Islam and advocating total separation of the races in the United States.

BLOCKBUSTING. Inducing property owners in a segregated

area to sell because of the expected purchase of property in the area by a member of the barred group.

BRAINWASHING. The process by which individuals are so conditioned that they no longer can express their own real thoughts but merely repeat, parrot-like, the thoughts or ideas which have been implanted in their minds by others. Endless interrogation, constant exposure to intense lighting, deprivation of sleep and food are some of the conditioning methods used. See COLD WAR, PSYCHOLOGICAL WARFARE, THOUGHT CONTROL.

BRINKMANSHIP. The art of conducting foreign policy in such a way as to move to the brink of war without becoming involved in war. ". . . the ability to get to the verge [of war] without getting into the war is the necessary art. . . . If . . . you are scared to go to the brink, you are lost." (John Foster Dulles, Secretary of State, January 1956.)

CADRE(s). A French military term denoting the important personnel of a military unit, as, for example, the staff. Nowadays, in a political sense, the term usually signifies members of a well-trained group who are training or manipulating larger numbers in order to achieve a defined goal. Often used in the plural.

CAPTIVE NATIONS. The nations of Eastern and Central Europe which have fallen under Kremlin control. Exiles from nine of these nations have set up in the United States the Assembly of Captive European Nations: Albania, Bulgaria, Czechoslovakia, Estonia, Hungary, Latvia, Lithuania, Poland, and Rumania. Exiles from Yugoslavia and East Germany are not represented in the Assembly. The purpose of the Assembly is to remind the free world of the fate of, and keep it informed of developments affecting, the exiles' fellow nationals behind the IRON CURTAIN (q.v.).

CASTROISM. The program and actions of Fidel Castro.

CENTO. Central Treaty Organization, which takes its name from the fact that the member states occupy a central area between the territories of the NATO and SEATO powers, some of which are also members of CENTO. CENTO originated in the signature of the Baghdad Pact on February 24, 1955, by representatives of Iran, Iraq, Pakistan, Turkey, and the United Kingdom. Following the withdrawal of Iraq, the name was changed to Central Treaty Organization. The United States is not a signatory of the treaty but has sent observers to meetings of the Baghdad Pact Council and the CENTO Council. See REGIONAL SECURITY ARRANGEMENTS.

CIVIL RIGHTS MOVEMENT. The movement to obtain for the Negro the civil rights guaranteed to the individual by the Constitution of the United States.

COLD WAR. A term invented in the West since the Second World War to designate the conflict, short of armed conflict, being waged by the Soviet Union and other communist-controlled states against the free world. The conflict is carried on in the ideological, political, economic, and diplomatic arenas; it involves, at times, espionage, bribery, kidnaping, and similar activities. The cold war is the reverse side of the coin whose obverse side is labeled PEACEFUL COEXISTENCE (q.v.). With some justification it may be contended that the cold war really began with the issuance on November 8, 1917, of the first foreign policy document by the new government in Petrograd on the day after the Bolshevik leaders seized power—the oft-cited but misleadingly dubbed "decree on peace." Its "cold war" passages are usually not men-

tioned by present-day communist writers and spokes-
men, including fellow travelers. The decree contained
not only an appeal to "all belligerent peoples and their
governments immediately to begin negotiations for a
just, democratic peace"; it contained, in effect, an appeal
to the class-conscious workers of Germany, England,
and France to armed revolt against their governments
during wartime, which is an act of treason.

COMECON. A Western abbreviation for the Council of
Mutual Economic Assistance established under the
terms of a treaty signed at Moscow in January 1949 by
representatives of Bulgaria, Czechoslovakia, Hungary,
Poland, Rumania, and the Soviet Union. The treaty was
adhered to by Albania in February 1949 and by the
German Democratic Republic in September 1950.
Critics have asserted that the Council has been used by
the Kremlin to control and "milk" the economies of the
satellites.

COMMON MARKET. Usually the term applies to the six
states comprising the EUROPEAN ECONOMIC COMMUNITY
(q.v.). However, it is also at times applied to the Central American states as a result of their 1958 agreement
for "Central American Free Trade and Economic Integration" and their 1960 treaty providing for the establishment of a customs union at the end of a five-year
transition period. See EUROPEAN FREE TRADE ASSOCIA-
TION, INNER SIX, OUTER SEVEN.

COMMUNISM. In communist theory, the second or final
phase of the development of a communist society; it is
preceded by a first or lower phase, SOCIALISM (q.v.).

Communism, victorious on a world scale, will differ in a
number of traits and peculiarities from communism constructed in a single or in several countries. In developed

communism, finally established on a world scale, there will be no state, and national differences will gradually disappear. In this situation the path to the dying away of the state under communism lies not through its weakening but, on the contrary, through its strengthening by every means. In the same way the path to the fusion of nations and national cultures lies through the maximum development of the socialist nations and their cultures, national in form and socialist in content. Communism is the final goal of the struggle of the toilers of all countries. (*Political Dictionary*, Moscow, 1958.)

The word *communism* is frequently used in the free world to designate the existing political structure in the Soviet Union which is based on the dictatorship of the leaders, or leader, of the Communist Party of the Soviet Union.

CPSU. Communist Party of the Soviet Union.

Conventional War (Arms). Non-nuclear.

Cosa Nostra. The group in control of an extensive criminal or gangster organization in the United States.

Cosmonaut. The Soviet equivalent of the Western term Astronaut (q.v.); literally, a cosmos traveler. According to unofficial estimates Soviet astronauts have penetrated into space a distance of 307.5 miles above the surface of the earth.

Cult of Personality. A communist-coined phrase generally used in a derogatory sense of a leader's deliberate effort to magnify out of all reason his own talents and accomplishments and simultaneously to reduce the role of the Communist Party and of the people's masses in matters affecting the country. Both Stalin and Khrushchev have been accused by communist critics of having practiced this cult. Communist leaders, particularly so-called Stalinists, have been similarly criticized in other communist-controlled countries.

CULTURAL EXCHANGE AGREEMENT. Usually a bilateral agreement providing for the exchange, on temporary visits, between the signatory states of individuals and groups representing various segments of the cultural life of each country, such as actors, musicians, dancers, singers, writers, publishers, scientists, economists, educators, parliamentarians, and the like.

DEMOCRACY. In the upside-down language of the communists *democracy* is a favorite term. They are for it and, one is supposed to believe, that is what they have given the people of the communist-controlled states. They are not for "bourgeois democracy," but their own type of democracy—which, in fact, is dictatorship by communists.

A new, higher type of democracy is proletarian, socialist democracy. The dictatorship of the proletariat, comprising the basic political content of the period of transition from capitalism to socialism, is in essence government by the people. Realizing the governance of society by the state, the working class and its Communist Party attract all toilers to the directing of the state, create conditions for the development of economic and political self-activity of the masses in the interests of the construction of socialism and communism. . . .

In the Soviet Union socialist democratism [*sic*] has found its realization in the practice of constructing the Soviet State and has legally been strengthened by the Constitution of the U.S.S.R. In the countries of PEOPLE'S DEMOCRACY [q.v.], proletarian democratism is realized in the form of people's democracy. (*Political Dictionary*, Moscow, 1958.)

DEVIATIONISM. Any criticism of, or departure from, the line established at any given moment by the topmost leader, or leaders, of the Communist Party of the Soviet Union. Today's leader in good standing may tomorrow be a right- or left-deviationist in the event he should disagree with or has disagreed with such leader or leaders, on the need for a more rapid or less rapid expansion of heavy industry, or of the consumer goods industry, etc., etc. See DOGMATISM, REFORMISM, REVISIONISM, and SECTARIANISM.

DOGMATISM. A term used by communists to denounce other communists opposed to the Kremlin line of the moment. Dogmatists in the eyes of the denouncers fail to take into account the "creative" and "truly revolutionary" character of Marxism-Leninism. *The Programme of the Communist Party of the Soviet Union,* adopted October 31, 1961, states that dogmatism and sectarianism

lead to the dissociation and isolation of Communists from the masses, doom them to passive expectation or incite them to Leftist adventurist actions in the revolutionary struggle and hinder a correct appraisal of the changing situation and the use of new opportunities for the benefit of the working class and all democratic forces.

See DEVIATIONISM, REFORMISM, REVISIONISM, SECTARIANISM.

DOVE. A peacefully inclined person. Compare HAWK.

ESCALATION. The act or process of expanding into something of a larger dimension. There exists a fear that a brush war, or conventional war, may escalate into a nuclear war.

EURATOM. European Atomic Energy Community, established under the terms of the treaty signed at Rome on March 25, 1957, by the Foreign Ministers of Belgium, France, the Federal Republic of Germany, Italy, Luxemburg, and the Netherlands. The treaty states:

It shall be the aim of the Community to contribute to the

raising of the standard of living in Member States and to the development of commercial exchanges with other countries by the creation of conditions necessary for the speedy establishment and growth of nuclear industries. (Article 1.)

The treaty provides for a variety of procedures and institutions to accomplish the aim stated.

European Economic Community. Established by a treaty signed at Rome on March 25, 1957, by the Foreign Ministers of Belgium, France, the Federal Republic of Germany, Italy, Luxemburg, and the Netherlands. The treaty states:

It shall be the aim of the Community, by establishing a Common Market and progressively approximating the economic policies of Member States, to promote throughout the Community a harmonious development of economic activities, a continuous and balanced expansion, an increased stability, an accelerated raising of the standard of living, and closer relations among its Member States. (Article 2.)

The treaty provides for a variety of procedures and institutions to accomplish over a period of years the purposes indicated. See COMMON MARKET, INNER SIX, EUROPEAN FREE TRADE ASSOCIATION, OUTER SEVEN.

European Free Trade Association. An organization established by the signing in Stockholm on January 4, 1960, of a convention by representatives of Austria, Denmark, Norway, Portugal, Sweden, Switzerland, and the United Kingdom. The purposes were to expand economic activity, full employment, increased productivity and the rational use of resources, financial stability, and continuous improvement in living standards; to promote fair competition in trade between Member States and the expansion of world trade and the progressive removal of barriers to it. The motivation was to protect

Member States against feared competition from the EUROPEAN ECONOMIC COMMUNITY or COMMON MARKET (q.q.v.). Known as the OUTER SEVEN (q.v.).

EYEBALL TO EYEBALL. A phrase used by Secretary of State Dean Rusk on learning that Soviet ships, approaching Cuba after President Kennedy's imposition in October 1962 of a naval quarantine against the importation of offensive weapons into Cuba, had turned back. "We're eyeball to eyeball, and I think the other fellow just blinked," he said.

FELLOW TRAVELER. A pro-communist who is not a member of the Communist Party.

FOREIGN AID. The term applies to a great variety of programs under which United States government agencies have extended and are now extending assistance to foreign countries.

Loans of various kinds, the teaching of technical skills, gifts of food to help people in emergencies, grants of equipment to foster economic development, and the transfer of military weapons for the common defense of the free world . . . "foreign aid," whatever you call it, carries with it the built-in concept that our programs aid others and aid us, too, because they and we have common interests. (Thorsten V. Kalijarvi, Deputy Assistant Secretary of State for Economic Affairs, October 25, 1956.)

Under the Marshall Plan, aid was extended to Western European countries to assist them to recovery from the Second World War and to forestall possible communist takeovers. President Truman's Point Four Program initiated broad-scale aid to the UNDERDEVELOPED COUNTRIES (q.v.). Other countries, notably the Western European countries, the Soviet Union and Communist China, also extend aid to foreign peoples.

FREEDOM RIDER. A person who travels from the North to the South to test the scope of desegregation.

FRONTLASH. Defection of anti-Goldwater Republicans to the Democratic Party in the 1964 election.

GATT. General Agreement on Tariffs and Trade, signed at Geneva on October 30, 1947, by 23 nations, including the United States. As of July 1965 there were 66 full members, six provisionally accepted members, and seven other participating or de facto associated states. The basic purpose of the agreement is to facilitate the expansion of international trade by the lowering of tariffs. Meetings at which representatives of the signatories negotiate mutual tariff concessions are termed *rounds*. The "Kennedy round" (sponsored by the late President) was not then completed. The General Agreement is supplemented by an agreement of March 10, 1955, providing for the establishment of the Organization for Trade Cooperation.

GREAT SOCIETY, THE. The announced, but undefined, goal of President Lyndon B. Johnson, designed to give the American people an ever more abundant life.

HAWK. A militant, aggressive individual: someone willing to resort to military action to attain his goal. Compare DOVE.

INFILTRATION. The act or process of entering, or becoming a member of, an organization for purposes detrimental to the reasons for which the organization exists, probably with the intention of gaining control of, or obtaining secret information about, the organization. In the period of the COLD WAR (q.v.), this tactic is engaged in by both communists and anti-communists.

INNER SIX. The six states comprising the EUROPEAN ECONOMIC COMMUNITY (q.v.).

IRON CURTAIN. The mechanism which prevents the enjoyment (as between the Soviet Union and its satellites, on the one hand, and the countries of the free world, on the other) of the types of relationships and intercourse normal among peoples and governments of the free world.

> From Stettin in the Baltic to Trieste in the Adriatic, an iron curtain has descended across the Continent. Behind that line lie all the capitals of the ancient states of central and eastern Europe. (Winston Churchill, March 5, 1946.)

The iron curtain consists not only of a censorship and control of the content and flow of information, news, and ideas across the frontiers of the communist-controlled countries of Europe; it consists also of watchtowers, barbed wire, searchlights, plowed fields, masonry, and arms and ammunition used to prevent people from crossing those frontiers, in particular to prevent people east of the curtain from escaping to the West. See BERLIN WALL.

KGB (kah-gay-bay). Komitet Gosudarstvennoi Bezopasnosti, or Committee of State Security, attached to the Council of Ministers of the USSR. This organization is the lineal descendant of the first Soviet secret police organization, the so-called Extraordinary Commission (Cheka) to Fight Counter-Revolution and Sabotage, and its intervening successors: the GPU, the NKVD, and the MVD (or, successively, the State Political Administration, the People's Commissariat for Internal Affairs, and the Ministry of Internal Affairs).

KNEEL-IN. A civil rights movement term, designating the posture assumed by a group to protest an act of an official, or to favor a proposed action. It may take place out-of-doors or indoors. See LIE-IN, SIT-IN, TEACH-IN.

KREMLINOLOGIST. An expert on Soviet affairs.

LIBERAL. In the AESOPIAN LANGUAGE (q.v.) of the communists, a fellow traveler or communist sympathizer.

LIBERATION. A deceptive communist propaganda term. "Armed conquest of free people is called 'liberation.'" (President Dwight D. Eisenhower, January 7, 1960.)

LIE-IN. A civil rights movement term, designating the posture assumed by a group to protest an act of an official, or to favor a proposed action. Entry into a building, or approach to a building, is sometimes effected before the intention of the group to stage a lie-in becomes known to the authorities. See KNEEL-IN, SIT-IN, TEACH-IN.

LUNIK. Applied to a Soviet rocket bound for the moon. (From the Russian *luna* meaning moon.)

MEGALOPOLIS. A very large city. Currently the word has been used to designate the area which embraces Washington on the south and Boston on the north and constitutes the most industrialized region of the globe.

NATO. North Atlantic Treaty Organization which was created by the North Atlantic Treaty signed at Washington on April 4, 1949, by representatives of Belgium, Canada, Denmark, France, Iceland, Italy, Luxemburg, the Netherlands, Norway, Portugal, the United Kingdom, and the United States. Turkey and Greece adhered to the treaty on February 18, 1952, and the Federal Republic of [West] Germany on May 6, 1955.

The parties to the treaty agreed that an armed attack against one or more of them in Europe or North America shall be considered an attack against them all and that, if such an attack should occur, they will individually and in concert with the other parties take defensive action, including the use of armed force. Under the terms by which Greece and Turkey became parties, the area of operation of the treaty was extended to include their territories. The treaty was designed to deter possible aggression by the Soviet Union. See REGIONAL SECURITY ARRANGEMENTS.

NEGRO REVOLUTION. A term used to describe the current CIVIL RIGHTS MOVEMENT (q.v.) in the United States.

NEIGHBORHOOD YOUTH CORPS. An organization sponsored by the federal government to participate in the national antipoverty program; ideologically based on the PEACE CORPS (q.v.).

NEW FRONTIER. A term given currency by the late President John F. Kennedy, who expressed the view that the United States stood at a "new frontier . . . of unknown opportunities and of perils."

NEW FRONTIERSMAN. An ardent supporter of the philosophy of the NEW FRONTIER (q.v.).

NO-SHOW. Nonappearance; absenteeism; something in the nature of a strike.

OAS. Organization of American States, the Charter of which was signed at the Ninth International Conference of American States at Bogota, March 30–May 2, 1948. The Charter mentions, *inter alia,* the following purposes of the Organization: to strengthen the peace and security of the continent; to provide for common action on the part of Member States in the event of aggression.

The Pan-American Union remains in existence as "the central and permanent organ of the Organization of American States and the General Secretariat of the Organization." See REGIONAL SECURITY ARRANGEMENTS.

OAU. Organization for African Unity, established on September 10, 1964.

OECD. Organization for Economic Cooperation and Development; a European organization which is a successor to the Organization for European Economic Cooperation, the executive organization for carrying out the Marshall Plan.

OPERATION HEAD START. The program, sponsored by the United States government, to give instruction and training to pre-kindergarten-age children, particularly retarded children, in impoverished areas.

OUTER SEVEN. The seven states comprising the EUROPEAN FREE TRADE ASSOCIATION (q.v.).

OVERKILL. In general, the military capacity to destroy more than the total population or resources of an enemy. More specifically, this term describes our surplus of nuclear weapons; that is, the number of weapons in excess of those needed to destroy all key Soviet targets.

PEACE CORPS. An organization financed by the United States Government; its members are recruited, at very nominal compensation, for service in the UNDERDEVELOPED COUNTRIES (q.v.) to impart to their peoples a variety of knowledge and know-how. See NEIGHBORHOOD YOUTH CORPS.

PEACE, DEMOCRACY, AND SOCIALISM. A communist-invented trilogy designed to mislead the uninitiated. In the Aesopian language used by communists, *peace* often means PEACEFUL COEXISTENCE (q.v.) which is an alias for COLD WAR (q.v.); *democracy* means democracy of the Soviet type, that is, dictatorship and tyranny; and *socialism* means either *communism* or the political-economic-social structure which prevails in the Soviet Union.

PEACEFUL COEXISTENCE. A communist propaganda slogan designed to mislead the uninitiated. Essentially, it is an alias for COLD WAR (q.v.). As early as February 1920,

Lenin spoke to a foreign correspondent of "peaceful cohabitation (*sozhitel'stvo*) with the peoples, with the workers and peasants of all nations." Significantly, he did not mention other elements of the population. In January 1922 a resolution of the Ninth All-Russian Congress of Soviets used the term "peaceful and friendly coexistence (*sosushchestvovaniye*)." The term does not mean "live and let live." Its meaning is clear from the following quotations:

Peaceful coexistence affords more favorable opportunities for the struggle of the working class in the capitalist countries and facilitates the struggle of the peoples of the colonial and dependent countries for their liberation. . . .

The peaceful coexistence of states with different social systems does not imply any easing of the ideological struggle. The Communist Party will go on exposing the antipopular, reactionary nature of capitalism and all attempts to paint bright pictures of the capitalist system. (*Programme of the Communist Party of the Soviet Union,* adopted Oct. 13, 1961.)

Peaceful coexistence offers the most favorable premises for an intensification of the class struggle against the imperialist bourgeoisie in the developed capitalist countries and for the unification around the proletariat of all other sections of the people. (A. Sovetov, *International Affairs,* No. 1, January 1962.)

As far as relations between socialist and bourgeois ideologies are concerned, there can be no coexistence, and we do not conceal this. (Khrushchev, Nov. 28, 1959.)

The policy of peaceful coexistence, as regards its social content, is a form of intense economic, political, and ideological struggle of the proletariat against the aggressive forces of imperialism in the international arena. . . .

The path to socialism lies through proletarian revolution and the establishment of the dictatorship of the proletariat. As for the forms of transition to socialism, they will, as was pointed out by the 20th CPSU Congress, become increasingly diverse, and it is not essential that the transition to socialism everywhere and in all cases be connected with armed uprisings and civil war.

Marxism-Leninism proceeds from the view that the forms of transition to socialism can be of a peaceful or nonpeaceful nature. Revolution by peaceful means is in keeping with the interests of the working class and the masses. But if the ruling classes counter revolution with force and are unwilling to bow to the will of the people, the proletariat must break their resistance and start a resolute civil war. (Khrushchev, Jan. 6, 1961.)

PEACE-LOVING. In the AESOPIAN LANGUAGE (q.v.) of communists, the communist-controlled states aligned with Moscow; a member of the Communist Party anywhere acknowledging Moscow's dominance in the communist world and pro-communists similarly oriented.

PEKINOLOGIST. An expert on Chinese Communist affairs.

PEOPLE'S DEMOCRACY. A term invented by Moscow to apply to the new communist-controlled dictatorships set up under the protection of Soviet arms in the countries of Eastern Europe after the Second World War. The *Political Dictionary* (Moscow, 1958) defines the term as "a form of political organization of society whose content, depending upon concrete historical conditions, is either a dictatorship of the proletariat and the peasantry or a dictatorship of the proletariat." Use of the term has since been broadened by Moscow to include communist-controlled regimes in Asia. "Police states are called 'people's democracies.'" (President Dwight D. Eisenhower, January 7, 1960.)

PHASE OUT. The completing of an undertaking by stages according to plan.

POLYCENTRISM. A term used to denote the breakup of the

former monolithic, Kremlin-dominated communist bloc into an area having many centers, each exercising authority in its own sphere, supposedly along Marxist lines, but not necessarily along the same path of development that was followed in the Soviet Union.

POSITIONS OF STRENGTH. A phrase that by the process of double translation (into and from the Russian) has been changed from the expression originally used by Secretary of State Acheson (February 16, 1950): "The only way to deal with the Soviet Union, we have found from hard experience, is to create situations of strength."

PROGRESSIVE. In communist terminology, a communist, a communist sympathizer, or a fellow traveler.

PSYCHOLOGICAL WARFARE. An international war of propaganda, threat, and coercion by means of which the wagers seek, at the least, to create confusion and arouse, on the part of the nationals of the given opponent, distrust toward their own rulers and, at the best, to win over the minds of such nationals to the side from which the propaganda emanates. A civil war of an analogous type, waged domestically by the governing authority against its own subjects. See BRAINWASHING, COLD WAR, THOUGHT CONTROL.

PURGE. The expulsion on a large scale of members of an organization by its leaders, a phenomenon frequently encountered in communist-controlled organizations.

REACTIONARY. In the communist dictionary, anyone or any organization opposed to communism.

REENTRY. The return from space of a SPACECRAFT (q.v.) to the atmosphere of the earth.

REFORMISM. A term long used by Marxists to castigate the view maintained by socialists that socialism may be attained gradually by peaceful means, without armed revolution, along the path of bourgeois democracy. The *Political Dictionary* (Moscow, 1958) defines the term as "A political tendency in the workers' movement which substitutes petty reforms which do not touch the bases of the exploiters' regime for the struggle of the working class against capitalism [and] for the dictatorship of the proletariat and socialism." See DEVIATIONISM, DOGMATISM, REVISIONISM, SECTARIANISM.

REGIONAL SECURITY ARRANGEMENTS. In an effort to deter further Soviet expansion, the countries of the free world, led by the United States, beginning in 1949, entered into several regional defensive military agreements and set up corresponding military organizations. Of these the most important at present are ANZUS, CENTO, NATO, OAS, SEATO (q.q.v.).

In order to counter NATO, the Soviet Union has set up a nominally analogous organization in Eastern Europe under the WARSAW PACT (q.v.). The Arab League States have concluded the ARAB DEFENSE TREATY (q.v.). All of the above-mentioned arrangements have been made under the provisions of the United Nations Charter.

REVISIONISM. A term defined in the *Political Dictionary* (Moscow, 1958) as follows:

A tendency in the workers' movement which, to please the bourgeoisie, seeks to debase, emasculate, destroy Marxism by means of revision, that is, reconsideration, distortion, and denial of its fundamental tenets. . . . Contemporary revisionism seeks to defame the teaching of Marxism-Leninism, declares it antiquated, allegedly to have lost, at present, significance for social development. Revisionists seek to undermine the faith of the working class and toiling people in socialism.

The *Programme of the Communist Party of the Soviet Union,* adopted October 31, 1961, devotes some space to the subject:

Revisionism, right-wing opportunism, which is a reflection of bourgeois influence, is the chief danger within the Communist movement today. The revisionists, who mask their renunciation of Marxism with talk about the necessity of taking account of the latest developments in society and the class struggle, in effect play the role of pedlars of bourgeois-reformist ideology within the Communist movement. They seek to rob Marxism-Leninism of its revolutionary spirit, to undermine the faith which the working class and all working people have in socialism, to disarm and disorganize them in their struggle against imperialism. The revisionists deny the historical necessity of the socialist revolution and of the dictatorship of the proletariat. They deny the leading role of the Marxist-Leninist party, undermine the foundations of proletarian internationalism, and drift to nationalism. The ideology of revisionism is most fully embodied in the programme of the League of Communists of Yugoslavia.

Another view of revisionism has been supplied by Khrushchev (speech of January 6, 1961):

We must always keep our powder dry and wage implacable war on revisionism which tries to wipe out the revolutionary essence of Marxism-Leninism, whitewash modern capitalism, undermine the solidarity of the Communist movement, and encourage Communist Parties to go their separate national ways.

See DEVIATIONISM, DOGMATISM, REFORMISM, SECTARIANISM.

RIDE-OUT. The movement of Negroes from the South to the North usually with one-way transportation paid by segregationists; also a Negro who is thus subsidized.

SATELLITE. A state subordinate to another state. "States formally independent but in fact subordinate to a large imperialist power are called satellites." (*Political Dictionary*, Moscow, 1958.) This definition is acceptable to persons who consider the Soviet Union "a large imperialist power."

SEATO. Southeast Asia Treaty Organization, which was created by the Southeast Asia Collective Defense Treaty (Manila Pact), signed at Manila on September 8, 1954, by representatives of Australia, France, New Zealand, Pakistan, the Philippines, Thailand, the United Kingdom, and the United States. See REGIONAL SECURITY ARRANGEMENTS.

SECTARIANISM. In its nonreligious meaning, a term used by communists to denounce other communists opposed to the Kremlin line of the moment. The *Political Dictionary* (Moscow, 1958) supplies these "characteristic peculiarities of political sectarianism": "a negative attitude toward the struggle for the unity of the working class and the tactic of the Popular Front, undervaluation of the significance of work in the reformist trade unions, parliaments, etc., supercilious, mistrustful attitude toward rank-and-file Social-Democrats and non-Party workers." This source states further: "Sectarianism gives birth to dogmatism, gives birth to striving to quit the masses and to enclose oneself in a narrow circle, and throttles down the initiative of the toiling masses." See DEVIATIONISM, DOGMATISM, REFORMISM, SECTARIANISM.

SIT-IN. A civil rights movement term, designating the posture assumed by a group to protest an act of an official, or to favor a proposed action. See KNEEL-IN, LIE-IN, TEACH-IN.

SOCIALISM. In communist theory, the first or lower phase of development of a communist society; the second or higher or final phase which follows is COMMUNISM (q.v.). Officially, socialism has been attained in the Soviet Union: classes and private ownership in the means of production have been abolished. Inasmuch as socialism is less offensive to Western minds than communism, communist propaganda frequently uses the term *socialism* instead of *communism*. Soviet propaganda classes the Soviet Union along with other communist-controlled countries as a member of the socialist camp. See PEACE, DEMOCRACY AND SOCIALISM.

SPACECRAFT. A vehicle, manned or unmanned, which moves beyond the earth's atmosphere in space.

SPLASHDOWN. The landing of a spacecraft on the sea.

SPUTNIK. A Soviet earth satellite; also means FELLOW TRAVELLER (q.v.).

SUMMIT CONFERENCE. A meeting of chiefs of state and/or heads of government.

SUPERPOWERS. In present circumstances, due to their massive and unequaled nuclear power, the United States and the Soviet Union.

TEACH-IN. A prolonged meeting, usually taking place in a building on, or near, the campus of an educational institution at which, at the request of the student organizers of the meeting, the speakers, as a rule, present a point of view that opposes a policy or action of constituted authority. Impassioned criticism often appears to dominate over objectivity in the organization and presentation of the program and the selection of speakers.

THOUGHT CONTROL. The conditioning or indoctrinating of the human mind by dictators as a result of which their subjects are expected to accept and/or do, without question, whatever they are told. For this purpose an elaborate and strict censorship and incessant propaganda involving protracted use of the mass media for purposes of repetition are utilized. See BRAINWASHING, COLD WAR, and PSYCHOLOGICAL WARFARE.

TITOISM. A word derived from the assumed name of the Yugoslav communist leader, Tito, whose real name was apparently Josip Broz. Titoism may be defined as the Yugoslav brand of communism. The Kremlin has blown hot and blown cold with regard to Tito since he attained power in Yugoslavia. In 1948 Stalin had Yugoslavia expelled from the group of countries which adhered to the Cominform (Information Bureau of the Communist and Workers Parties). Subsequent to Stalin's death, Khrushchev visited Belgrade and a partial reconciliation was reached. Later relations again became less friendly. Tito and Titoism are frequently denounced by Communist China.

TOKENISM. The acceptance, in previously all-white schools, of a very small number of Negro students with a view to qualification for federal financial aid. The term also applies to employment, housing, society gatherings, etc.

TROIKA. A three-man administration proposed by the Soviet Union to replace the Secretary General of the United Nations. The composition was to be one representative from the communist-controlled states, one from the Western states, and one from the nonaligned nations. Unanimity was to be the requirement for decision, a feature which would have given the communist representative the power to prevent a decision from being reached. From the Russian.

UNDERDEVELOPED COUNTRIES. Countries that do not have a highly developed, industrialized economy. Most of the countries normally included in this classification are located in Asia, Africa, and Latin America.

USSR. Union of Soviet Socialist Republics.

WARSAW PACT. The "treaty of friendship, cooperation, and mutual assistance" signed at Warsaw on May 14, 1955, by representatives of Albania, Bulgaria, Czechoslovakia, Hungary, the German Democratic Republic, Rumania, and the Union of Soviet Socialist Republics. Inasmuch as Kremlin dominance over the satellites was unquestioned at the time, this act was mere window-dressing on the part of the Kremlin, nominally necessitated by "the creation of a closed military grouping of the Western powers," as a result of which "the peace-loving, democratic countries were required to adopt measures for the guaranteeing of their own security." (*Political Dictionary*, Moscow, 1958.) See REGIONAL SECURITY ARRANGEMENTS.

WARS, KINDS OF. In communist theory there are only two kinds of wars: just wars and unjust wars. The *History of the Communist Party of the Soviet Union (Bolsheviks): Short Course* (1938) defines these two kinds of wars as follows:

(a) Just wars, wars that are not wars of conquest but wars of liberation, waged to defend the people from foreign attack and from attempts to enslave them, or to liberate the people from capitalist slavery, or, lastly, to liberate colonies and dependent countries from the yoke of imperialism; and

(b) Unjust wars, wars of conquest, waged to conquer and enslave foreign countries and foreign nations.

Wars of the first kind [the comment goes on to say] the Bolsheviks supported. As to wars of the second kind, the Bolsheviks maintained that a resolute struggle must be waged against them to the point of revolution and the overthrow of one's own imperialist government.

Any war in which the Soviet Union engages is a just war, as well as a defensive war, no matter who fires the first shot.

VETO. A term used loosely to apply to a negative vote in the United Nations Security Council by one of its permanent members (China, France, the Union of Soviet Socialist Republics, the United Kingdom, and the United States); there are also ten nonpermanent members elected for a term of two years. Article 17 of the United Nations Charter provides:

1. Each member of the Security Council shall have one vote.

2. Decisions of the Security Council on procedural matters shall be made by an affirmative vote of seven members.

3. Decisions of the Security Council on all other matters shall be made by an affirmative vote of seven members, including the concurring votes of the permanent members, provided that, in decisions under Chapter VI, and under Paragraph 3 of Article 52, a party to a dispute shall abstain from voting.

CHAPTER **15**

Between Sense and Spirit

The Language of Psychology

ADAM MARGOSHES

Psychology is a discordant discipline, embracing rival schools with radically different, often flatly contradictory, views. These divergences are reflected in the various terminologies, which differ so radically that sometimes the same word has quite different meanings. For example, *transference* in psychoanalytic terminology refers to the transfer to the analyst of feelings the patient originally experienced toward his parents; while in neobehaviorist terminology, it refers to the transfer of benefits or hindrances that occurs when one shifts his attention from one task to another. This example is typical, because the two major trends in scientific psychology in the English-speaking world are the psychoanalytic influence, as exerted in clinical, medical, and counseling psychology, and the behaviorist or neobehaviorist influence, as exerted in experimental and academic psychology.

Of these two streams of thought, there is no question that the one better known to the general public is the psychoanalytic. Its concern with the vital questions of life, love, and death, and its dramatic formulations, have extended its influence far beyond the confines of the doctor's office. Its ideas and the vocabulary in which the ideas are expressed have percolated into the consciousness of the educated public through many channels, particularly through the novel, the play, and the short story. This influence of psychoanalysis on literature has been reciprocal, for the psychoanalytic vocabulary strongly reflects Freud's deep grounding in the humanistic culture of ancient and modern Europe, the most obvious example of which is the name he gave to his central concept, the *Oedipus complex*.

Freud, of course, considered himself primarily a scientist. From his earliest days his guiding ambition was to model psychology after the successful older natural sciences, especially physics. His mentor here was Brücke, a distinguished physiologist whose life's work consisted in establishing physiology on purely mechanistic principles, and Freud deliberately set out to do for psychology what Brücke had done for physiology. His ambition was to erect a conceptual structure that would embrace the discipline within a comprehensive set of principles grounded on the great cornerstone principle of nineteenth-century physics, the conservation of energy. This influence of physics is apparent throughout the psychoanalytic vocabulary in such terms as *dynamic psychology, cathexis, sublimation, transference*, etc.

One other fertile source of the psychoanalytic lexicon is rooted in Freud's personal fascination with military figures, Moses and Hannibal, and their campaigns. His writing is rich in military metaphors, some of which have supplied names for psychic processes: for example, *defenses, aggression, repression*.

Neobehaviorist psychology stems from an entirely different tradition, branching out from the laboratories of Pavlov in Russia, and Thorndike and Watson in America.

Pavlov was originally a physiologist, and throughout his life he viewed psychology as a branch of physiology. This view continues to be influential in America and is, of course, dominant in Russia, and its traces are clearly discernible in the psychological languages of both countries, which include the terms *conditioned reflexes, unconditioned reflexes, inhibition, activation,* and *stimulus generalization.* The classic American behaviorists were interested in explaining man as essentially a very complicated mechanism, and their language and that of their numerous followers has a markedly mechanistic strain: *positive reinforcement, negative reinforcement, trial-and-error learning, discrimination apparatus, Skinner box, feedback, homeostasis.* The British school, as well as certain American psychologists, has been traditionally preoccupied with tests, measurements, and statistics, and a large number of terms from this field have not only entered the scientific psychological vocabulary, but are even heard occasionally in everyday speech: *factor analysis, correlation, validity, reliability, IQ,* etc.

One of the dominant trends in scientific psychology during recent years has been in the direction of a rather loose eclecticism, with a resultant blurring of the distinctions between the two schools. This is of course reflected in their increasing practice of borrowing from each other's vocabularies. An outstanding example is found in the writings of Cattell, a leading experimentalist of the British-American statistical school, closely related to the neobehaviorists. He has hatched a whole brood of neologisms, but he has also adopted the Freudian *id, superego,* etc. Other contributors to this psychological *lingua franca* of the new eclecticism are members of the small but influential group of Gestalt psychologists, most of whom came to this country from Germany around the time of World

War II. They introduced many terms borrowed from the German tradition of Kantian and post-Kantian philosophy: *Gestalt* itself, for instance, and *closure,* and *isomorphism.*

In general, psychoanalytic terminology (of the neo-Freudians as well as the orthodox) is closer to everyday speech, as its ideas are closer to everyday concerns. Neobehaviorist terminology is more technical in its vocabulary, since its ideas are mainly concerned with more technical questions. Thus, Freud typically uses the term, *happiness,* which he defines as "the fulfillment of repressed childhood wishes," while Skinner, perhaps the leading contemporary neobehaviorist, speaks of *schedules of reinforcement,* which refers to the number of times a rat will press a lever when rewarded with pellets of food. Both vocabularies, of course, like most scientific vocabularies, draw heavily on Greek and Latin roots, but this tendency is more marked in the language of the neobehaviorists than in that of the psychoanalysts.

The scope of the following vocabulary excludes the possibility of exhaustiveness; those selected are what seem to be the most frequently used and most important terms in the literature.

WORD LIST

ABLATION. Destruction of part of the brain or other part of the body. A research technique for studying animal behavior.

ADAPTATION LEVEL or **AL.** The neutral level used by each person in making judgments. For example, in a series of weights the AL is neither heavy nor light, but the weights above it are heavy and the weights below it are light. Expressed in a mathematical formula by H. Helson.

AFTERIMAGE. The image seen after looking at a bright light.

ALPHA WAVE. The normal type of brain wave in the waking state.

AMBIVALENCE. Simultaneous love and hate.

ANAL CHARACTER. In Freudian theory, a character marked by extreme stinginess, orderliness, and stubbornness.

ASSOCIATION VALUE. The ability to evoke associations. A word has high association value if reading it or hearing it causes many other words to be remembered.

AUTOKINETIC MOVEMENT. The apparent movement of an actually stationary light in an otherwise completely dark room.

BEHAVIORISM. The school of psychology, founded by John Watson, that confines itself to the study and measurement of overt behavior in man and animals. Radical behaviorist doctrine denies the existence of mind as well as soul.

CATHEXIS. In Freudian theory, the investment of a thing or process with psychic energy.

CEPHALOCAUDAL PROGRESSION. The tendency in man and animals for development to begin at the head end of the body and progress toward the tail end.

CLOSURE. The tendency to perceive incomplete figures as complete or imperfect figures as perfect. For example, a circle with a small gap in it is often perceived as an unbroken circle.

COGNITIVE DISSONANCE THEORY. Festinger's theory that the need to reduce incongruities or conflicts in knowledge is an important motivational principle. An example is the case of the fox who decided the grapes were sour, because his desire for them was dissonant with his inability to get them.

CONDITIONED RESPONSE. The response evoked by conditioning.

CONDITIONED STIMULUS. The stimulus to which a new response becomes related through conditioning, as the bell in Pavlov's experiment to condition a dog to salivate at the sound of the bell (by ringing it just before feeding him).

CONDITIONING. Associating a response with a stimulus by presenting the stimulus just before the presentation of another stimulus that already elicits the response. The dog salivates at the sight of meat; therefore he can be conditioned to salivate at the sound of a bell by ringing the bell just before showing him the meat.

CONVERSION REACTION. A hysterical symptom, such as blindness or paralysis, in the absence of organic defect.

COUNSELING. A kind of psychotherapy. Psychoanalysts have patients; counselors have clients. Counseling is used most extensively by people with mild disturbances or normal people in need of advice.

CRITICAL FLICKER FREQUENCY or CFF. The frequency at which a light must flicker on and off in order to appear to be continuously on.

DEFENSE MECHANISM. Techniques people use, mostly unconsciously, in defending themselves against things in themselves they fear or disapprove. The defense mechanisms include: repression, regression, reaction formation, projection, and identification with the aggressor.

DELTA WAVES. The normal type of brain wave in the sleeping state.

DISTRIBUTED PRACTICE. A training procedure in which successive trials are separated by long intervals, such as twenty-four hours.

ECTOMORPHY. A tendency to skinniness in body type.

EGO. In Freudian theory, the part of the personality that deals with reality. The ego is the part of the personality that each person feels is his true self.

EIDETIC IMAGE. A memory image as intense and fresh as actual perception. Eidetic imagery is most common in young children.

EINSTELLUNG. A mental set, or condition, which predisposes the organism toward a particular activity.

ELECTROENCEPHALOGRAPH or **EEG.** A record of brain waves. The technique for recording brain waves was discovered by Berger.

ENDOMORPHY. A tendency to fleshiness in body type.

EQUIPOTENTIALITY. The principle that, in regard to most functions, any part of the cerebral cortex can substitute for any other part.

EXTINCTION. The tendency of a response to disappear if the conditioned stimulus is presented many times without being paired with the unconditioned stimulus. Thus, if we condition the dog to salivate at the sound of a bell and then ring the bell many times without feeding the dog, his tendency to salivate at the sound of the bell will eventually disappear.

EXTRASENSORY PERCEPTION or **ESP.** Perception without the use of eyes, ears, or other sense organs.

FACTOR ANALYSIS. A mathematical technique for describing a great number of simultaneous correlations. When dealing with many things, this technique is used to indicate which things tend to cluster together.

FEEDBACK. The process in which a response to a stimulus becomes, in turn, part of the stimulus to ongoing action; the effect of behavior on the continuation of the same stream of behavior.

FREE ASSOCIATION. The patient's report of everything that is passing through his mind, no matter what it is, no matter how intimate, no matter how embarrassing, and no matter how unimportant or irrelevant. This is a fundamental technique of psychoanalysis.

FUNCTIONAL AUTONOMY. The tendency for activities to become ends in themselves, even though they were originally adopted to serve other ends. For example, a boy may run away to sea in order to escape his father's authority, but in this way he learns to love a sailor's life and continues in it long after his conflict with his father is resolved.

FUNCTIONAL FIXEDNESS. The tendency to perceive an object as fixed in a given function. Functional fixedness is a hindrance to good problem-solving, which often depends upon seeing a familiar object in a new way.

GALVANIC SKIN RESPONSE or GSR. A change in the electric potential of the skin. This occurs during emotional excitement and recordings of the GSR are an important part of the so-called "lie detector."

GENERALIZATION. The tendency to give a response to a stimulus similar to, but not identical with, the stimulus that originally elicited the response. For example, the dog, conditioned to salivate at the signal of a green light, may generalize this response when he sees a blue light.

GENITAL CHARACTER. In Freudian theory, a character marked by normality, independence, decisiveness.

GESTALT. Form, figure, or configuration.

GESTALT PSYCHOLOGY. A school of psychology that stresses the integrated nature of psychic functioning.

HIGHER-ORDER CONDITIONING. Conditioning to a stimulus which has already been conditioned. For example, if the dog is conditioned to salivate on hearing a bell, higher-order conditioning can be established by associating a flashing light with the bell.

HOMEOSTASIS. The maintenance of a steady state through self-regulation. A thermostat operates homeostatically, and so does an organism which eats exactly what it needs.

ID. In Freudian theory, part of the personality; a bundle of sexual and aggressive instincts; the source of the unconscious.

IDIOT SAVANTS. Idiots who have one mental aptitude very highly developed. There have been idiot savants of below average intelligence with extraordinary ability to calculate arithmetically; there have also been cases of idiots with great musical gifts.

INCUBATION PERIOD. In creative thought, a time during which no conscious effort is made to think of the problem. After the incubation period, the solution to a problem sometimes emerges as though from nowhere. The incubation period is believed to be marked by intense unconscious mental activity.

INSIGHT. Learning through sudden understanding.

INSTINCT. Innate patterns of behavior. Behaviorism has tended to minimize the role of instinct in psychology. The study of instinct, especially in animals, has been revived by the ethologists, such as Lorenz and Tinbergen, who study animals in the wild.

INTELLIGENCE QUOTIENT or **IQ.** An exact quantitative measurement of intelligence.

INCIDENTAL LEARNING. Learning that occurs without any definite intention of learning. For example, if one sets out to learn a list of words and some of them are printed in red, one may remember which ones are printed in red. The words one has learned are an example of intentional learning, but the knowledge of their color is an example of incidental learning.

INTENTIONAL LEARNING. Learning that occurs as the result of a decision to learn the given material. See INCIDENTAL LEARNING.

JAMES-LANGE THEORY. The theory that bodily movement causes emotion. According to this theory, we are sad because we cry and happy because we laugh.

LASHLEY JUMPING STAND. An apparatus used in studies of visual discrimination. A rat jumps from a platform to a stimulus card. If he chooses the correct card he lands in food, if he chooses the wrong card he falls into a net.

LATENCY. The time between the stimulus and the response.

LATENT LEARNING. Learning that is not manifested till after a lapse of time.

LAW OF EFFECT. Thorndike's fundamental law of learning —reward stamps in and punishment stamps out.

LAW OF EXERCISE. In a series of responses, the response most likely to occur is the one which has occurred most frequently and most recently.

LIBIDO. Sexuality. In Freudian theory, the basic psychic energy.

LIFE-SPACE. The individual's psychic world, past, present and future, real and unreal.

MASKING. The effect of a stimulus in reducing the effect of any other stimulus presented at the same time.

MASSED PRACTICE. A training procedure in which successive trials are separated by very short intervals. Reading a list of words over and over again at one sitting is an example of massed practice. See DISTRIBUTED PRACTICE.

MEMORY DRUM. An apparatus used in learning and memory experiments. It enables the experimenter to show the subject one word at a time.

MESOMORPHY. A tendency to muscularity in body type.

NEURASTHENIA. A neurosis characterized by chronic fatigue, boredom, and laziness.

NONSENSE SYLLABLE. Meaningless combinations of letters used to study learning and memory. Invented as psychological tool by Ebbinghaus.

OBSTRUCTION METHOD. A technique for measuring the strength of drives. An electrified grid must be passed in order to reach a goal. It has been found that a rat will show greatest persistence in the satisfaction of the maternal drive.

OEDIPUS COMPLEX. In Freudian theory, the universal unconscious desire to mate with the parent of the opposite sex and to murder the parent of the same sex.

ORAL CHARACTER. In Freudian theory, a character marked by extreme dependence.

OVERLEARNING. Study that continues after the material has been learned. For example, if one must read a list of words ten times in order to learn all the items on it, overlearning occurs when one reads it more than ten times. Overlearning makes for more permanent retention.

PARALLEL PLAY. Simultaneous play by several children, each of whom ignores the others.

PARANOIA. A form of insanity characterized by delusions of grandeur and of persecution.

PHANTOM LIMB. The feeling of a limb which has been amputated.

PLATEAU. A time during the learning process when there is no improvement.

PREACTIVE INHIBITION. The prevention of memory by the interference of material learned before the material being remembered.

PROJECTION. The defense mechanism of attributing to others the evils that are within us but that we cannot accept.

PSYCHOANALYSIS. The school of psychology invented by Sigmund Freud. Psychoanalysis stresses the role of unconscious sexual motivation in human life.

PSYCHODRAMA. A kind of psychotherapy in which the patients dramatize their emotional problems. Invented by Moreno.

PSYCHONEUROSIS. Any one of the milder forms of emotional disturbance.

PSYCHOPHYSICS. The exact measurement of psychic sensations. The oldest branch of scientific psychology, founded by Fechner and Weber in the nineteenth century.

PSYCHOSIS. One of the more serious forms of emotional disturbance; insanity.

REACTION FORMATION. A defense mechanism. Unconscious tendencies are fought by the adoption of a mode of behavior that expresses exactly the opposite tendency. The reaction formation usually covers a great area of personality, and is a regular pattern of behavior. Thus, according to Freudian theory, pacifism may be a reaction formation against aggressiveness, and aggressive behavior a reaction formation against fear.

REACTIVE REINFORCEMENT. The tendency of a conscious process to generate an opposing unconscious process. This is more a reaction against than a reaction to; for example, conscious love may generate unconscious hatred.

REFLEX. A simple, unlearned response to stimuli.

REGRESSION. A defense mechanism consisting of a return to a more primitive mode of functioning. For example, if a grown person reacts to frustration by throwing a tantrum, he is acting regressively.

REINFORCEMENT. Strengthening of a response tendency by pairing the conditioned stimulus with the unconditioned stimulus. Thus if one conditions the dog to salivate at the sound of a bell by ringing a bell just before showing it meat, every time the bell rings and the dog is shown meat, the salivating response is reinforced.

RELEARNING. A technique for measuring memory. The number of trials needed to relearn a task is compared to the number of trials needed for the original learning. The difference is called the *savings*.

REPRESSION. In Freudian theory, the most fundamental form of defense mechanism, which consists of making unacceptable experience unconscious and keeping it unconscious.

RETICULAR FORMATION. Part of the brain stem, believed to be the seat of waking consciousness.

RETROACTIVE INHIBITION. The prevention of memory by the interference of material learned after the material being remembered.

RORSCHACH TEST. A personality test in which the testee is asked to report what he sees in a series of ten standard-ized ink blots.

SAVINGS METHOD. See **RELEARNING.**

SCHIZOPHRENIA. The most common form of insanity, char-acterized by withdrawal, thinking disorders, and bizarre behavior.

SELF-ACTUALIZATION. A basic human tendency to actualize our potential. According to Maslow and Rogers, the touchstone of psychic health.

SET. A readiness to make a given response or series of re-sponses.

SHAM RAGE. Rage behavior exhibited by decorticate ani-mals, some of the cortical substance of whose brains had been stripped away. This differs from real rage in being evoked by almost any stimulus, and in disappearing as soon as the stimulus is withdrawn.

SIBLING RIVALRY. Feelings of competition among brothers and sisters. Stressed as a motivational factor by Adler.

SOMATOTYPE. Body type in Sheldon's typology of ecto-morphy, endomorphy, mesomorphy.

SPAN OF APPREHENSION. The largest number of objects that can be perceived at one time without actually counting them. The normal limit of the span of apprehension in the human being seems to be eight objects.

SPONTANEOUS RECOVERY. The return of a response after its extinction.

STANFORD-BINET TEST. One of the most widely used intel-ligence tests.

STRONG VOCATIONAL INTEREST BLANK. A test to measure vocational interest. The most widely used of such tests.

SUBLIMINAL PERCEPTION. Perception beneath the threshold

of consciousness, as when someone sees something but does not know he has seen it.

SUPEREGO. In Freudian theory, the part of the personality corresponding to the popular concept of conscience.

SYNESTHESIS. One sense modality functioning along lines usually belonging to another. For example, some people have a tendency to see certain colors when they hear certain sounds.

TACHISTISCOPE. An instrument that can flash images on a screen as quickly as desired. It can flash these images so quickly that the eye cannot see them.

TIME-AND-MOTION ANALYSIS. A technique for analyzing motor performance.

TRANSFER. The effect on the learning of a task by the learning of a prior task. If one learns B more easily because he has already learned A, this is called *positive transfer*. If one learns B with more difficulty because he has already learned A, this is called *negative transfer*.

TRANSFERENCE. In Freudian theory, transference to the analyst by the patient of the feelings he originally experienced toward his parents. An indispensable step in the process of a successful psychoanalysis.

TRIAL-AND-ERROR LEARNING. Learning by discovering and repeating the correct response in a situation that permits a number of responses.

TROPISMS. Unlearned movements of an organism in response to a particular stimulus or class of stimuli. Typical tropisms are a moth's phototropism toward light, and a flower's heliotropism toward the sun.

UNCONDITIONED RESPONSE. The original response evoked by an unconditioned stimulus. For example, the salivation of a hungry dog at the sight of meat.

UNCONDITIONED STIMULUS. An object in the environment that evokes a response without any training. For example, a piece of meat is an unconditioned stimulus that evokes salivation in a hungry dog or a hungry man.

WEBER'S LAW. The oldest quantitative law of scientific psychology, it states the exact relationship that determines the barely noticeable difference in any judgment. For example, one may be able to tell the difference between a twenty-pound weight and a thirty-pound weight, but not between a twenty-pound weight and a twenty-one-pound weight. Weber's Law expresses the fact that what counts here is not the absolute difference, but the relative difference. Thus, one could tell the difference between a one-pound weight and a two-pound weight.

WECHSLER ADULT INTELLIGENCE SCALE or WAIS. A more recent intelligence test, which is gradually overtaking the Stanford-Binet in popularity.

ZEIGARNIK EFFECT. The tendency to recall an uncompleted task better than a completed task.

CHAPTER 16

Money and the Marketplace

The Language of Business

JAMES J. FLYNN

The business vocabulary has found its major source in the law, as would be expected. With the contract as the cornerstone of the everyday give-and-take of business, it was inevitable that legal terminology would play a leading part in its language. But man-to-man daily contacts have also contributed many words of the street.

As the business community became more and more important in the daily life of Americans, the language grew with it and is still growing, with words drawn from many sources. Some are nothing more than a series of initials used to tell a complete story, such as *LIFO*—last in, first out—a method of valuing merchandise in inventory from one fiscal period to the next so that a company's physical working-capital position will be unimpaired. A word more familiar in gambling comes up frequently in business: *hedging*, offsetting one kind of risk with another. For example, if a manufacturer buys a large quantity of a commodity, he may simultaneously sell the same quantity for future delivery in a commodity futures market. Then, if the price of the actual goods falls, he will make a contract on his futures short sale. Business even goes into the kitchen for some of its vocabulary, as for instance with *frozen assets,* assets that cannot quickly be converted into cash. Nor is the vocabulary derived exclusively from our English forebears, as for example *agio,* from the Italian, the difference in value between bank notes and gold, or between one kind of paper money and another. The family touch enters with *ship's husband,* one who takes care of a ship's repairs while in port, and all the other chores preparatory to a voyage.

Latin naturally gives much to the business vocabulary. One of the most commonly used Latin phrases is *caveat emptor,* let the buyer beware, warning the buyer that he purchases at his own risk. Some of the more usual business phrases such as *per contra,* to the opposite side of an account, *bona fide,* in good faith, *ad valorem,* according to the value, are accepted without the realization that they were used by the Romans hundreds of years before the birth of Christ.

In business, as in all types of endeavor, it is most natural that the times add to the vocabulary. The expression *lame duck* is usually political, but in business it is stockbrokers' slang for one unable to meet his liabilities. A person who served time in the armed forces never forgets a muster, and business uses the word *muster* for a collection of samples. Short cuts in language are not new to Americans, and they apply in business as in other fields. For example, *ten forties* are United States Government bonds which could be redeemed by the government in ten years or could be allowed to run for forty. *Featherbedding* in labor-management indicates the request for more workers than the job demands. *Straddling* has many meanings, but it has been adopted by business to mean buying a futures contract in one month and selling a contract in another. In the monetary area the word *seigniorage,* taken from medieval times, identifies the charge levied on bullion brought by private persons to the mint to be coined.

These few sample expressions will give you some general conception of the diversity of sources from which everyday business language has been drawn. All this jargon, at times applicable to other fields, has a meaning all its own to everyone in finance, commerce, and industry.

WORD LIST

ABATEMENT. The amount deducted from a bill for any cause; removal of a nuisance; lessening of intensity. (The dress was soiled, so the price was cut by five dollars.) (The court has ordered John Brown to remove his noisy juke box.) (The storm has abated in fury.) The word comes from the French *abatre, abattre,* to beat down.

AGGREGATE DEMAND. Aggregate demand, in the National Income Division figures for the United States, is equal to gross national product. It is the dollar amount of the demand for our national output. (Aggregate demand has increased by $100 million in 1965 over 1964.)

ARBITRAGING. Taking advantage of differing prices for the same security or commodity. (Smith was arbitraging with United States Steel common stock, by purchasing in London at $103.00 and selling in New York at $126.00.) The word comes from the Latin *arbitror,* to make a decision. The word *arbitrator* is used, and is well known, in labor-management. Taft-Hartley set up a federal arbitrator. He is one who makes a decision.

ACTUARY. Expert in vital statistics. An expert in the mathematics of insurance. (The actuary for Acme Insurance determined the life span of professional employees.) From the Latin *actuarius,* clerk.

ADVENTURE. Shipment of goods on shipper's own account. A commercial venture; speculation. (Apex Company keeps a debit and credit account with all companies with which they do business in Brazil. This account is called an adventure.) Comes from the Latin *advenio,* to come.

AFFREIGHTMENT. To hire a ship to transport goods. (Dale Company entered into an affreightment with the Cunard Line.)

ALLONGE. A paper attached to a note or bill of exchange to allow more endorsements than the bill has room for. From the French *allonger,* to make long. (This bill of exchange needs an allonge before being sent for endorsement.)

ATTORN. To agree to become a tenant to another as landlord or owner. (His attornment was declared legal in the civil courts.) Taken from feudal law where it had the meaning of transferring homage to another lord.

BALANCE OF PAYMENTS. The fact that the total of all payments made by parties in the United States to parties in the rest of the world during any period must balance with the total of all payments by parties in the rest of the world to parties in the United States during that period. (President Johnson is doing everything possible to keep the balance of payments in our favor.)

BANCO. The difference between bank value and current value of money. (The banco at present is slight in comparison to one year ago.)

BASIS. A term used in the cotton trade to describe the spread or difference between the price for futures cotton as established in a futures contract on an exchange and the price for any kind of spot cotton as established in a spot transaction. (The basis for futures and spot purchases is too great for a purchase today.)

BIELBRIEF. In European maritime law, it is a document furnished by the builder of a vessel, containing a register of her measurements. (The bielbrief of the new vessel indicates it is larger than the *Queen Mary*.) This is taken from the German.

BIENES. Goods; property of every description, including real and personal property. (Smith's bienes was considerable after taxes.) This is taken from Spanish law.

BILLS OF RIGHTS. The business bill of rights includes freedom of contract, the rights of a business in properties it owns, the right to a fair trial and equal treatment— treatment equal to that accorded other businesses of the same nature—and freedom from restrictive retroactive legislation, wide freedom of expression, and a somewhat circumscribed freedom of association. (As an American businessman you have the right to own property and make a contract.)

BINDER. A preliminary agreement to provide immediate insurance until a policy can be written, either by an agent or company. (Always get a binder when buying a piece of property until you can get all other matters settled.)

BLUE-SKY LAW. A popular name for acts providing for the regulation and supervision of investment companies, for the protection of the community from investing in fraudulent companies. (Prior to the Securities and Exchange Commission, Delaware had no blue-sky laws.)

BOOK VALUE. Book value is the value of an item of property as shown on the balance sheet of the owner. It may also be the value of an obligation of a business enterprise or other party as shown on the balance sheet of that party. In general, the book value of a building or a piece of equipment at any date is its historical cost minus the accumulated reserve for its depreciation as of that date. The book value of a share of stock in a corporation that has only one kind of stock outstanding is the net worth of the corporation divided by the number of shares of stock outstanding. (The stock in Apex, Inc., had a book value of $50.00 and a market value of $38.50.)

BUCKET SHOP. An office or place where persons engage in pretended buying and selling of commodities or securities. (Until state laws made it a crime, many bucket shops existed which fraudulently took people's money without executing their orders.)

BULGE. A small but sudden advance in prices. (United States Steel stock bulged in the early hours of trading.)

BULL. Stock exchange slang for a broker who believes that the value of stocks will rise and speculates for a rise; "goes along" on a stock. (Smith is bullish on Acme Fast Freight stock.)

BY-BIDDER. One employed by the seller or his agent to bid on property with no purpose to become a purchaser, so that bidding thereon may be stimulated in others who are bidding in good faith. (Adams always acted as a by-bidder when Smith was attempting to push up the price on poor property.)

COINSURANCE. A policy provision or endorsement specifying that the property owner will carry insurance to at least a stated percentage of the value of the property in consideration of a reduced rate. (The coinsurance rate will be 65 percent of the value of the property at a premium showing a 10 percent reduction.)

COLLECTIVE BARGAINING. Negotiations between representatives of a trade union or organization of trade unions on the one hand and representatives of an employer or an employers' association on the other are called collective bargaining. The agreement arrived at in regard to the terms of employment of the union members, and often other employees as well, is referred to as a collective bargaining agreement or contract. (The Wagner Act made it possible for all workers to set up collective bargaining agreements with management.)

CONSOLS. Term originally applied to consolidated loans of governments, such as 3 percent consolidated annuities of Great Britain. (Charles Jones purchased a number of British consols.)

CORNER. A situation in which more shares of stock or more units of a commodity have been sold than the sellers can deliver. (John Smith has created a corner for himself in his recent sale of typewriters to Liberia.)

DEL CREDERE. Extra commission given an agent in consideration of his warranting the solvency of the purchaser. (For your kindness to our concern we are sending you your del credere in the next mail.) This comes from the Italian.

DEMURRAGE. Forfeit money for detention of vessels or freight cars beyond the time allowed by a charter-party. (Your demurrage has increased by an additional day because of your failure to notify us by wire.)

DEPLETION. Depletion is the result of removing valuable minerals from a mineral deposit by mining or by some other extractive operation. It is the dollar amount deducted because of such removal from the operating revenues and other credits to the income account of a business for purposes of computing its net income for a period. (The Ivin Gold Mine Corporation showed a depletion of $800,000 in 1965.)

DEPRECIATION. Depreciation is the dollar amount by which the book value of a building or an item of equipment decreases during a year (or other accounting period). This amount is determined according to a procedure adopted at the time the asset was acquired. Depreciation is charged as an expense in computing the net income for the period, and added to the depreciation reserve. The standard asset value rule for such an asset is that its book value at any date equals its historical cost minus the accumulated depreciation reserve at that date. (The government permits a 10 percent depreciation in equipment for mining corporations in any fiscal year.)

DOUBLE PATENTING. The test respecting double patenting is whether the claims of both patents, when properly construed in the light of the descriptions given, define essentially the same things.

DOWER. The provision which the law makes for a widow out of the lands or tenements of her husband, for her support and the nurture of her children.

DUNNAGE. Pieces of wood placed against the sides and bottom of the hold of a vessel, to preserve the cargo from the effect of leakage. (Pack the cargo in #1 Hold with sufficient dunnage.)

EASEMENT. A right in the owner of one parcel of land, by reason of such ownership, to use the land of another for a special purpose not inconsistent with the general property of the adjacent owner.

ELASTICITY. The price elasticity of demand is a measure of the response of the buyers in the market for goods or services to a small change in the price of the goods or services. It is equal to the ratio of the percentage increase in the physical quantity of the goods or services buyers will buy in response to a small decrease in the price to the percentage decrease in price. (Salt has what the economist calls inelastic demand. As you raise or lower the price a great deal, the demand changes little.)

ENTERING SHORT. When bills not yet due are paid into a bank by a customer, it is the custom of some bankers not to carry the amount of the bills directly to his credit, but to enter them short, as it is called.

ENTREPOT. A place where goods are deposited without paying duty, to await transportation elsewhere; a free port. (England was the entrepot for goods shipped from the Colonies to ports in Europe.)

FINANCIAL ASSET. A financial asset of one party is a debt or obligation of someone else. A party's financial assets may include cash on hand, accounts receivable, loans and securities owned, and any other claims that are debts of other parties. (Jones's financial asset was increased when he acquired two new parcels of land.)

FLOAT. Credit extended by the Federal Reserve to reserves of member banks to cover checks delayed in collection. (The long weekend increased the size float carried by the New York Federal Reserve.)

GROSS NATIONAL PRODUCT (GNP). The precise definition of GNP involves a great many technical, detailed questions. However, the general nature of the GNP can be quite simply indicated. The GNP, during any period, represents the total value of all final products turned out by the economy during that period—that is, the total value of all products other than "intermediate products" such as raw materials and supplies used up in producing the final products. The GNP consists of four main components: (1) personal consumption expenditure, (2) gross private domestic capital formation (fixed capital formation plus the inventory increment), (3) government GNP purchases, and (4) the export surplus. GNP equals AGGREGATE DEMAND (q.v.). (The gross national product of the United States has increased each year since 1945.)

INFLATION. Inflation means a somewhat widespread price increase. The amount of inflation during any period is measured by the upward movement of some price index. The most commonly used monthly index is the Consumer Price Index, published by the Bureau of Labor Statistics. A more comprehensive index, available quarterly, is the GNP price index. The term inflation should not be taken to suggest anything about what causes price increases. (The cost of living has gone up 3 percent since 1963 because of the inflation trend.)

INSIDE FUNDS. Inside funds are funds becoming available from the operations of a business during a particular period to finance its capital formation. The total of such funds available to finance a quarter's private capital formation, as shown by the national income and product accounts for our economy, is equal to total quarterly depreciation and other provisions for capital consumption plus the quarter's retained corporate income. (United States Steel, because of its large inside funds, has been able to expand greatly.)

INVENTORY INCREMENT. In computing the gross national product, the increase (or decrease) during the year in the physical quantity of goods held in a business inventory is valued at the average price for the year. The inventory increment is the sum of the values of all physical quantity increases minus the sum of the values of all physical quantity decreases. This algebraic total is a component of gross private capital formation and a component of aggregate demand. (The GNP must take into account the physical quantity of goods that General Motors holds in its inventory at an average price for the year.)

LABOR FORCE. The civilian labor force consists of all employees (except members of the armed forces), active sole proprietors of and active partners in unincorporated business enterprises, and unemployed persons who want employment. (Our labor force is greater because we also include the unemployed who are seeking employment.)

LONG. Indicates a trading position in which the trader owns more securities or commodities than he has contracted to deliver. By extension, one who has a long position, a bull. (Charles Jones found himself in a long position in steel stocks when the market closed.)

MARGIN. Money deposited with a broker to protect trades made, or to be made; the difference between the market value of collateral and the amount that a bank will lend against the collateral. (The Federal Reserve has set the margin for the purchase of stocks and bonds at 50 percent.)

MARGINAL COST. The marginal cost of any goods or services produced by any business is the estimated additional cost per unit of added output that would be involved in increasing the output of those goods or services during a year (or during some other fiscal period). (Jackson Company decided not to produce another 100,000 typewriters because the marginal cost of these machines would be $83.50. This would increase the cost of the entire production from $72.00 to $79.75.)

MARKUP. The amount by which the original selling price

is increased. If an item is offered for sale at $10 and then the price is changed to $11, the markup is $1. (The markup in automobiles is extremely high.)

MONOPOLISTIC COMPETITION. There is said to be monopolistic competition between business firms that are selling similar but not identical goods or services when each firm, by virtue of owning a brand name or because of other circumstances, has a monopoly of the particular goods or services it is selling, but has to sell them in competition with the similar goods or services that are substitutes for it. (General Motors, Ford, and Chrysler have a monopolistic competition setup in the American automobile industry.)

MONOPSONY. A trader is said to have a monopsony in his market, or to be a monoposonist, when he is the only trader on the demand side of a market for goods or services, and the nearest competing demander is interested in buying somewhat different goods or services. (Smith can be said to be a monopsonist in New York City because he is the only one who buys elephant tusks.)

MORAL HAZARD. The possibility of loss being caused or aggravated by dishonesty or carelessness of the insured, his agents, or employees. (The young man, driving his father's car after three accidents, was refused insurance as a moral hazard.)

NET WORTH. Net worth is the dollar amount by which the total assets of a business enterprise or of any other party exceed the total liabilities or debts of that party. In the case of a corporation, the liabilities include all obligations to pay money sums to creditors of all sorts; they do not include the obligations of a corporation to its stockholders. (Jackson's net worth is $100,000 after deducting his total liabilities.)

OPEN MARKET. One in which supply and demand are unhampered by any arbitrary interference. (The sale of sugar is not in an open market.)

OVER THE COUNTER. A market outside the registered exchange. While most of their business is in securities not listed on any exchange, on occasion they handle listed securities. (ABC Corporation is on the over-the-counter listing and not on the New York Stock Exchange.)

PARITY. In broad terms parity means equality. Today it is most commonly heard in connection with an endeavor by the farmer in line with that of the rest of the country. (Wheat is now at 90 percent of parity, when parity was $2.25 per bushel.)

PARTICIPATING BOND. A bond that, in addition to paying a fixed rate of interest, has the privilege of participating or sharing in the earnings of the issuer.

PAYABLE IN EXCHANGE. Meaning that a draft or other instrument must be paid in funds of the place where issued.

PEG. To hold prices or quotations at a fixed level. (In World War II the government attempted to peg the price of sugar.)

POOL. In financial circles, a group of persons who combine their resources for a purpose. A stock pool (now illegal) was a combination of persons working together to manipulate a stock. (All the steel companies pooled their resources to study the new open-hearth method.)

PRIMARY RECEIPTS. The aggregate receipts of cotton and grains at the principal primary points, namely, the large cities that receive such shipments direct from the country.

PRICE INDEXES. A price index such as the Consumer Price Index (CPI) is a ratio of averages; it relates the average level of prices during each month (or each year or other period) to the average level in some comparison base period, for example, to the average level in 1957-1959. Nearly all present price indexes are of the aggregative type. The computation of such an index for a series of successive months (or other periods) involves three main steps: (1) determining what are called the weights, (2) computing what are called value aggregates, and (3) converting these aggregates into index number form. (The price index is given to us every three months by the Bureau of Labor Statistics.)

PROCURATION. A general letter or power of attorney. (Mrs. Axel gave her procuration to Attorney Smith.)

PRODUCTION. Production or gross national product (GNP) is measured as the total value of all final goods and services turned out by our economy during a year or quarter, the goods and services of the various years and quarters all being valued at the same set of prices, that is, the prices prevailing at some one time, so that changes in the total reflect physical quantity changes, not changes in prices. Final goods and services are distinguished from intermediate goods and services, that is, from goods and services used up in producing other goods and services. The National Income Division publishes figures on our GNP valued at 1954 prices. Total GNP is also referred to as aggregate demand. There are four main components of GNP: personal consumption expenditure, gross private domestic capital formation, government GNP purchases, and the export surplus.

(Production must be looked at from the standpoint of GNP. All the goods and services turned out by our economy during a year.)

PROFIT MAXIMIZATION. Under the profit system, maximizing profit is the primary objective of the management of a business enterprise. The plan for the activities of a business enterprise has come to have two main parts, the current budget and the capital budget. Maximizing the current year's profit is the main objective of the current budget. The primary longer-term objective of the capital budget can be thought of as maximizing the present value of planned profits. This involves a planning discount rate. Let this be "r." The discount rate r is used for discounting next year's planned profit by dividing the profit by $1 + r$, for discounting the profit planned for the year after that by dividing it by $(1 + r)^2$, and so on. A more precise way to state the primary longer-term objective is to say that it is to maximize the amount by which the present discounted value of planned cash receipts exceeds the present discounted value of planned cash disbursements. (It is standard procedure to maximize profit, if you are a good businessman.)

PUBLIC POLICY. There is no simple way to state what is good public economic policy. In general, it is in accord with good public policy to have those goods and services produced in those quantities that best express the preferences indicated by the dollar ballots cast by final product purchasers. It is in accord with good public policy, too, to have each employed member of the labor force employed in the job he finds most attractive, assuming this means employment in the job in which he can make a maximum contribution to the economy's total product. And it is in accord with good public policy to have the economy's plant and equipment attracted into the uses that offer the most attractive compensation, assuming this means the uses in which these items of fixed capital are most productive. (You will produce under good public policy only those products that the people want to buy.)

Put. A contract giving the right to deliver to the maker a set amount of stocks or commodities at a named price during the time of the contract. (The put was worked out to the satisfaction of all.)

Realizing Sales. Sale made to cash-in on profits in "long" accounts.

Recession. Business cycles or business fluctuations consist of alternating periods of successive quarters of increase in aggregate demand and periods of successive quarters of decrease in aggregate demand. Once a period of increase is inaugurated, it tends to continue for a time; the same is true of a period of decrease. A recession is a period of decrease. (The unemployment figure rose to a point when the Bureau of Labor Statistics indicated a recession.)

Rediscount Rate. The interest rate at which the Federal Reserve System will lend to member banks. The banks may borrow on commercial paper that they have previously discounted, and the Federal Reserve will discount the paper again. In England, this rate is called the *bank rate*.

Refunding. The issuing of a new security to replace one about to fall due. (Alexander Hamilton refunded the national debt, thereby saving the credit rating of the United States.)

REVERSION. Right to possess property after the happening of some event, as the death of a person. (There was a reversion of Jones's property when his daughter, in violation of his will, married young O'Toole.)

SECTOR. The economy of the United States is regarded as consisting of groups of transactors; businesses, governments, households and single individuals, and so forth. However, each business is thought of as a kind of dual personality; one personality is in the producing sector, the other is a final purchaser of the economy's output. (Each person in the nation has a sector to handle. He is in the producing sector as well as the consuming sector.)

SERIAL BONDS. Those payable in installments according to a series of fixed maturities. The serial payment procedure effects a systematic reduction in the principal of the loan, and is used extensively in state and municipal financing.

SHORT. A person who has sold securities or commodities that he does not own, in the hope of being able to buy them later at a lower price. (Smith was selling short and was caught by a rising market.)

SINKING FUND. Fund or reserves into which certain designated sums are set aside at specified intervals by the issuer, to be used for the acquisition, either by calling at a fixed price or by purchase in the market, of a specific amount of the particular bond issue. (The sinking fund for Ace Company bonds calls for $50,000 each quarter.)

SPLIT. The process of exchanging the number of outstanding shares of a corporation for an increased number with a proportionate reduction of the par or stated value of the shares. (Polaroid stock has split three times since it was originally issued.)

SPREAD. A general term applied to the differential between various security quotations. Denotes differences between bid and asked prices. (The spread in Acme Freight was as much as three points in today's market.)

SQUEEZE. A market condition in which buyers are forced to cover their requirements at sharply rising prices. In the money market, a temporary shortage of funds resulting in a jump in current interest rates. (Jones was caught in a squeeze when he attempted to borrow from his bank.)

SUBROGATION. The legal process by which an insurance company seeks from a third party who may have caused the loss, recovery of the amount paid to or in behalf of the policyholder. (Smith discovered the Apex Insurance Company seeking to get him by subrogation to pay them for money given to Brown for an accident.)

SUTLER. One authorized to sell goods to an army. (The sutler used inferior goods during the Civil War.)

TENDERING. The process of delivering a commodity sold through a futures contract; also the submission of bids for the purchase of security offerings. (The tendering date for our wheat purchase is next Tuesday.)

TIME DEPOSITS. Time deposits consist of deposits in mutual savings banks and deposits in commercial banks that are legally subject to an advance notice requirement prior to withdrawal. (Savings banks can make you wait for the withdrawal of your deposits under the regulation that they are time deposits.)

TURNOVER. The number of shares, bonds, or commodities bought and sold in a market over a given period. (The turnover in electrical stocks for June was exceptionally low.)

ULLAGE. What a cask lacks of being full. (The ullage on the one-hundred-gallon casks was two gallons.)

WAIVER. Relinquishment of a legal right or privilege. (Adams waived his right to immunity when he went before the grand jury.)

WAY BILL. List of goods given to a carrier. (The way bill given to American Railway Express was missing many items.)

CHAPTER 17

Words about Words

The Language of Linguistics

JOHN HUGHES

The terminology of descriptive linguistics—as distinct from that of traditional grammar—has grown up with its field in approximately the last forty years. Much of it was invented by Leonard Bloomfield, originally a professor of German at the University of Chicago and, since 1940, the country's first professor of linguistics (at Yale). Some is translated or borrowed from European languages. Linguistic terminology is still very much in flux: different schools have different terms, sometimes designating the same thing, and there are linguists whose only distinction is the invention of a new term. The early linguists were usually well grounded in Latin, Greek, and Sanskrit (the forerunner of linguistics in the strict sense having been comparative philology, which essentially aimed at reconstructing the Indo-European language from its ancient and modern descendants). And since the terminology of descriptive linguistics began to be developed at a time when the classical languages were still fairly strong in American schools, the linguistic vocabulary is based upon Latin and Greek more than any of the other scientific vocabularies, except those (like chemistry and medicine) which had their first significant development in the nineteenth century.

When a scientist is looking for a new word to express a new concept, there are several clear advantages in turning to Latin and Greek roots. If he gives a new meaning to a word already in English use, there is danger of ambiguity: in a number of linguistic terms, one may be uncertain whether a word is used linguistically or in the ordinary sense, and if the scientist tries to limit the term with English qualifiers, he will probably arrive at a compound or phrase of unwieldy length. If he picks a Latin or Greek root, however, he has a short word which he can make mean exactly what he wishes it to, which fits harmoniously into the structure of most European languages (many of them actually derived from Latin), and which already has an internationally recognized general meaning which can suggest the special scientific meaning. A good many of the terms of linguistics, therefore, are directly or indirectly derived from Greek and Latin, sometimes through modern languages, such as a term in French formed from Latin and then borrowed into English.

On the other hand, many younger linguists have not studied Latin and Greek, and must develop their terminology entirely in English, with the disadvantages mentioned above.

From the vocabulary that follows, terms of traditional grammar have generally been excluded, except for some which have continued into linguistics or which express concepts still current in linguistics. The vocabulary is, so far as space permits, a representative survey of the terminology of contemporary descriptive linguistics.

WORD LIST

ABLAUT. Alternation of stem vowels (see STEM) in different tenses of a verb (e.g., drive, drove, driven) and elsewhere. Generally characteristic of strong verbs in Germanic languages. The root of the Latin word *toga* is an ablaut-form of the verb root *teg-*, to cover. From the German, meaning change of sound. Synonym: apophony. See UMLAUT.

AFFIX. A syllable attached to a root either at the front or at the end, usually with the purpose of modifying the meaning of the root either by INFLECTION or by DERIVATION (q.q.v.). An affix may be a prefix or a suffix. From the Latin *ad + fixare*.

AGGLUTINATING. A type of language structure; a language in which independent or semi-independent elements are added to a root to form words, often quite long, whose identity is often maintained by vowel harmony. Usually the MORPHEME-FORMANT (q.v.) ratio tends to be 1:1. From the Latin *glutino*, to glue together.

ALLOMORPH. Alternative forms of a MORPHEME (q.v.) which have the same meaning. In English, *will* and *I* are allomorphs, because *I will* and *I'll* mean the same. From the Greek *allos*, other, and *morphē*, form.

ALLOPHONE. On the same principle, this means alternative forms of a PHONEME (q.v.) which do not have different meanings. In English, we have different *p*'s in the words *pit* and *spit:* the *p* in *spit* is really p + h. This difference is not significant in English, but in many languages there is a whole series, *p* vs. *ph, t* vs. *th, k* vs. *kh.* (See ASPIRATION.) But in English, *p* and *ph* are allophones of the phoneme /p/. From the Greek *allo–*, other, and *phonē*, sound.

ANALYTIC. A type of language structure in which certain things are expressed by independent words instead of by parts of other words, or by other devices. For instance, in Latin, *mater Dei* means "mother of God"; what is expressed in English by the word "of" is expressed in Latin by the *-i* at the end of the word *dei* (contrasting with other forms such as *deus, deo, deum*). Originally from Greek, but a standard word in English before it acquired a linguistic meaning.

APOPHONY. See **ABLAUT.**

ARCHIPHONEME. In the Prague or European school of linguistics, the actual phoneme realized when there is **NEUTRALIZATION** (q.v.). It may be one allophone or the other, or a third distinct from either. In standard German, for instance, the opposition of voice is neutralized in favor of the voiceless phoneme in final position; thus, to a German, *rise* and *rice* would be the same word. From the Greek *archi-*, chief, and *phonema,* unit of sound.

ASPECT. When a language has two verb forms in the same tense, the different forms are different aspects. Thus, English has a present progressive and a present habitual: "Do you read French novels?" implies habitual reading; "Are you reading a French novel?" implies action now going on—but both are in the present time. A standard English word to which a special meaning has been given.

ASPIRATION. Many consonants are pronounced with such force that there is actually a puff of air after them; the puff of air could be called an *h*. In Germanic languages initial consonants normally have this aspiration, so that the English word *pot* should really be written *phot*.

Romance languages do not usually have aspirated initial consonants. From the Latin *aspiratio*, a breath.

ASSIMILATION. Alteration of a phoneme to make it more like a neighboring phoneme; it is progressive assimilation if the phoneme to which the assimilation is made follows, regressive if it precedes, the phoneme assimilating. The derivation of *affix* from *adfixum* is an example of progressive assimilation. From the Latin *assimilatio*, becoming more like.

AUSLAUT. Final position. From the German *auslaut*, a finishing or closing sound.

BOUND FORM. A term invented by Bloomfield, designating a linguistic form that cannot occur independently (i.e., as a word) but only as part of a word. (See FREE FORM.)

CHAIN OF SPEECH. A term invented by the Swiss linguist De Saussure, who likens speech to a chain in which one link follows another, so that speech can be conceived of as horizontal. But at each point in the chain the form actually produced is selected from a certain number of possibilities, any of which could have fitted into the chain at that point: this is the vertical aspect of speech. Originally from French.

CLICKS. In Indo-European languages, all the sounds of speech are produced in the process of expelling air from the mouth. If air is drawn into the mouth, the same positions give a completely different set of sounds—the implosive sounds or clicks. Clicks are used in English, though not as sounds of speech: the click-sound corresponding to *T* is used for disapproval, written tsk-tsk or tch-tch, and that corresponding to *l* is used to signal horses, usually written *cluck-cluck*. A standard English word, probably applied to the click sounds by onomatopoeia.

COMMUTATION. Replacing one phoneme in a word by another, or one word or form by another. If this results in the formation of a different word or a sentence of different meaning, the two phonemes or words are in MINIMAL CONTRAST (q.v.). From the Latin *commutare,* to exchange.

CORRELATION. In European or Prague-school linguistics, a series of oppositions based on the same feature. Thus *p* is opposed to *b* by the opposition voiceless/voiced, but so is t/d, k/g, s/z, and so on. This series of oppositions is called a correlation. Ultimately from Latin, probably through German (the term may have been invented by Troubetzkoy).

DERIVATION. The process of forming one word from another, as distinct from INFLECTION (q.v.), the formation of various cases of the same word. Thus, the noun affliction is derived from the verb afflict by the addition of a suffix. Ultimately from the Latin *derivare,* to draw off (water).

DIGRAPH. When a single sound is expressed in writing by two letters, the two letters are called a *digraph.* In English, the letters *t + h* usually express a single sound, *th.* From Greek *di-,* two, and *graph,* letter.

DIPHTHONG. A sequence of a vowel and a semivowel (or the reverse) making only one syllable. If the vowel comes first, it is a falling diphthong (*ai, au,* etc.); if the semivowel comes first, it is a rising one (*ya, wa,* etc.). From the Greek *di-,* two, and *phthongos,* sound.

DISTRIBUTION. The positions in which a phoneme occurs. Some phonemes, e.g., English /h/, occur only at the beginning of a syllable, not at the end of one. Of two allophones, if one occurs only where the other one does not, the allophones are said to be in *complementary dis-*

tribution. A standard English word to which a special linguistic meaning is given.

ENDOCENTRIC STRUCTURE. In Bloomfield's terminology, a construction which belongs to the same form-class as one or more of its constituents: thus *poor John* belongs to the same form-class as *John; boys and girls* belongs to the same form-class as *boys* and *girls*. In effect, endocentric structures are those which are less than sentences. From the Greek *endo-,* within, and Latin *centrum,* center.

EXOCENTRIC STRUCTURE. A construction which belongs to the form-class of none of its immediate constituents. A sentence is an exocentric construction, but so is the relation-axis construction: *with me, in the house.* From the Greek *exo-,* outside, and Latin *centrum,* center.

FREE FORM. Another Bloomfield term, defined by him as follows: "A linguistic form which is never spoken alone is a *bound* form; all others (as, for instance, *John ran* or *John* or *run* or *running*) are free forms."

FRICATIVE. See SPIRANT.

FUNCTIONAL YIELD. The number of words kept distinct from each other by a given opposition. Thus, in English, some speakers distinguish *wh* from *w,* and keep distinct such words as *where* and *wear, wheel* and *weal, whoa* and *woe, which* and *witch, what* and *watt;* other English speakers pronounce *wh* and *w* alike, and for them all the words cited are HOMONYMS (q.v.).

GEMINATION. Doubling of a consonant; a sequence of two of the same consonant. This term is now preferred to *doubling.* From Latin *geminare,* to pair; to twin (cf. Gemini, a sign of the Zodiac, and Project Gemini, ultimately designed to have two astronauts rendezvous in space).

GENERATIVE GRAMMAR. A theory largely identified with Professor Noam Chomsky of the Massachusetts Institute of Technology, according to which a KERNEL (q.v.) of the sentences in a language is analyzed by immediate-constituent analysis, and all other sentences are derived (generated) from these by rules of transformation.

GLOSSEMATICS. A theory of language largely identified with Professor Louis Hjelmslev of the University of Copenhagen. It is defined by him as follows: "Linguistics . . . must see its main task in establishing a science of the expression and a science of the content on an internal and functional basis. . . . Such a linguistics . . . would be one whose science of the expression is not a phonetics and whose science of the content is not a semantics." From the Greek *glossa,* tongue: *glossemes* (Greek *glossemata,* although the word was probably coined by Hjelmslev), the minimal forms which the theory leads us to establish as bases of explanation.

GLOTTOCHRONOLOGY. A theory largely identified with the linguist Morris Swadesh. It holds, in general, that as one language changes into another, the amount of vocabulary which changes is measurably proportional to the time elapsed, so that a study of the amount of vocabulary change can give an indication of the chronology of change. From the Greek *glotta* (a dialect alternative of *glossa*), tongue, and *chronos,* time, plus the suffix *-ology* (Greek *logos*), science.

HIATUS. Essentially, a sequence of two (usually different) vowels, especially when one is at the end of a word and the other begins the following word. Many languages abhor hiatus and employ special devices to avoid or remove one. From the Latin *hiatus,* an opening (of the mouth).

HOLE IN THE PATTERN. If a language has a series of phonemic oppositions but one possible opposition does not occur, it is called a hole in the pattern. Thus, if a language had *p/b*, *t/d*, *k/g*, *sh/zh*, but no *z* opposing *s*, the *z* would be a hole in the pattern.

HOMONYMY. The situation which arises when two words, with different meanings, have the same sound: like *gait* and *gate*. From the Greek *homo-*, similar, and *onyma*, name.

HYPERTAGMEME. In the theory of linguistics known as TAGMEMICS (q.v.), a sentence, looked at as a series of *tagmemes*. From the Greek *hyper*, large, and *tagmema*, unit of arrangement.

IMMEDIATE CONSTITUENT. Traditional grammar assumed that a sentence was composed of words. One of the most important discoveries of modern linguistics is that the immediate constituents of a sentence are not words but groups of words (sometimes single words), and that at each level of analysis, the immediate constituents are normally two. The first division is into subject-group and predicate-group (this much was known to Aristotle), and then each of those groups is broken into two, and each of the resultants into two, until eventually we get to the individual words.

INFIX. An element introduced into the middle of a word, sometimes within a root, usually with the purpose of modifying its meaning, and much like a prefix or a suffix except for its position. Thus Latin had a root *sac*, and in Latin *sacer* meant sacred; but the insertion of the infix *-n-* changed the adjective to *sanctus*, holy, and the verb to *sanctificare*, to sanctify. From the Latin *in* + *fixare*.

INFLECTING. A type of language structure in which the

grammatical process of INFLECTION (q.v.) plays a dominant part. Derivation: Latin *in* + *flecto,* bend.

INFLECTION. Alteration of a word by exchange of suffixes to express its function in a sentence; thus Latin *servus* meant a slave, subject of sentence; *servum* meant a slave, object of sentence; *servi* meant of a slave, and so on. See INFLECTING.

ITEM-ARRANGEMENT. A term originated by the linguist Hockett to indicate one type of grammatical description in which the implication is not made that one form is prior to another.

ITEM-PROCESS. Hockett's term for conventional grammatical description, which assumes that some forms are derived from others—that the *item* has been subjected to a *process.*

JUNCTURE. Essentially, a signal of the boundaries between structures, corresponding in a general way with marks of punctuation. For instance, the voice-cadence and pause used to indicate the end of a sentence is called the *double-cross juncture.* Originally from Latin *junctura,* a joining.

KERNEL. In GENERATIVE GRAMMAR (q.v.), the set of sentences produced by applying obligatory transformations to the terminal strings of the constituent-analysis grammar.

LABIODENTAL. Articulated with the lips and teeth. From the Latin *labium,* lip, and *dentes,* teeth.

LARYNGEAL THEORY. A theory largely identified with Professor Jerzy Kurylowicz of Poland. It holds that the Indo-European language at an early stage had laryngeal sounds, the dropping of which accounts for certain developments in the vocalism.

LENITION. Change of a stop to a spirant in medial position, or at the beginning of a word if it is really medial in speech. In some dialects of Italian, for instance, *la casa* becomes *la hasa.* From the Latin *lenitio,* softening, from *lenis,* soft.

MECHANICAL TRANSLATION. Translation from one language to another by means of computers. Research has been going on in this area since World War II, and a machine has been programmed which can translate Russian to English, if the Russian text has no more than four grammatical constructions and no more than 200 different words.

MEDIAL. In the middle of a word. From the Latin *medius,* middle.

METATHESIS. Exchange of position, usually of phonemes: for instance, many people say *revelant* instead of *relevant.* From the Greek *meta,* after, and *thesis,* putting.

MINIMAL CONTRAST or **MINIMUM OPPOSITION.** When the exchange of one phoneme for another in a word produces a different word, all other phonemes remaining the same, it proves that the opposition between those two phonemes is meaningful (phonemic) and hence significant in the language. Changing *pit* to *bit* makes a new word, hence the opposition p/b is phonemic in English.

MOOD. The ordinary implication of speech is that the speaker is saying what is true, or what he believes to be true. If he is conscious that what he says may not be true—a wish, for instance, which may not come true, or a condition, known to be contrary to fact—he may use special verb forms to indicate this: subjunctive, optative, or conditional moods.

MORPHEME. In the most general usage, the smallest unit of word formation: in the word *dogs*, for instance, *dog* is one morpheme and *-s* is another, expressing plurality. The morpheme is the smallest bit of speech that conveys a meaning. A PHONEME (q.v.) does not in itself have meaning, but it affects meaning. From the Greek *morphema*, unit of form.

MORPHOLOGY. The branch of grammar which describes the principles governing the construction of words. From the Greek *morphē*, form, *-ology*, science.

NASALIZATION. Pronouncing a sound or word with accompanying resonance from the nasal passage, by not closing the soft palate during the articulation.

NEUTRALIZATION. A phonemic opposition may not be employed in all positions; if there are some in which it is not employed, the opposition is said to be neutralized there.

OPPOSITION. The contrast between one phoneme and another: *p* is opposed to *b*, because replacement of *p* by *b* in a word would produce a different word. And *p* is also opposed to *f*, but in a different way.

PALATALIZATION. Pronouncing a sound with the blade of the tongue instead of the tip or back, giving a characteristic quality. Thus French has an *n* and a palatalized *n* (*gn*).

PARADIGM. A table presenting certain related grammatical forms, like the inflection of a noun, the conjugation of a verb, etc. From the Greek *paradeigma*, a demonstration.

PATTERN DRILL. A method of language teaching developed from linguistics, in which, instead of memorizing paradigms, the student memorizes meaningful sentences as patterns and manipulates them.

PHONE. The speech sound as the subject of the science of phonetics; a particular speech sound.

PHONEME. The unit of word-structure in language is an idea of a speech sound, rather than an actual speech sound or PHONE (q.v.). The actual sounds produced by speakers may or may not be recognized as phonemes of the language, according as they do or do not fulfill the norms which that language sets up for a particular phoneme. A given phone may be a phoneme in one language and an ALLOPHONE (q.v.) in another. From the Greek *phonema,* unit of sound, from *phonē,* sound.

PHONEMICS. That branch of linguistics which endeavors to determine the phonemes of a language. From *phoneme* and *-ics,* a suffix meaning the science of, as in *physics* (originally from Greek *-ika*).

PHONETICS. The science which investigates speech sounds, endeavoring to describe them according to either their articulation or their acoustic properties. From the Greek *phonetika,* things pertaining to sound, from *phonē,* sound.

PHONOLOGY. The branch of grammar which describes the sounds and pronunciation of a language. From the Greek *phonē,* sound, and *-logy,* science.

PLOSIVE. See STOP.

POLYSYNTHETIC. A type of language structure in which every utterance is a sentence. From the Greek *poly,* much, many, and *synthetikos,* putting together.

PREFIX. An affix attached before the root. From Latin *prae,* before, and *fixare,* to fix.

PROSODIC FEATURES. Features observable in an utterance which do not ordinarily convey or affect meaning: accent, pitch, voice cadence, pauses. From the Greek *prosodia*, a song sung to music, or the tone or accent of a syllable.

PSYCHOLINGUISTICS. The area in which psychology overlaps linguistics. Psychology studies human thought and thinking, but thought is conveyed only through language. From the Greek *psyche*, the soul.

REALIZATION. The actual speech sound uttered, viewed as an actualization or realization of the concept of a speech sound (the phoneme).

RELEVANCY. The relevancy of a feature is whether or not it affects meaning.

ROOT. The part of a word which expresses the word's meaning, as distinct from elements which modify this meaning and convey information about the grammatical functioning of the word.

SANDHI. The assimilatory changes undergone by sounds in connected speech, especially when final in one word and initial in the next; originally in Sanskrit but by analogy in any language. From Sanskrit *san-dhi*, putting together.

SHWA. The name of a Hebrew letter—more strictly, a masoretic point—which expressed an obscure vowel like that in the second syllable of English *tartan, linen, robin, button;* hence, such a vowel in modern languages, and the phonetic symbol for such a vowel, [ə].

SEMANTICS. The study which concerns itself with the meanings of words, particularly the fact that different people mean different things by the same words. From the Greek *semantica*, things concerning the expression of meaning, from *semaino*, to signify.

SERIES. The list of consonants in a language which have the same articulatory location, e.g., the labial series; the dental series.

SPIRANT. A consonant in the pronunciation of which there is a passage of air, in contrast to the stops, during which there is momentarily a complete stoppage of air. From the Latin *spirare,* to breathe.

STEM. Sometimes a syllable is added to a root, apparently without meaning, before the root combines with suffixes or endings; such a lengthened root is called a stem.

STOP. A consonant during the production of which there is momentarily a complete stoppage of air, as in *p, t, k.*

STRESS. A syllable pronounced more loudly than the other syllables in a word is said to have stress.

SUBSTRATUM. A language which was spoken in a given area before the now dominant language was brought in, or which is spoken by a small number of speakers in an area where there is a much more widespread language, speakers of the substratum generally being able to speak the dominant language. From the Latin *sub,* under, and *stratum,* layer.

SUFFIX. An affix added to the root or stem; generally distinguished from an ending, which expresses inflection. From the Latin *sub,* under, and *fixare,* to fix.

SUPRASEGMENTAL. A term used by Trager and Smith (the Continental school of linguistics prefers *prosodic features*) to designate stress, pitch, and juncture. From the Latin *supra,* above, and *segmentum,* a piece (of the chain of speech); in other words, features over and above those normal to the chain of speech.

SYNTAX. That part of grammar which deals with the principles governing the construction of sentences (in traditional grammar, usually compound or complex sentences). From the Greek *syn-*, together, and *taxis*, arrangement.

TAGMEME. In the theory of grammar known as *tagmemics*, a tagmeme is defined as a slot-class correlation, or a substitution point along with the class of words found at that point. In other words, at practically every point in a sentence, a number of words could be substituted for the word actually used without changing the structure. Such a substitution point, with the words which could be substituted there (as a class), is a tagmeme. From the Greek *tagmema*, a unit of arrangement.

TERMINAL STRING. In the theory of grammar known as GENERATIVE GRAMMAR (q.v.), a terminal string is defined as the last string of a terminated derivation, resulting from the successive application of instruction formulas to a finite set of initial strings.

TONE LANGUAGE. A language in which variation of tone in speech is significant for meaning. Thus, in Chinese, a syllable is two or more different words depending on the tone on which it is spoken.

UMLAUT. A change of the stem vowel in German nouns, generally to indicate the plural; also, the mark ·· which indicates this change. From the German *um*, around, and *laut*, sound, i.e., transformation of sound.

VOWEL HARMONY. In some languages the affixes and endings which can be added to roots have variable vowels, one or the other of which is used according to what the root vowel is, so that all the vowels in the word are of the same class (i.e. front or back, sometimes middle). Thus in Hungarian, *ember*, man, takes a plural suffix *-ek* (*emberek*), but the suffix for *ház*, house, is *-ak* (*házak*).

CHAPTER 18

That Man May Live

The Language of Medicine

DONALD G. COOLEY

Medical language is as old as Hippocrates and as new as Gemini and Apollo spacecraft. When doctors speak of *cranium*, *thorax*, and *pharynx*, they are using terms that were familiar to Hippocrates nearly 2,500 years ago. When we speak of "penicillin" and "antibiotic," we use terms that were coined within the last few years. Hippocrates would have been puzzled by *antibiotic*, which literally means "against life." He might have construed it to be some kind of device for killing, as, in a sense, it is. Antibiotics are highly selective toxins, deadly to disease germs but generally quite innocuous to patients who harbor them. Antibiotics are *against* the life of disease germs but *for* the life of the patient.

There were no antibiotics, nor any need of a word for them, a generation ago. With the development of penicillin, streptomycin, and other chemical substances of general safety to the patient but deadly to infection-causing bacteria, there arose a need for a descriptive word, and "antibiotic" entered our vocabularies and dictionaries. Tens and hundreds of new medical terms are coined as new discoveries and needs unfold, so that scientific language, which includes medical language, comprises the majority of words incorporated into new editions of dictionaries.

Along with medical advances and burgeoning terminology there has come increasing sophistication of the ordinary citizen. We see and hear hundreds of medical (and sometimes quasi-medical) words in newspaper stories, magazine articles, books, and radio and television programs. Programs about doctors are very popular and a good deal of information about disease, along with words of the profession, can be picked up from the portrayed travails of internes and nurses. Advertisers have been known to coin words for horrendous ailments they have a pill for, and to show ingenious animations of alarming physiological events, such as hammers pounding inside the skull, not known to occur in living persons. However, much of the educational material on health and medicine that reaches the public through physicians, public health officials, voluntary organizations, and professional science writers comes from highly responsible and authentic sources. Inevitably, many fairly difficult medical words filter into the common language. But not all physicians indulge in esoteric trade-talk all of the time.

Like the rest of us, physicians have more than one vocabulary: a speaking vocabulary and the vocabulary of the written word. There is also a reading vocabulary of words we recognize but rarely speak or write. The papers doctors write for each others' eyes in medical journals tend to be most generously larded with technical terms—a truism applicable to all occupations. There are at least two reasons for this. In the first place, specialized training gives rise to specialized knowledge and specialized terms to fit it. A man familiar with *canthook* and *peavy*

knows something about logging, a man familiar with
rongeur knows something about surgery. In the second
place, a technical word is often more precise, concise, specific. *Hysterectomy* is a more economical word than
"surgical removal of the uterus." To know the special
words of a vocation is not, to be sure, to be qualified to
practice it. But comprehension widens and insight deep-
ens with every new word we understand. This is strik-
ingly true of medical words which encompass all life
processes.

It would be a mistake to assume that medical language
is totally bereft of pithiness and simplicity. On the contrary, everyday medical English is full of sturdy Anglo-
Saxonisms: *gall, heart, lung, gut, knee, skull, skin, tooth,
tongue, throat, mouth.* These are so simple that we rarely
think of them as medical words unless, perhaps, we go to
a doctor complaining of a sore throat. The doctor probably calls it a sore throat too until he collects enough
cases to do a treatise on *pharyngitis. Pock,* meaning
"pustule," derives from Anglo-Saxon and leaves its imprint on the disease we know as "small" pox, originally to
distinguish it from the "great" pox, or syphilis. Anglo-
Saxon words are mostly limited to a relatively few terms
of anatomy and function, generally suspect of vulgarity or
at best of unseemliness. Another handicap is that every-
body understands Anglo-Saxon words; nothing need be
learned. A British gastroenterological journal is titled, simply, *Gut,* but *gut* and *belly* are widely considered to be
lowbrow. Many people erroneously use *stomach* as a
synonym for *belly,* or worse yet, bowdlerize *stomach*
into *tummy.* The best euphemism for delicate matters
of anatomy and physiology is a foreign language. As a
practical matter, understanding the majority of medical
terms is a matter of understanding words that have come

down to us, been modified, or coined from aristocratic
languages other than our own.

A fair estimate is that three-fourths of the words in
medical dictionaries derive from the Greek and the rest
from Latin. There are a few infusions from the Arabic
—*elixir, alkaloid,* and *alcohol,* for example. *Alcohol* derives from Arabic *al koh'l,* a fine powder. "Kohl" is still a
term for preparations used by Oriental women to darken
their eyelids. Its transformation into "alcohol," which is
hardly a powder, is an instance of changes that affect
words as they migrate through history. Some medical
words sojourned in France and acquired Gallic modifications. *Migraine,* the word for a splitting one-sided headache, is vaguely recognizable in the parent form, *hemi-
crania,* meaning "half skull." Eponyms which memorialize
the first describer of a disorder—Bright's disease, Addison's
disease, Graves' disease—are historically interesting but of
dwindling importance as medical terms. Descriptive,
rather than eponymic, labels take over as research dis-
closes the nature of disease. For instance, Bright's disease
is now usually referred to as *chronic nephritis.*

Although medical English contains its quota of mav-
erick words, almost all of its scientific terms have a Greco-
Roman heritage. This parallels the history of medicine.
Greek medicine was adopted and adapted by the Romans
who added Latin terms to professional vocabularies. For
a time after the decline of Rome, Arabian medicine made
great strides but we have relatively few Arabic terms to
remind us of it. The overwhelming predominance of
Greek and Latin in the medical language of Western civilizations was a fact in ancient times as it is today.

The oldest and least changed medical words tend to be
those concerned with anatomy. After all, a foot is a foot
and remains so in Anglo-Saxon, or as Latin *pes.* Many

words express a fancied resemblance of parts of the body to familiar objects. The *thyroid* gland which straddles the windpipe gets its name, which means "like a shield," from its resemblance to the armament of Homeric warriors. *Gland* derives from Latin *glans*, meaning "acorn"; with a little imagination, lymph nodes resemble acorns. Some terms express measurement. *Duodenum*, the word for the first part of the small intestine, means "twelve fingerbreadths long." The outlet of the stomach is surrounded by muscles which constrict or relax to retain or release stomach contents. This is appropriately called the *pylorus*, Greek for "keeper of the gate." Sounds, too, enter into medical nomenclature. The classic example is *borborygmus*, imitative of the sound of belly-rumbling or intestinal gurgling.

Most new medical words, except chemical terms which describe molecular structures, are coined from long-familiar Greek or Latin roots. The discovery of penicillin required that the drug be named. Inspiration came from the Latin *penicillus*, meaning paintbrush or pencil, descriptive of the mold which yields the drug. Occasionally, a newly minted word combines a Greek and Latin root in a miscegenation which exasperates classicists but almost nobody else.

Anyone equipped with a few dozen Greek and Latin roots can make a good show of translating unfamiliar medical words and with practice gain considerable expertise. One need not tangle with syntax, irregular verbs, or become a classical scholar. All that is necessary for a beginning is a vocabulary of basic root forms. If you know that *ortho* means "straight," and *pnea* means "breathing," you can infer that *orthopnea* means "straight breathing." You might not guess that orthopnea is a condition in which the patient breathes most comfortably when sitting straight or upright. It is always necessary to consult a dictionary for precise meanings. But, with root forms and a fair guess in mind, it is likely that a confirmed meaning will stick in your memory and you will never have to look up the word again.

This brief article cannot serve the purpose of a medical dictionary with many thousands of entries. However, it is possible to list some of the more important combining units so that many-jointed words can be dissected into their individual meanings.

WORD LIST

A- or **AN-**. Greek; without, lacking. An *afebrile* patient is one without fever. *Anesthesia* means without sensation (Greek *aisthesis*).

ANTI-. Greek; against. *Antihistamine* drugs are *against* histamine in that they deter its release from cells.

ADEN-. Greek; gland. *Adenoid* means like a gland.

-ALGIA. Greek; pain. From this we get *analgesia*, a condition of being without pain. The many *-algia* words locate the site of pain by their prefixes: nerves in *neuralgia*, ears in *otalgia*, etc.

ARTHR-. Greek; a joint. *Arthritis* is an inflamed joint.

BI-. Latin; or **DI-**. Greek; two, double. *Binaural* hearing requires two good ears.

BRADY-. Greek; slow. *Bradycardia* means slowness of the heart.

CARDIO-. Greek; heart. *Cardiac* has become part of the common language.

-CELE. Greek; a swelling. Indicates fluid accumulation or abnormal protrusion: *Hydrocele*, collection of fluid in the testicles; *rectocele,* hernial protrusion of part of the rectum.

CHOLE. Greek; bile. *Chole + cyst = cholecyst,* the gallbladder.

COSTAL. Latin; rib. *Intercostal* means between the ribs.

CRANIUM. Greek; skull. The combining form is *cranio-.* *Cranial* pertains to the skull.

CYST-. Greek; bladder. *Cystitis* is inflammation of the urinary bladder. However, the root word is not limited to that organ. Any normal or abnormal sac, especially one filled with a liquid or semisolid, is a cyst.

-CYT-. Greek; cell. *Erythrocytes* are red blood cells (Greek *erythros,* red).

DERM-. Greek; skin. The Latin word for skin, *cutis,* persists in "cuticle," but has almost lost the nomenclature battle. It is permissible to call a condition of inflamed skin *cutitis,* but all dermatologists (there are no cutologists) and most patients call it *dermatitis.*

DIA-. Greek; through. *Dia + rrhea = diarrhea,* a flowing through.

DUODENUM. Latin; *duodeni,* twelve. The first part of the small intestine, twelve fingerbreadths long.

DYS-. Greek; difficult, bad. *Dyspnea* is difficult breathing; *dysuria,* difficult urination; *dyspepsia,* difficult digestion.

-ECTOMY. Greek; cutting out. A very familiar suffix, as in *tonsillectomy.* Preceded by name of the organ that is surgically removed: *hysterectomy,* uterus; *pneumonectomy,* lung; *splenectomy,* spleen.

ENDO-. Greek; within. *Endocardium* is the lining membrane inside the heart.

Entero-. Greek; intestine. The province of *gastroenterology—gastro* (stomach) + *entero* (intestine) + *logy* (science).

Epi-. Greek; on, upon. An *epidemic* is upon the people.

Eu-. Greek; good, well. A *eupeptic* patient enjoys good digestion (Greek *pepsis*).

Gastro-. Greek; stomach.

Glossa. Greek; tongue. *Glossitis* bespeaks a sore tongue.

-gogue. *Greek;* eliciting, leading. An *emmenagogue* stimulates the menstrual discharge.

-gen. Greek; producing. A *goitrogen* is an agent that produces goiter.

-gnath. Greek; jaw. *Prognathous,* having abnormally projecting jaws.

Hepar. Greek; liver. *Hepatitis,* inflammation of the liver.

Hem-. Greek; blood. Prefix of scores of medical words associating blood with specific organs or conditions; e.g., *hematoma,* a blood-containing tumor or swelling. The *h* is sometimes missing as in *anemia,* literally "without blood." *Hemostatis,* halting the flow of blood from a wound.

Hyper-. Greek; over, above, beyond the ordinary. The prefix usually signifies excessive production or amount; e.g., *hypertension,* elevated blood pressure; *hyperacidity,* too much acid.

Hypo-. Greek; less, below. The two meanings, "underneath" and "less than," can be confusing. A *hypodermic* injection is given "under" the skin; *hypoglossal* means "under" the tongue. But a *hypothyroid* patient produces "less than" normal amounts of thyroid hormone. *Hypochondriac,* the word for a person morbidly anxious about his health, is puzzling until its history is considered. The word refers to rib cartilages (G *chondros*) "under" which lies the upper abdomen, anciently thought to be the seat of melancholy.

-ITIS. Greek; inflammation. *Tonsillitis, appendicitis, conjunctivitis,* and innumerable other *itises* make this inflammatory suffix familiar to all.

LEUKO-. Greek; white. *Leukocytes* are white blood cells.

MAMMA. Latin; MAST-. Greek; the breast. Applicable to both sexes. The Latin root is obvious in "mammal" and "mammary gland," but the Greek root is more common in medical words: *mastitis,* inflammation of the breast; *mastectomy,* excision of the breast.

MELANO-. Greek; black. *Melanocytes* are cells that produce pigments and give us freckles or a suntan.

MYO-. Greek, muscle. *Myalgia* is muscle pain.

NEPHRO-. Greek; REN-. Latin; kidney. Two word roots, perhaps appropriate to two kidneys. Doctors speak of *renal* disease and *adrenal* or *suprarenal* glands (on or above the kidney) but not of *renitis*. The word for inflammation of the kidney is *nephritis* and for the condition of having kidney stones, *nephrolithiasis* (Greek *lithos,* stone).

NEURO-. Greek; nerve.

OCULUS. Latin; OPHTHALMO-. or OPT-. Greek; eye. An *oculist* or *ophthalmologist* is a physician who specializes in diseases of the eyes. *Ophthalmology* is the science of the eye, and an *optician* makes *optical* goods.

ODONT-. Greek; tooth. It is perfectly correct to call a dentist an *odontologist*. It will surprise him. Among other things, he deals with *periodontal* structures (surrounding a tooth).

-OID. Greek; like, resemblance. *Eunuchoid,* like a eunuch. *Typhoid* was so named for its resemblance to typhus.

OLIGO-. Greek; scanty, few. *Oligospermia* signifies scarcity of spermatozoa in semen.

-OMA. Greek; tumor or swelling. The suffix does not necessarily signify a malignant tumor.

ORTHO-. Greek; straight. *Orthodontists* straighten teeth. The prefix also indicates "correctness."

-OSIS. Greek; a chronic condition. *Tuberculosis* is a condition of tubercle formation; acidosis; diverticulosis.

OSTEO-. Greek; bone. *Periosteum* is the membrane surrounding bone surfaces.

-OSTOMY. Greek; *stoma,* mouth. Indicates the making of a "mouth" or opening, as in *colostomy,* the formation of an artificial anus in the abdominal wall.

OTO-. Greek; ear. *Otitis media* means inflammation of the middle ear.

-OTOMY. Greek; a cutting. Not to be confused with *-ostomy.* The suffix indicates that an incision was made, as in *laparotomy,* incision through the abdominal wall, or *phlebotomy,* incision of a vein (Greek *phelps*).

PARA-. Greek; beside. *Parathyroid* glands lie beside the larger thyroid.

PATHO-. Greek; feeling, suffering. *Pathology* = suffering or disease + *logos,* science or study.

-PENIA. Greek, poverty. Denotes scarcity or starvation; e.g., *leukopenia,* reduction in number of white blood cells.

PEPSIS. Greek; digestion. *Dyspepsia,* meaning "difficult digestion," is outmoded among doctors, who seek a specific lesion such as *peptic* ulcer.

Peri-. Greek; around. This prefix appears in scores of medical words, such as *pericardium,* tissue which encloses the heart.

Paid-. Greek; child. Commonly *ped-,* as in *pediatrics.* Can be confused with the Latin word for "foot."

Pharynx. Greek; throat. The "x" turns to "g" in combining forms; e.g., pharyngeal; also **Larynx**—*laryngeal* or *laryngal.*

-plasty. Greek; to form. Hence, "plastic" surgery. The name of an organ followed by *-plasty* tells what is given form. Surgical molding of the nose is *rhinoplasty.*

Procto-. Greek; anus. *Proctitis,* inflammation of the rectum.

Pulmo-. Latin; **Pneumo-.** Greek; lung. Custom dictates which root is used in word constructions. Patients may have *pneumonia* but they do not have *pulmonia* although they do have *pulmonary* disease.

Rhino-. Greek; nose. *Rhinorrhea,* sometimes obviously, is a flowing from the nose.

-rhagia. Greek; a breaking forth. The familiar word *hemorrhage* means a burst of blood.

-rhoea. Greek; to flow. The meaning is obvious in *diarrhea,* less so in *catarrh,* copious flow from a mucous surface.

Sclero-. Greek; hard. *Arteriosclerosis* is a concise word for the condition of hardening of the arteries. *Scleroderma* means "hard skin." The tough supporting tunic of the eyeball ("white of the eye") is called the *sclera;* some medical words refer to this specific tissue.

Soma. Greek; the body. *Psychosomatic,* involving both mind and body.

Stoma. Greek; the mouth. *Stomatitis,* inflammation of the mouth.

Thrombo-. Greek; a clot. *Thrombosis* is a condition of clot formation.

Tachy-. Greek; fast. *Tachycardia* means rapid heartbeat.

-ur-. Greek *ouron,* urine. Appears in many words: *uremia,* presence of urinary constituents in the blood; *hematuria,* blood in the urine; *diuresis,* increased secretion of urine.

Of course hundreds of medical words contain elements other than those listed. Nevertheless, a brief list gives some useful tools for breaking down formidable words into their components. For instance, *cholecystogastrostomy* is a real jawbreaker. But break it into its components: *chole* (bile) + *cyst* (bladder) + *gastr-* (stomach) + *ostomy* (to make a mouth); thus, forming a communication between gallbladder and stomach. Greek and Latin roots are so abundant in English that the common language and medical language illuminate each other in many ways. *Oliguria* means "scanty urine." The same root in *oligarchy* gives us "government by a few." *Sympathy* is *syn* (with) + *pathos* (suffering), an everyday word for suffering together. Is a *pedagogue* a schoolmaster? Literally, he leads children: *ped* (child) + *gogue* (eliciting, leading). And what of the anatomy of *melancholy?* Etymologically, it is *melan* (black) + *chole* (bile). Anciently, a melancholy person was thought to suffer from an excess of black bile.

Medicine has its share of phrases which may qualify as jargon but are more like a form of verbal shorthand. G. I., as in *G. I. Series,* is short for "gastrointestinal tract," as *G. U.* is short for "genitourinary." A *BMR* (basal metabolic rate) is a breathing test for diagnosis of thyroid diseases. *D&C* is dilation and curettage, a scraping of the interior of the cavity of the uterus. An *ECG* is an electrocardiogram, a "writing" of electrical activities of the heart. A *Pap smear* abbreviates the name of Dr. George Papanicolaou who developed cytological (cell science) techniques of screening for the presence of cancer cells in body fluids "smeared" on glass plates for examination under a microscope.

Doctors are sometimes charged with using highly technical language to keep their arts secret and hide the truth from the patient. But most doctors, in explaining matters to intelligent patients, use simple language. Ordinary English is itself a rich medical language, not to be scorned. Any medical word can be translated into plain English. But often it takes many more words to do so, not to say effort. Technical medical words are not used for purposes of secrecy, but for precise professional communication. In them is wrapped the fascinating history of medicine (Anglo-Saxon: *leechcraft*).

CHAPTER 19

Water, Fire, the Wheel, and Now....

The Language of Computers

CHARLES A. VELDON

The field of computer science has been plagued with ambiguous words, misconstrued terminology, or downright conjecture. The flood of written material in the daily presses and magazines has not only done little to dispel this erroneous picture but has served to solidify it. Cartoons, automation "terror" articles in magazines, and union fights against computer-directed operations have all introduced us to a new science in a superficial and confusing manner, and have led the public to assume a simple definition for a given word or thing. Even the interested and affected reader is often misled and makes assumptions which he later finds incorrect. Such failings are the natural result of incomplete knowledge.

When the public was first introduced to a large-scale electronic computer via television in the 1952 presidential election, an "electronic brain" was being used to compile the returns. As a result of such a performance, a machine with blinking lights and the capacity to calculate became a *UNIVAC* to the viewing public. Thus the confusion began and has been perpetuated so that the terms *UNIVAC*, *electronic brain,* and *computer* are now believed inter-changeable. This is one of many examples of erroneous definitions, and in order to appreciate fully the signifi-cance of the vast data-processing industry, it is important to know the real significance of the words.

While automation by computers evolved as a solution for producing faster information to help conduct ballistic experiments during World War II and whittle down the ever higher mountains of records accumulating in govern-ment and business, it is now used to run production plants as well as to save time, effort, and money for the average person whose life is becoming more and more enmeshed in a complex world. Yet one who has had little or no oppor-tunity to become familiar with computers and their appli-cations usually believes that knowledge of these electronic wonders is restricted to the federal government and the industrial and commercial firms directly served by them.

The first all-electronic computer, *ENIAC,* was built by the University of Pennsylvania in 1946. It was an electric culmination of advances upon the mechanical computing devices invented by many of the famous math-ematicians of the seventeenth century. From here the variation and function of electronic computers rapidly spread, as more and more manufacturers entered the de-velopment field to meet the demand for their production and myriad uses.

There are two basic types of computers—analog and dig-ital. *Analog computers,* which evolved first, measure phys-ical magnitudes such as pressures, temperatures, voltages, etc., and in turn report or transmit adjustments. Obvi-ously, they are most applicable to engineering and process control problems. The *digital computer* creates a numeric analogy of the problem such as formulae and accounting procedures, receives data represented as numbers, and outputs information as numbers. Digital computers are actually automatic adding machines with the additional ability to change the calculating sequence by recognizing certain decisions, such as numbers being odd or even, greater than, less than, or equal to zero.

Since electronic computers were first used in scientific and engineering computation, solving primarily mathematical problems, many of the terms came from this mathematical background. Another source was the subject of translation of directions from the human to the machine. Translation meant language, and language meant words. Now the definition of a *computer word* is "an ordered set of characters which is treated as a unit in processing," versus the definition we know of a *word* in any language being "a sound or a combination of sounds, or its written or printed representation, used in any language as the sign of a conception." In addition, when translating computer programs from the programmer's language to machine language, an internal dictionary is first created, and the computer then proceeds with the language conversion based upon a fixed list of vocabulary with a prescribed set of grammatical rules.

So we see that a concise language is important as a means of more rapidly translating human endeavor into a recognizable form for both human and machine. Such languages were called *software* by some anonymous electronic computer manufacturer, programmer, or user. *Software* was defined as anything and everything related to an electronic computer that is not present in *hardware*, which is considered the actual equipment and associated data processing machines. So *software* was adopted as the converse of *hardware* and became an elastic term.

In order to better comprehend some of the mystery behind the terminology associated with these machines, one must understand how they function by tracing through a problem as processed by a digital computer. Initially all program instructions are entered on standard punched cards whose size is said to be that of the old dollar bill, supposedly set for banking purposes. Here information is recorded as small rectangular or round holes punched in specific locations. These holes are electrically sensed during the reading process, automatically converted to an electronic language, and entered into the machine. In most large computer centers these card images are first written on a magnetic tape in the form of magnetized spots. This process, called a *card-to-tape*, is handled by a small computer, and is done not only because the data on a magnetic tape can be read into storage 50 to 75 times as fast as punched cards, but because of the ease with which the tape can be handled along with its tremendous storage capacity. A reel of tape one half inch wide and 2400 feet long weighs four pounds and can contain data equivalent to 200,000 fully punched cards. To protect the data on the tape from being written over accidentally, there is a removable plastic ring on the back of the tape called a *file protection device*, which is removed as a safety measure during computer processing.

This input tape is attached to one of the tape drives of a larger computer system and read into core storage. Storage can be made up of magnetic cores, which are small rings of ferromagnetic material. These cores are strung on a grid of fine wires, and when some are magnetized in one direction and some in the other, they represent items of information which can be made ready for processing in a few millionths of a second. This restricted ability of being magnetized in only one direction has dictated the computer's internal language called the *binary mode*. This binary mode of operation of the components provides signals to the computer, just as the presence or absence of light from an electric light bulb tells a person it is either on or off. Hence we see that the binary system of notation can only use two symbols, zero or one, to represent all quantities, and therefore we say it has a base two. These symbols, 1 and 0, are commonly called *bits*, from the contraction of *b*inary dig*it*. The 1 is designated a *bit*, and the 0 is designated a *no bit*. The *octal* or base 8 system is a sort of shorthand method for grouping three binary bits to form an *octal digit*, and programmers find it a convenient way to handle binary conversions into our decimal, or base 10 system.

While this binary system seems restricted to numbers, it is not. A code, or method of representing numeric as well as alphabetic characters, was devised and standardized by the computer manufacturers. This is called the *Standard BCD* (Binary Coded Decimal) *Interchange Code* and consists of 64 different bit combinations to provide 69 different characters. As the input is read into storage, addresses are assigned to each word, or piece of information. Storage is arranged somewhat like a group of numbered mailboxes in a post office, where each box is identified and located by its number or address. Once all the input is in storage, the CPU (Central Processing Unit) takes control and supervises the entire computer system performing the actual arithmetic and logical operations on data. Assisting the CPU are registers capable of receiving information, holding it, and transferring it as directed by control circuits.

The *output*, or results generated by the computer, is written on another magnetic tape, printed on a printing device called an *on-line*, or punched into cards. In most cases the output is written on magnetic tape, and this tape is printed using a smaller computer system to convert the tape symbols to numbers and letters.

Underlying all this processing is the human, guiding and controlling the flow of information into, through, and out of the computer by means of a plan called a *program*. Once a problem is defined, an *analyst* breaks down the steps that must be followed and constructs a system *flow chart* showing what job is to be done from the viewpoint of the data processing equipment, and then makes a program flow chart to show how it is to be done by pointing out the detailed decisions and operations to be performed. The programmer uses this program flow chart during the coding of the program as a guide to the sequence in which logical and arithmetic operations occur, as well as the relationship of one portion of a program to another. Programming is not simply a coding task. It involves many different jobs such as taking care of the *housekeeping* or allocation of storage locations to data, instructions, etc.; setting up a system of handling tables, files, along with the plan for editing input data; specifying operator and error messages; deciding upon the best mathematical technique of handling the processing of data; and outputting the results in a clear manner so that they are usable by the people responsible for their application. The programming language may take the form of convenient equivalents of machine instructions called *mnemonics* having symbols such as ADD for add, SUB for subtract, DIV for divide, etc. The computer, using a previously written language program called a *processor*, translates these mnemonics into equivalent machine instructions in the binary mode, its own internal language.

While the program written by the programmer is called the *source program*, the translated machine language program is called the *object program*. In essence, the programmer produces the cards for the human part of the program and checks their punching veracity on a listing, while the machine produces a deck of cards in binary and edits the human endeavor by giving out *diagnostics,* or error messages, that disclose human errors made in the source program which are unacceptable to its internal processing system. This translation process is done when a source deck is entered into a computer for translation into machine language during the *assembly* or *compiler* stage. After the program has been assembled properly and the obvious bugs have been worked out by the programmer (based on the diagnostics), the program is ready to be executed to obtain output.

Analog computers also require a program to instruct the computer to take certain readings from machinery in a processing plant and to react according to the logic as prescribed by the flow chart. The output in this case is a direction to close or open valves, adjust the rate of flow of fluids, voltage, etc., or print out a message to the console operator to perform a certain action based upon the disclosed results. Both analog and digital computers can operate on problems in *real time,* that is, making instantaneous decisions and executing them in a fixed period of critical time to prevent a delay or interruption to the process or guidance of an aircraft or astronaut.

WORD LIST

ADDRESS. A number, label, or name which defines or identifies, for the computer, a specific location in its memory where information is stored.

ALPHAMERIC. Characters which may be letters of the alphabet, numerals, or special symbols that are recognized by a computer.

ALPHANUMERIC. See **ALPHAMERIC.**

ANALYST. A person who can define and break down problems into an orderly set of routines which can then be processed through a computer for solution.

ASSEMBLY PROGRAM. A computer routine which translates a source language program from mnemonics into machine language, i.e., substitutes binary coding for symbolic instructions and may assign storage locations.

BASE. A unique quantity that is the total number of distinct integers that define a number system. For example, in the decimal system the base, or radix, is 10, i.e., it uses 10 symbols. The binary notation uses 2 symbols— 0 and 1. For a full explanation of binary numbers, see chapter on Electronics.

BIT. A contraction of *b*inary dig*it*. A binary digit is either 1 or 0.

BLOCK. A packaged grouping of words or records which is handled as a unit.

BUFFER. An intermediary device which collects and transfers data between the I/O (Input/Output) units and core storage, devised to compensate for the variance of transmission speeds between units.

BURST. To separate along the perforated lines each individual sheet of printed output.

CARD COLUMN. A punching field which is a vertical line on a standard input card.

CARD FIELD. Consecutive columns on an input card, or input form, which contain a specific piece of information.

CARD-TO-TAPE. The process of transcribing the information on punched cards to a magnetic tape.

CHANNEL. A circuit path in computers along which input or output information flows.

CHECK-OUT. The same as debugging, i.e., the testing of a finished program to determine its veracity under all possible combinations of input data.

COBOL. *CO*mmon *B*usiness *O*rientated *L*anguage, which makes use of English language statements and is used mostly for commercial, or business, applications.

CODE. A series of symbols which represent a language acceptable to both the programmer and computer.

COMPILER. A program which will translate a source program in a MACRO (q.v.) language, such as COBOL or FORTRAN (q.q.v.), into mnemonics and, in turn, equivalent machine language.

COMPUTER. A device capable of performing calculations or carrying out transformations of information by means of internally stored instructions and outputting these results.

CONSOLE. A unit of the data processing or computer equipment which contains the button lights indicating the internal operations and which is the operator's external control over the computer operation.

CONTROL PANEL. A circuit assembly wired in a fixed manner on a panel board which is inserted into a computer unit to interpret, direct, and execute a standard program.

DATA. A collection of facts, such as numeric, alphabetic, or analog values, which is processed by a computer. The word is used either singularly or plurally in the field of automation.

DATA PROCESSING. A general term used to describe all computer operations on business or commercial data.

DEBUG. To locate, correct, and remove any errors in a computer program, or routine, as well as in the computer itself.

DENSITY. The number of magnetic bits stored on a linear inch of magnetic tape.

DIAGNOSTIC. A message output by the compiler or processor, indicating an error in a program.

DICTIONARY. An internal list of mnemonic code names along with the stored addresses and cross-references created by a compiler or processor for each individual program.

DISCLAIMER. A statement, rubber stamped on the program write-up, stating that the originator of a program has subjected it to an intensive checkout, but it may contain errors which he did not discover and, henceforth, he is not responsible for errors incurred by users.

DUPLICATE. To punch an exact reproduction of an original punched deck of cards.

DUMMY. A repeatedly used storage word which is tagged for multiple usage for varying bits of information during the execution of a program.

DUMP. The data included in, and the printing of, the contents of the entire core storage area along with information in selected registers.

EDIT. Checking data for unwanted symbols, correct magnitude and proper format, as well as rearranging blocks of data for ease of processing and transmission.

EDP. Electronic Data Processing, or the abbreviation describing processing of data by electronic means via a computer.

ERASE. Removal of information stored on a magnetic tape, or clearing out information within a computer by making all bits equal to zero.

EXECUTE. To perform to completion the logical steps dictated by a program or an instruction.

FILE. An organized collection of records, usually referring to information written on a magnetic tape.

FLOATING POINT. An arithmetic system in which a numerical quantity is represented by a number multiplied by a power of the number base.

FLOW CHART. A line diagram or outline using standard blocked figures with brief verbal descriptions to represent the logical steps involved to produce the completed computer program.

FORMAT. A fixed order or arrangement of input or output data, as well as interpretation of internally handled numbers or symbols.

FORTRAN. *FOR*mula *TRAN*slation. A macro language used primarily for programming scientific problems.

GARBAGE. Undecipherable or meaningless information produced or included in computer output or retained within the computer memory.

HANDS ON. A term used when a programmer or analyst is present and immediately involved with processing a program on the computer system.

HOUSEKEEPING. The programmer's or compiler's task of setting up storage areas, constants, buffer areas, etc., prior to execution of a program.

INTERPRET. To print on the top of a punched card the symbols which the punched holes represent.

KEY PUNCH. A typewriter machine which punches holes representing data into a standard computer input card.

LIBRARY. A standard group of programs and subroutines which can be incorporated into new routines, and usually are contained as part of a compiler program.

LIST. To print, by means of a data processing machine, the information punched on a deck of program cards.

LOOP. A sequential series of programmed instructions that is repeated through a number of iterations either planned through programming or erroneously encountered.

MACRO. A programming word that is translated by a compiler to generate a series of mnemonics and machine instructions.

MEMORY. The internal storage capacity of a computer.

MICR. *M*agnetic *I*nk *C*haracter *R*ecognition. A system used primarily in banks whereby special properties of the ink printed on documents, such as checking account numbers, can be given small charges of electricity which are recognized by data processing equipment.

OBJECT PROGRAM. A program which is a translation of a source program into the language of the computer used to process the basic program.

OCTAL. A number system founded on base, or radix, eight. Useful as a shorthand notation of binary numbers, where groups of three binary numbers are interpreted as base eight, or octal.

ONLINE. Reference to an operating function, such as input or output, of or on the main frame computer.

ORIGIN. The fixed address in storage where a program or block of data begins or is referred.

OUTPUT. Internally processed data which is sent out from the computer, or the act of extracting data from the central processor.

Overflow. To produce more digits than a register is capable of indicating; also the number of digits exceeding a register's capacity.

Pack. To include several pieces of data in one computer word.

Patch. A group of instructions inserted into a program to modify the routine or correct an error.

Processor. A program, or piece of data processing equipment, which translates, compiles, or assembles a source program into machine language, or the desired object program.

Programmer. A person who prepares programs for translation by the computer.

Radix. See **Base.**

Raw Data. Input information which must be processed by a computer to arrange it in a fixed order so that it can be handled by a program.

Reader, Card. A piece of data processing equipment which converts the holes in a punched card into electrical pulses which, in turn, are fed into a computer.

Real-Time. The processing time required to permit effective control of an action as it occurs, without seriously interrupting the continuous flow of the operation under computer direction.

Record. A unit of data which is considered an entity in data processing and is considered a separate subdivison of a file.

Redundancy Check. A system of checking the number of binary bits (or ones) in a coded character or piece of data, either on magnetic tape or a punched card.

Run. The actual processing of an operating program on a computer.

Set-Up. The procedure involved in readying a computer for processing a program, such as mounting magnetic tapes, loading the card hoppers, etc.

Shot. A scheduled period of time during which a person has access to a computer to process his program.

Simulator. A routine which translates or represents a program written for one computer so that it can be executed and processed on another computer.

Sophisticated Routine. An intricate series of programmed instructions that perform calculations in an absolute minimum of time, as well as showing a high degree of programming proficiency.

Source Program. A program written in an artificial language, i.e., a language other than machine language which must be input to a processor for machine language translation.

Storage. Magnetic tape, drums, discs, cards, etc., attached to a computer where units of information can be entered and held until retrieved at a later time.

Sub-Routine. A group of program instructions which perform a fixed operation, such as extracting a square root, that can be referred to repeatedly throughout a main program or routine.

Symbolic Language. A system of mnemonics which represents a form of language which facilitates the programmer's translation from human to machine language.

Tape Drive. A piece of data-processing equipment connected to a computer which has the facility of reading or writing data on a magnetic tape.

Trap. An interruption in a computer program indicating

the attempt to process some impossible mathematical procedure such as dividing by zero.

UNIVAC. A name given to one of a series of computers developed by the Sperry-Rand Corporation. From *UNI-Versal Automatic Computer.*

VERIFIER. A key-punch type machine which is used to check the original punched data on a card. This is accomplished when the key punch operator inserts the punched cards in a verifying machine hopper and retypes the same symbols. When the sensed holes in the card differ from the correct value, a light goes on, and the card is rejected for repunching. Correctly punched cards get a notch on the side to indicate verification.

WORD. A group of characters within a computer which are contained in one storage location or address.

WRITE-UP. Documentation of a computer program explaining its function, as well as its logical construction.

CHAPTER 20

Outside Our World
The Language of Space Research
JULIE ANN FARRER

Much of the vocabulary of space and space exploration is understandably of very recent vintage because of the tremendous advances made almost daily in the field. Here, perhaps more than in any other area at the present time, one is able to watch the English language actually in the process of dramatic growth and change. A language which has taken centuries to evolve into its present usage, with comparatively few modifications from generation to generation, is suddenly experiencing dynamic expansion. Each impressive launch of a new space vehicle brings literally dozens of new terms into the language. But the vocabulary of space is unlike that of most fields where "shop talk" is only understood by those associated with it. Aerospace advances are given detailed coverage by mass communication, and the result is that atmospheric drag, perigee, and escape velocity are now becoming part of the layman's conversation.

The coining of new terms in any field is likely to be the result of shortened descriptions for a particular process, experience, device, etc., and the same holds true for the

new terminology in space exploration. However, many of
the new terms, and especially proper names in the area,
have far deeper roots. Classical mythology accounts for
most of the names of the various space projects, the individual vehicles, and some of the major component parts.
The classical languages also contribute many prefixes and
root words to the field. This influence probably stems
from the heavy reliance upon Greek and Latin for the vocabularies of both astronomy and mathematics. A large
percentage of space terminology comes from words already in the language, but for the new field they are given
new and sometimes unrelated meanings. The majority of
the words, however, are products of twentieth-century
America. Some are humorous, some descriptive, and all
are necessary and useful.

The goal of the glossary section of this particular chapter is to give the reader a more complete knowledge of
the vocabulary of the field, without losing him in the involved scientific formulas and without needlessly repeating widely known terms. Thus, most of all, it is hoped the
glossary will prove useful and valuable to any reader.

WORD LIST

ABLATION. The elimination of excess heat from a vital
part through its absorption by a less important part.

ABSOLUTE ALTITUDE. Altitude above the actual surface of
a planet or natural satellite, either land or water.

ABSOLUTE ZERO. The theoretical temperature at which all
molecular motion ceases; also expressed as $0°$ Kelvin,
equal to about $-273.16°$ Centrigrade or $-459.7°$ Fahren-
heit.

ACQUISITION. 1. The process of locating the orbit of a

satellite so that tracking data can be gathered. 2. The process of pointing an antenna or telescope to allow gathering of tracking data from a satellite or space probe.

AEROBIOLOGY. The study of the distribution of living organisms which are freely suspended in the atmosphere.

AERONOMY. 1. The study of the upper regions of the atmosphere where physical and chemical reactions due to solar radiation take place. 2. Science dealing with theories of planetary atmospheres.

AEROPAUSE. A region of indeterminate limits in the upper atmosphere, considered as a boundary between the denser portion of the atmosphere and space. From a functional point of view, it is that region in which the atmosphere is so tenuous as to have a negligible, or almost negligible, effect on men and aircraft, and in which the physiological requirements of man become increasingly important in the design of aircraft and equipment.

AEROTHERMODYNAMIC BORDER. An altitude at about 100 miles, above which the atmosphere is so rarefied that the motion of an object through it at high speeds generates no significant surface heat.

AFTERBODY. 1. A companion body that trails a satellite. 2. A section or piece of a rocket or missile that reenters the atmosphere unprotected behind the nose cone or other body that is protected for reentry. 3. The aft part of a vehicle.

AIRGLOW. The quasi-steady radiant emission from the upper atmosphere as distinguished from the sporadic emission of the aurorae.

AIR SHOWER or **CASCADE SHOWER.** A grouping of cosmic-ray particles observed in the atmosphere.

AIR SOUNDING. The act of determining atmospheric conditions by means of apparatus carried by balloons or rockets.

AMBIENT. Pertaining to the environment about a flying aircraft or other body but undisturbed or unaffected by it, as in "ambient air," or "ambient temperature."

ANGSTROM. (Å). A unit of length, used chiefly in expressing short wavelengths. Ten billion angstroms equal one meter.

ANOXIA. A complete lack of oxygen available for physiological use within the body. Compare HYPOXIA.

ANTIGRAVITY. A hypothetical effect that would arise from some energy field's cancellation of the effect of the gravitational field of the earth or other body.

APHELION. That orbital point farthest from the sun when the sun is the center of attraction. See PERIHELION.

APOGEE. In an orbit about the earth, the point at which the satellite is farthest from the earth; the highest altitude reached by a sounding rocket. See PERIGEE.

ASTROBALLISTICS. The study of the phenomena arising out of the motion of a solid through a gas at speeds high enough to cause ablation; for example, the interaction of a meteoroid with the atmosphere.

ASTROBIOLOGY. The study of living organisms on celestial bodies other than the earth.

ATMOSPHERIC DRAG. The retarding force produced on a satellite by its passage through the gas of the high atmosphere.

ATTITUDE. The position of an aircraft, spacecraft, etc., as determined by the relationship between its axis and some reference line or plane such as the horizon.

BIRD. A colloquial term for a rocket, satellite, or spacecraft.

BLACK BODY. A hypothetical "body" which absorbs all of the electromagnetic radiation striking it; that is, one which neither reflects nor transmits any of the radiation. No actual substance behaves as a true black body, although platinum black and other soots rather closely approximate this ideal.

BLACK BOX. Colloquially, any unit, usually an electronic device such as an amplifier, which can be mounted in a rocket, spacecraft, or the like, as a single package.

BREAKOFF PHENOMENON. The feeling which sometimes occurs during high-altitude flight of being totally separated and detached from the earth and human society. Also called the "breakaway phenomenon."

CHEMICAL ROCKET. A rocket using chemical fuel, fuel which requires an oxidizer for combustion, such as liquid or solid rocket fuel.

CHEMOSPHERE. The vaguely defined region of the upper atmosphere in which photochemical reactions take place. It is generally considered to include the stratosphere (or the top thereof) and the mesosphere, and sometimes the lower part of the thermosphere.

CHROMOSPHERE. A thin layer of relatively transparent gases above the photosphere of the sun. It is most easily observed during a total solar eclipse.

CISLUNAR. Pertaining to projects or activity in space between the earth and the moon, or between the earth and the moon's orbit. Latin, *cis*, on this side.

CLOSED ECOLOGICAL SYSTEM. A system that provides for the maintenance of life in an isolated living chamber such as a spacecraft cabin by means of a cycle wherein exhaled carbon dioxide, urine, and other waste matter are converted chemically or by photosynthesis into oxygen, water, and food.

Console. An array of controls and indicators for the monitoring and control of a particular sequence of actions, as in the checkout of a rocket, a countdown action, or a launch procedure. A console is usually designed around desklike arrays. It permits the operator to monitor and control different activating instruments, data recording instruments, or event sequencers.

Data Reduction. Transformation of observed values into useful, ordered, or simplified information.

Debug. 1. To isolate and remove malfunctions from a device, or mistakes from a computer routine. 2. Specifically, in electronic manufacturing, to operate equipment under specified environmental conditions in order to eliminate failures.

Destruct. The deliberate action of destroying a rocket vehicle after it has been launched, but before it has completed its course. Destructs are executed when the rocket gets off its plotted course or functions in a way so as to become a hazard.

Drogue Parachute. A type of parachute attached to a body, used to slow it down; also called "deceleration parachute," or "drag parachute."

Ecological System. A habitable environment, either created artificially or occurring naturally, in which man, animals, or other organisms can live in mutual relationship with each other.

Effective Atmosphere. That part of the atmosphere which effectively influences a particular process or motion, its outer limits varying according to the terms of the process or motion considered. Also called "sensible atmosphere."

ESCAPE VELOCITY. The radial speed which a particle or larger body must attain in order to escape from the gravitational field of a planet or star.

EXOBIOLOGY. The study of living organisms existing on celestial bodies other than the earth.

EXOSPHERE. The outermost or topmost portion of the atmosphere.

EXPLOSIVE BOLT. A bolt incorporating an explosive which can be detonated on command, thus destroying the bolt. Explosive bolts are used, for example, in separating a satellite from a rocket.

EYEBALLS IN, EYEBALLS OUT. Terminology used by test pilots to describe the acceleration experienced by the person being accelerated. Thus the acceleration experience by an astronaut at lift-off is "eyeballs in" and the experience when retrorockets fire is "eyeballs out."

FIXED SATELLITE. An earth satellite that orbits from west to east at such a speed as to remain constantly over a given place on the earth's equator.

FREE FALL. 1. The fall or drop of a body, such as a rocket not guided, nor under thrust, nor retarded by a parachute or other braking device. 2. Weightlessness.

G or G. An acceleration equal to the acceleration of gravity, approximately 32.2 feet per second at sea level; used as a unit of stress measurement for bodies undergoing acceleration.

GARBAGE. Miscellaneous objects in orbit, usually material ejected or broken away from a launch vehicle or satellite.

GENERATION. In any technical development, a period that is marked by features not existent in a previous period of development, as in "second-generation rocket."

Geo-. A prefix meaning "earth," as in "geology," "geophysics."

Giga-. A prefix meaning multiplied by one billion.

G-Tolerance. A tolerance of a person or other animal, or piece of equipment, to an acceleration of a particular speed.

Gyro. A device which utilizes the angular momentum of a spinning rotor to sense angular motion of its base about one or two axes at right angles to the spin axis. Also called "gyroscope." From Greek *gyros* meaning circle.

Hardness. Of X-rays and other radiation of high energy which will penetrate a 10-centimeter thickness of lead. Compare Soft Radiation.

Heterosphere. The upper portion of a two-part division of the atmosphere according to the general homogeneity of atmospheric composition; the layer above the homosphere. The heterosphere is characterized by variation in composition, and mean molecular weight of constituent gases. This region starts at 49 to 63 miles above the earth.

Homosphere. The portion of the two-part division of the atmosphere opposed to the heterosphere. The region in which there is no gross change in atmospheric composition. It includes all the atmosphere from the earth's surface to about 49 to 63 mi. and includes the troposphere, stratosphere, mesosphere, ozonosphere, and part of the chemosphere.

Hot Test. A propulsion system test conducted by actually firing the propellants.

Hypoxia. Oxygen deficiency in the blood, cells, or tissues of the body in such degree as to cause psychological and physiological disturbances.

IMPACT BAG. An inflatable bag attached to a spacecraft or reentry capsule to absorb part of the shock of landing.

INERTIAL GUIDANCE. Guidance by means of acceleration measured within the craft.

IONOSPHERE. The atmospheric layer above the MESOSPHERE (q.v.).

LAUNCH WINDOW. An interval of time during which a rocket can be launched to accomplish a particular purpose, as "lift-off occurred 5 minutes after the beginning of the 82-minute launch window."

LOX. 1. Liquid oxygen. Used attributively as in "lox tank," "lox unit." Also called "loxygen." 2. To load the fuel tanks of a rocket vehicle with liquid oxygen. Hence, "loxing." Opposed to "gox" or gaseous oxygen.

MACH NUMBER. A number expressing the ratio of speed of a body with respect to the surrounding air or other fluid, or the speed of a flow, to the speed of sound in the medium; the speed represented by this number. If the Mach number is less than one the flow is called "subsonic," and if the Mach number is greater than one the flow is called "supersonic." After Ernst Mach, 1838-1916, Austrian scientist.

MAGNETIC STORM. A world-wide disturbance of the earth's magnetic field. Magnetic storms are frequently characterized by a sudden onset in which the magnetic field undergoes marked changes in the course of an hour or less, followed by a very gradual return to normality which may take several days. Magnetic storms are caused by solar disturbances, though the exact nature of the link between the solar and terrestrial disturbances is not understood. Sometimes a magnetic storm can be linked to a particular solar disturbance. In these cases, the time between solar flare and onset of the magnetic storm is about one or two days, suggesting that the disturbance is carried to the earth by a cloud of particles thrown out by the sun.

MAIN STAGE. 1. In a multistage rocket, the stage that develops the greatest amount of thrust. 2. In a single-stage rocket vehicle, powered by one or more engines, the period when full thrust is attained. 3. A sustainer engine, considered as a stage after booster engines have fallen away.

MEGA-. A prefix meaning multiplied by one million as in "megacycles."

MEMORY. The component of a computer, control system, etc., designed to provide ready access to data or instructions previously recorded so as to make them bear upon an immediate problem, such as the guidance of a physical object, or the analysis and reduction of data.

MESOSPHERE. A layer of atmosphere between the STRATOSPHERE and the IONOSPHERE (q.q.v.). The mesosphere begins about 50 miles above the earth.

METEOROLOGICAL ROCKET. A rocket designed primarily for routine upper-air observation (as opposed to research) in the lower 250,000 feet of the atmosphere, especially that portion inaccessible to balloons, which is above 100,000 feet. Also called "rocketsonde." Compare RADIOSONDE.

MICRO-. 1. A prefix meaning divided by one million. 2. A prefix meaning very small, as in micrometeorite.

MODULE. 1. A self-contained unit of a launch vehicle or spacecraft which serves as a building block for the overall structure. The module is usually designated by its primary function as "command module," "lunar landing module," etc. 2. A one-package assembly of functionally associated electronic parts; usually a plug-in unit.

NEUTROSPHERE. The atmospheric shell from the earth's surface upward in which the atmospheric constituents are for the most part electrically neutral.

NOISE. Any undesired sound; any unwanted disturbance within a useful frequency band, such as undesired electric waves in a transmission channel or device. When caused by natural electrical discharges in the atmosphere noise may be called "static." If ambiguity exists as to the nature of the noise, a phrase such as "acoustic noise" or "electric noise" should be used.

OCCULTATION. The disappearance of a body behind another body of larger apparent size. When the moon passes between the observer and a star, the star is said to be occulted.

OUTGASSING. The evolution of gas from a solid in a vacuum.

OZONOSPHERE. A narrow layer of high ozone concentration about 20 miles up in the STRATOSPHERE (q.v.).

PARAGLIDER. A flexible-winged, kite-like vehicle designed for use in a recovery system for launch vehicles or as a reentry vehicle.

PAYLOAD. 1. Originally, the revenue-producing portion of an aircraft's load, e.g., passengers, cargo, mail, etc. 2. By extension, that which an aircraft, rocket, etc., carries over and above what is necessary for the operation of the vehicle during its flight.

PERIGEE. That orbital point nearest the earth when the earth is the center of attraction. See APOGEE.

PERIHELION. That orbital point nearest the sun when the sun is the center of attraction. See APHELION.

PHOTON ENGINE. A projected type of reaction engine in which thrust would be obtained from a stream of electromagnetic radiation. Although the thrust of this engine would be minute, it may be possible to apply it for extended periods of time. Theoretically, in space, where no resistance is offered by air particles, very high speeds may be built up.

PHOTOSPHERE. The intensely bright portion of the sun visible to the eye. The photosphere is that portion of the sun's atmosphere which emits the continuous radiation.

PICO-. A prefix meaning divided by one million million.

PRESTAGE. A step in the action of igniting a large liquid rocket taken prior to the ignition of the full flow, and consisting of igniting a partial flow of propellants into the thrust chamber.

PRIMARY BODY. The spatial body about which a satellite or other body orbits, or from which it is escaping, or toward which it is falling. The primary body of the moon is the earth; the primary body of the earth is the sun.

PROBE. Any device inserted in an environment for the purpose of obtaining information about the environment. Specifically, an instrumented vehicle moving through the upper atmosphere or space or landing upon another celestial body in order to obtain information about the environment.

RADAR ASTRONOMY. The development of powerful radar transmitters, large antennas, and very sensitive receivers allows the detection of high-frequency radio waves (radar) reflected off the nearby members of the solar system. Signals reflected from the moon were first detected in 1945, while the first signals from Venus were clearly received in 1961. A careful analysis of the reflected signal gives information as to the distance, velocity of approach or recession, surface roughness, rate of rotation, and dielectric constant of the planet. A large antenna under construction in Puerto Rico should allow radar detection of Mercury, Mars, some of the asteroids, the satellites of Jupiter, and the planet Jupiter itself.

RADIOSONDE. A balloon-borne instrument for the simultaneous measurement and transmission of meteorological data.

RADIO TELESCOPE. A device for receiving, amplifying, and measuring the intensity of radio waves originating outside the earth's atmosphere.

REACTION CONTROL SYSTEM. A system of controlling the attitude of a craft when outside the atmosphere by using jets of gas.

REAL TIME. Time in which reporting on events or recording of events is simultaneous with the events. For example, the real time of a satellite is that time in which it simultaneously reports its environment as it encounters it; the real time of a computer is that time during which it is accepting data.

RECYCLE. In a countdown: to stop the count and return to an earlier point in the countdown. Also called "holding." In testing: to repeat a group or a series of tests.

REENTRY WINDOW. The area at the limits of the earth's atmosphere through which a spacecraft can pass to accomplish a successful reentry.

ROLL. The rotational movement of an aircraft which takes place about the longitudinal axis. Any amount of such rotation is called "roll."

SELENOGRAPHIC. 1. Of or pertaining to the physical geography of the moon. 2. Specifically, referring to positions on the moon measured in latitude from the moon's equator and in longitude from a reference meridian.

Soft Radiation. Radiation which is absorbed by the equivalent of 10 centimeters of lead or less. Radiation which can penetrate more than 10 centimeters of lead is termed "hard radiation" or "hardness."

Solar Cell. A photovoltaic device that converts sunlight directly into electrical energy.

Solar Radiation. The total electromagnetic radiation emitted by the sun.

Sonic Boom. A noise caused by the shock wave from an aircraft or other object traveling in the atmosphere at or above the speed of sound.

Sonic Speed. The speed of sound. Sound travels at different speeds through different mediums and under different conditions of temperature, etc. In the standard atmosphere at sea level, sonic speed is approximately 760 miles per hour.

Sounding Rocket. A rocket designed to explore the atmosphere within 4,000 miles of the earth's surface.

Space-Air Vehicle. A vehicle that may be operated either within or above the sensible atmosphere.

Space Simulator. A device which simulates conditions existing in space and used for testing equipment, or in training programs.

Stationary Orbit. An orbit in which an equatorial satellite revolves about the primary at the same angular rate as the primary rotates on its axis. From the primary, the satellite thus appears to be stationary over a point on the primary.

Stratosphere. The region of the atmosphere lying on the average between about seven and 38 miles; it has a temperature which is either constant or increases with altitude, and is therefore stable against convection.

Subsonic. In aerodynamics, dealing with speeds less than the speed of sound, as in subsonic aerodynamics. See **Sonic Speed.**

Sunspot. A relatively dark area on the surface of the sun, consisting of a dark center surrounded by an area which is intermediate in brightness. Sunspots usually occur in pairs with opposite magnetic polarities. They have a lifetime ranging from a few days to several months. **Sunspot Cycle** is the term used to describe their quite regular recurrence, which is about every 11.1 years, but varies between seven and 17 years. The number rises from a minimum of 0-10 to a maximum of 50-140 about four years later, and then declines slowly.

Supersonic. Pertaining to speeds greater than the speed of sound. Compare **Ultrasonic.**

Sustainer Engine. An engine that maintains the speed of a vehicle once it has achieved its programmed velocity by use of a booster or other engine.

Thermonuclear. Pertaining to a nuclear reaction that is triggered by particles of high thermal energy.

Thermosphere. The region of the atmosphere, above the mesosphere, in which there is strong heating and increasing temperature. It extends roughly from an altitude of 55 to 373 miles.

Thrust. 1. The pushing force developed by an aircraft engine or a rocket engine. 2. Specifically, in rocketry, the product of propellant mass flow rate and exhaust velocity relative to the vehicle.

Tidal Drag. The damping of a planet or satellite's rotation produced by frictional losses associated with tides raised within the solid body or the planet or satellite, or in seas upon its surface.

TRAJECTORY. In general, the path traced by any body, as a rocket, moving as a result of externally applied forces. Trajectory is loosely used to mean flight path or orbit.

TRANSLUNAR. Of or pertaining to space outside the moon's orbit about the earth.

T-TIME. Any specific time, minus or plus, as referenced to "zero," or "launch" time, during a countdown sequence that is intended to result in the firing of a rocket propulsion unit that launches a rocket vehicle or missile.

TROPOSPHERE. The lowest six to 12 miles of atmosphere. The troposphere is characterized by decreasing temperature with height, appreciable vertical wind motion, appreciable water vapor content, and weather.

ULTRASONIC. Of or pertaining to frequencies above those that affect the human ear, which is more than 20,000 vibrations per second. Ultrasonic may be used as a modifier to indicate a device or system intended to operate at an ultrasonic frequency. Supersonic was formerly used synonymously with ultrasonic, but this usage is now rare.

UMBILICAL CORD. Any of the servicing electrical or fluid lines between the ground or a tower and an upright rocket missile or vehicle before the launch. Often shortened to "umbilical."

UPPER-AIR OBSERVATION. A measurement of atmospheric conditions aloft, above the effective range of a surface weather observation. Also called "sounding" or "upper-air sounding."

VAN ALLEN BELT or VAN ALLEN RADIATION BELT. The zone of high-intensity radiation surrounding the earth beginning at altitudes of approximately 621.4 miles. For James A. Van Allen, 1915-.

WEIGHTLESSNESS. A condition in which no acceleration, whether of gravity or other force, can be detected by an observer within the system in question. Any object falling freely in a vacuum is weightless, thus an unaccelerated satellite orbiting the earth is weightless, although gravity affects its orbit. Weightlessness can be produced within the atmosphere in aircraft flying a parabolic flight path.

YAW. 1. The lateral rotation of an aircraft, rocket, or the like, about a transverse axis. 2. The amount of this movement is the angle of yaw.

ZENITH. That point of the celestial sphere vertically overhead. The point 180° from the zenith is called the **NADIR.**

ZERO G. Weightlessness.